D1446590

Translating for Singing

DISCARDED

Bloomsbury Advances in Translation Series

Series Editor: Jeremy Munday, Centre for Translation Studies, University of Leeds, UK

Bloomsbury Advances in Translation Studies publishes cutting-edge research in the fields of translation studies. This field has grown in importance in the modern, globalized world, with international translation between languages a daily occurrence. Research into the practices, processes and theory of translation is essential and this series aims to showcase the best in international academic and professional output.

Other titles in the series:

Corpus-Based Translation Studies
Edited by Alet Kruger, Kim Wallmach & Jeremy Munday
Community Translation
Mustapha Taibi
Global Trends in Translator and Interpreter Training
Edited by Séverine Hubscher-Davidson & Michał Borodo
Music, Text and Translation
Edited by Helen Julia Minors
Quality In Professional Translation
Joanna Drugan
Retranslation
Sharon Deane-Cox
The Pragmatic Translator
Massimiliano Morini
Translation, Adaptation and Transformation
Edited by Laurence Raw
Translation and Translation Studies in the Japanese Context
Edited by Nana Sato-Rossberg & Judy Wakabayashi
Translation as Cognitive Activity
Fabio Alves & Amparo Hurtado Albir
Translation, Humour and Literature
Edited by Delia Chiaro
Translation, Humour and the Media
Edited by Delia Chiaro
Translating the Poetry of the Holocaust
Jean Boase-Beier

Translating for Singing

The theory, art, and craft of
translating lyrics

RONNIE APTER
MARK HERMAN

Bloomsbury Advances in Translation

Bloomsbury Academic
An imprint of Bloomsbury Publishing Plc

B L O O M S B U R Y
LONDON · OXFORD · NEW YORK · NEW DELHI · SYDNEY

Bloomsbury Academic

An imprint of Bloomsbury Publishing Plc

50 Bedford Square	1385 Broadway
London	New York
WC1B 3DP	NY 10018
UK	USA

www.bloomsbury.com

BLOOMSBURY and the Diana logo are trademarks of Bloomsbury Publishing Plc

First published 2016

© Ronnie Apter and Mark Herman, 2016

Ronnie Apter and Mark Herman have asserted their right under the Copyright, Designs and Patents Act, 1988, to be identified as the Authors of this work.

All rights reserved. No part of this publication may be reproduced or transmitted in any form or by any means, electronic or mechanical, including photocopying, recording, or any information storage or retrieval system, without prior permission in writing from the publishers.

No responsibility for loss caused to any individual or organization acting on or refraining from action as a result of the material in this publication can be accepted by Bloomsbury or the author.

British Library Cataloguing-in-Publication Data
A catalogue record for this book is available from the British Library.

ISBN: HB: 978-1-4725-7189-2
PB: 978-1-4725-7188-5
ePDF: 978-1-4725-7190-8
ePub: 978-1-4725-7191-5

Library of Congress Cataloging-in-Publication Data
A catalog record for this book is available from the Library of Congress.

Series: Bloomsbury Advances in Translation

Typeset by Newgen Knowledge Works (P) Ltd., Chennai, India
Printed and bound in Great Britain

Dedicated to
Michael Spierman, founder and artistic director of the Bronx Opera
Company, who gave us our start, and our fathers, Joseph Herman
and Marvin Apter, who sang the songs of Gilbert and Sullivan to
us before we could even talk.

Contents

Figures

Tables

About this book

This book discusses the translation of singable lyrics for performance, that is, the creation of translated texts meant to be sung to the same music composed to set the original texts, or to music that has been changed only minimally. Further, the translations are intended for audiences who usually lack any other linguistic access to the texts translated. In particular, this book discusses translations of works for the musical stage from languages other than English into performable English. There is also some discussion of the translation of lyrics for which the music either no longer exists or exists only in fragmentary form. Word-music combinations employed on the musical stage and considered in this book range from spoken dialogue to dialogue spoken over music to speechlike and minimally accompanied *recitativo secco* to less speechlike *recitativo accompagnato* to non-speechlike aria to purely orchestral music without any words at all.

Dates of persons and works cited, if known, are usually given after their first mention.

Since boundaries between various genres—operas, operettas, *Singspiele*, musicals, musical comedies, choruses, and plays with songs—though more rigid or more porous depending on the era, have largely been erased by recent composers, in this book the word "opera" is sometimes used to generally mean any dramatic work for the stage or screen which is sung in whole or in part; the word "song" to mean a short piece lasting up to a maximum of about ten minutes, whether originally written as a stand-alone piece or as part of a larger work such as an opera. Where necessary, a distinction is made between an "aria," or a "duet," "trio," and so on, sung by the performer or performers while the onstage characters they are portraying are, by convention, speaking or thinking but not singing, and a "song," during which the characters as well as the performers are singing. Also, where necessary, a distinction is made between non-diegetic music and sounds, which are heard by the audience (and also obviously by the performers) but not, by convention, by the onstage characters; and diegetic music and sounds, which are also heard by the characters. In addition, music can acquire a life of its own and assume the function of another onstage character.

No part of this book may be reproduced, recorded, or performed without the express consent of the authors, except for brief excerpts quoted in reviews or covered under the doctrine of fair use.

Foreword

Jonas Forssell

Some years ago, I went to a performance of *Le nozze di Figaro* at *Folkoperan* in Stockholm with my youngest daughter, who was then 17 years old, very "punkish," and a bit obstinate. After the show she grabbed my shoulders and, while shaking them, said, or rather shouted: "Wow! How *fun* it was, and I understood it all! I want to see it again and bring some friends." At that particular point, I really felt that Mozart was giggling in satisfaction and jumping up and down while sitting there on his little cloud somewhere high up in the sky; similarly happy was Lorenzo Da Ponte, his famous librettist! The performance was not called *Le nozze di Figaro* but *Figaros bröllop*, and it was indeed a witty, congenial staging by the former artistic leader of *Folkoperan*, director Mira Bartov, together with an excellent cast consisting of the graduating class at the University College of Opera in Gothenburg. Their inspiring and energetic acting and singing was of course part of the success. The main reason, though, for my daughter's immediate happiness was her *understanding* of the words, and with that, her reception of the drama and thereby the intense impact the music made on her.

Da Ponte wrote in 1789, in a letter to the Burgtheater in Vienna probably about Mozart's and his collaboration on *Don Giovanni*, that *"in einem Land, wo die italienische Sprache eine Fremdsprache ist, ist es äußerst nötig, die Oper ins Deutsche zu übersetzen"* (in a land where the Italian language is a foreign language, it is extremely necessary to translate the opera into German) (Da Ponte, *Anweisung für den Theaterbetrieb [Instructions for Theater Operations]*, quoted in Tråvén, 1999: 2). Some readers may now object that *Figaro* premiered at the same Burgtheater on May 1, 1786—*in Italian*! But that was an occasion primarily for the Viennese court, and Italian was one of the languages spoken and understood by everyone there. Indeed, though we Swedes know the city under its German name—*Wien*, you in the English-speaking world use the Italian equivalent! Being a composer myself, mainly of operas, I cannot say how deeply I sympathize with the attitude of Da Ponte.

In 2010 I began a PhD project on opera and text, in order to find out, among many other things, if I were alone in my affinities. For inspiration I went, as I usually do in such a situation, to Berlin together with luggage containing a huge pile of books. Like many Swedes, I prefer to stay at a pension on Kantstrasse, close to Savignyplatz where I love to sit and contemplate in the sun at one of the many cafés and restaurants. When in Charlottenburg, you can feel the presence of the "Dead Poets', Philosophers' and Historians' Society," since they are all there: Mommsen(strasse), Goethe(strasse), and Leibniz(strasse), and you are not far from two of the main opera houses, *Staatsoper* at its temporary location *"im Schiller Theater" and Deutsche Oper*. Friedrich Carl von Savigny was himself a historian, and some blocks away from the square are the streets of Barthold Georg Niebuhr and Leopold von Ranke. Those three were among the most important persons in the development of Source Criticism as a method of Historical Research. So, in order to investigate to what extent the creative giants in the history of opera would be satisfied with the recent turn toward the use of only the "original language," I decided— inspired by the environment of Charlottenburg—to dig into the sources, a decision that led me into the field of opera translating and expanded that chapter of my thesis in a way I surely hadn't foreseen.

In his book *Opera in Crisis: Tradition, Present, Future*, Henry Pleasants tells us about his interview with the famous *La Scala* soprano Giuseppina Cobelli, made while he faced "a single full-length oil painting of Giuseppina as Isolde, her fully rounded arms outstretched, presumably singing the '*Liebestod*'—in Italian, of course" (1989: 108). (It is interesting to note that those very few Wagner recordings that Maria Callas made in the late 1940s, at the very beginning of her career, also were all sung in Italian!) The translation of *Tristano e Isotta* that Cobelli used was probably from the pen of Arrigo Boito who made it in 1876, the year before Verdi forced him to quickly translate the libretto of their *Otello* into French in order to induce the Paris Opera to perform it. As late as 1957, the first commissioned work in thirty years at *La Scala* in Milan, Francis Poulenc's *Dialogues des Carmélites*, was performed in an Italian translation. The translation, by Flavio Testi, was not forced by the opera house, but was made according to the expressed wish of composer-librettist Poulenc.   ·

According to the criteria of the recently founded Birgit Nilsson Prize, it can be awarded not only to a singer (Plácido Domingo was the first recipient of the Prize in 2009), or to a conductor (Riccardo Muti was the second recipient of the Prize in 2011), but also to "an institution with an outstanding record in opera or concert, such as an orchestra, a chorus, or an opera company, in recognition of an exceptional production which respects *the spirit of the composer.*" Looked at in historical perspective, "the spirit of the composer" hardly means performing in a language not understood by the audience, or worse, by the singers on stage, or, worst of all, by the stage director or the conductor. Not if we are talking about Mozart and Da Ponte, or Verdi, or Poulenc. Wagner?—Perhaps, but the young Wagner worked actively to have his operas translated. Puccini?—He supervised the first British performance of *La bohème* in Manchester in 1897 (in English!) and got most of his subjects from plays that were translated for him, just as most of us normally do. The practice of singing *Madama Butterfly* or *La fanciulla del West*, both based on works originally in English, in their "original" Italian for a Swedish audience would be regarded as quite odd if "transposed" into the field of spoken drama. Audiences at the Royal Dramatic Theatre in Stockholm would indeed be unfortunate if the plays they could attend by Molière, Pirandello, Schiller, or Shakespeare were "performed only in the original language." (Handel, then?—Well, there are always exceptions. Handel wrote Italian operas for the English stage, since, to paraphrase Edith Wharton [see Chapter 2 of this book], "an unalterable and unquestioned law of the London musical world in the 18th century required that the Greek text of German operas should be translated into Italian for the clearer understanding of English-speaking audiences.")

The attitude of opera composers toward translation is made clear by the fact that a surprisingly large number of them, such as Boito (a composer as well as a librettist), also worked as translators themselves, and not only for their own work but for operas by other composers. In Sweden, the clarinet virtuoso and composer Bernard Crusell (1775–1838) made the first Swedish versions of *The Marriage of Figaro* (1821), Rossini's *The Barber of Seville* (1825), and Boieldieu's *The White Lady* (1827). Composer Wilhelm Peterson-Berger (1867–1942) not only made the first Swedish translation of Wagner's *Tristan* (as Boito made the first Italian one), but also stage-directed its first performance in 1909. Finnish conductor and composer Armas Järnefelt (1869–1958) and the Swedish composer Ture Rangström (1884–1947) were both deeply engaged in several translations and text adaptions at the Royal Opera in Stockholm during the first decades of the twentieth century.

As for myself, primarily an opera composer and not a translator or linguist or with any special abilities to master a bunch of languages—I'm quite mono-lingual, using and understanding English only as most Swedes do—yet, surprise!, I actually have at least one translation to my credit. During my years as artistic director at the Northern Opera of Sweden in Umeå, we performed a small "Christmas-Opera" by Frank Bridge (the teacher of Benjamin Britten) based on a children's play by Margaret Kemp-Welch and Constance Cotterell called *The Christmas Rose*. There was no time to commission a proper translation—so I made one myself!

Why do composers actually care about singable translations? Basically because the whole idea of sitting several years together with a librettist, in a monk's cell with a piano and/or a computer, producing a-hell-of-a-lot-of material, collaborating with singers, directors, and conductors, rehearsing it and finally raising the curtain, is to create a "verbal/musical/rhetorical fusion . . . transmitted from a singer's mouth to a listener's ears as an interaction *realised in sound, sense and gesture"* (Golomb, 2005: 142). That's it, folks! No surtitling, however clever, can ever "possibly simulate the effect . . . as it functions in the original" (Golomb, 2005: 142).

The English-speaking world seems to have a quite strange and ambiguous posture toward singing in its own language. The Metropolitan Opera in New York was one of the first companies of its kind, not only in that it did not open the house with a commissioned opera work (but with a "French opera on a German text sung by a Swedish artist translated into Italian etc."), but also in that it preferred "musical communication with the composer to theatrical communication with the audience" (Golomb, 2005: 140), and perhaps the presence onstage of operatic superstars to both. This last seems, like many American concepts, to have wiped out all its competitors.

An obvious paradox of music theater is that the true English-language form—the *musical*—is almost always translated into the tongue of the audience, wherever in the world, and that operas for children are also always transmitted in a language that can be received by the young audience (anything else would be ridiculous!). One can sense, though, that lurking somewhere in here are judgments about whose meticulous work, forging music and words together into a powerful unit, is worth canonizing and whose is not. Engelbert Humperdinck's and Stephen Sondheim's are not, but Verdi's, Wagner's, and Puccini's are!

Another paradox is that most of the new contemporary operas that have been successful in finding an audience, both in terms of box office receipts and in numbers of productions, are all sung in English, composed by people with names such as Adams, Adès, and, most recently, George Benjamin. A plausible explanation is that, apart from the obvious skills and talents of the creators, Anglo-Americans have dominated popular music for about a 100 years, and television and films for at least 50. Therefore, future opera audiences all over the world will be well drilled in hearing and understanding sung English words and comprehending a dramatic context when expressed in the English language. I recently saw a performance at the Royal Opera in Stockholm of Benjamin's *Written on Skin* and, though I could raise some serious objections about the choice of subject, I must admit that the work is extremely well written and composed so that every single syllable pronounced on stage is audible and crystal clear. Just as my daughter put it, "I understood it all!" and without having any special competence in the English language. Perhaps the future of opera is *not* performance in Italian, French, or German with surtitling; it might well be opera in the *lingua franca* of our time—English! (I've already made one attempt myself: *Death and the Maiden*, an opera based on the play by Ariel Dorfman to my own libretto, 2008.)

My studies in the history of opera translation resulted, among many other good things, in the first course ever in opera translating at the Stockholm

University College of Opera, held during fall and winter 2013/14. During the course, we had the opportunity to invite Ronnie Apter and Mark Herman to guest-lecture. They had already made available to us their essays and papers, the collection of which probably constituted the most important textbook on the subject. The students also had the opportunity to work with, and put questions directly to, Ronnie and Mark, and, not surprisingly, all the students in the course passed the final test of the course and were accepted for the examination for the degree.

If one seeks other powerful arguments for using the vernacular in communicating, one can always go back to Dante, probably one of the inventors of the opera world's own *lingua franca*—Italian. In his *Convivio (The Banquet)*, he pleads that those

> who disparage our vernacular are possessed by an empty desire for glory. Many think they will be admired more for describing things in another language, and for praising it, than by doing so in their own. Certainly ability in learning a foreign language well is not unworthy of praise; but it is wrong to praise it beyond all truth in order to glory in its acquisition. (Dante Alighieri, *Convivio*, 1304–7, translated by A. S. Kline, 2008: 27)

However, quoting Dante about translation should be done with caution, since he also writes earlier in the same work: "Thus all should know that nothing harmonised according to the rules of poetry can be translated from its native tongue into another without destroying its original sweetness and harmony" (*Convivio*: 19). In this, his thoughts correspond perfectly with the many opera enthusiasts who look upon translation only as a kind of "unfavorable currency transaction," as the Geneva-based linguist Sergej Karcevski put it (referred to by Jakobson, 1959). There are, though, other opinions and theories about translation—for example, Walter Benjamin's, in his famous 1923 essay *"Die Aufgabe des Übersetzers"* ("The Task of the Translator")—concerned more about the new values that emerge from such a "transaction." Benedetto Croce (1866–1952), an influential Italian philosopher at the beginning of the twentieth century, said in *The Essence of Aesthetics*: "to translate with artistic skill is to create a new work of art" (1912: 75). The Finnish (but Swedish-speaking) literary translator Thomas Warburton looks upon his impressive lifework, in *Efter 30 000 sidor: från en översättares bord (After 30,000 Pages: From a Translator's Desk)*, with a little more modesty, describing himself as one of "the plumbers of literature.. . . without them all our water supply would not at all be what it is and what we need" (2003: 1).

Françoise Wuilmart, the Belgian translator who is also the Directrice of the *Centre Européen de Traduction littéraire*, in her essay *"Översättaren som förlossare ur den babyloniska språkförbistringen"* ("The Translator as a Redeemer from the Babylonian Confusion of Tongues"), calls translators

> *Idealistic*—because they struggle for the ideal, the perfect translation
>
> *Overambitious*—because they are fully aware . . . of their inability to achieve it
>
> *Obstinate*—because they still take on such a task
>
> *Frustrated*—because . . . [their efforts] can never satisfy them.
>
> But I would like to add another, more positive adjective . . . : *Altruistic.*
>
> (Wuilmart, 1995: 12)

Now that you know a little bit more about Ronnie Apter and Mark Herman, you should read their great text, made in the spirit of Donald A. Schön's *Reflective Practitioner* (1983), not because every single word in it is indisputably *The Truth, The Whole Truth, and Nothing But The Truth*, but because it emerges from the profound depths of experience, and because it is truly enjoyable to read.

Jonas Forssell
Rome, July 20, 2015

Copyright acknowledgments

Unless otherwise specified, everything in this book, including all translations (both performable and nonperformable), are by Mark Herman and/or Ronnie Apter and copyrighted by them. All material by or copyrighted by others is covered by the doctrine of fair use for scholarly or research purposes, is in the public domain, or is used by permission of those listed below, for which the authors and publisher are grateful. For those items requiring permission, for which the copyright holders either could not be traced or were inadvertently overlooked, the publisher will be pleased to make the necessary permission arrangements at the first possible opportunity after being contacted.

Author, Editor, Translator, or Adapter

Myrdene Anderson

Quotations from "The Saami Yoik: Translating Hum, Chant, or/and Song." Copyright © 2005 Editions Rodopi B. V., Amsterdam. Quotations used by permission of Koninklijke BRILL NV.

John Bloch

Quotations from THE ABDUCTION FROM THE SERAGLIO by W. A. Mozart. English translation by John Bloch. Copyright © 1962 (Renewed) by G. Schirmer, Inc. (ASCAP). International Copyright Secured. All Rights Reserved. Used by Permission.

Edward J. Dent

Quotations from "The Abduction from the Seraglio (Il Seraglio)." Music by Wolfgang Amadeus Mozart, words adapted by Gottlieb Stephanie from C. F. Bretzner, English version by Edward J. Dent. Copyright © Oxford University Press 1952. Extracts reproduced by permission. All rights reserved.

Stephen Fry

Two lines of an aria in *The Magic Flute*. Copyright © 2006 by Stephen Fry. Used by permission of Stephen Fry.

Tony Harrison

Quotations from *The Bartered Bride*, translated by Tony Harrison. Copyright © 1978 by G. Schirmer, Inc. (ASCAP). International Copyright Secured. All Rights Reserved. Used by Permission.

Mark Herman and Ronnie Apter (work copyrighted by others)

For further information about the work of Mark Herman and Ronnie Apter, please contact them at <mnh18@columbia.edu>.

1   Quotations from Herman and Apter's English translation of Donizetti's *Maria Stuarda (Mary Stuart)*. Copyright © 1997 by Casa Ricordi s.r.l.-Milano for the English translation. Quotations used by permission of Ricordi.

2   Quotations from Herman and Apter's English translation of Ferrero's *La figlia del mago (The Sorcerer's Daughter)*. Copyright © 1993 by Casa Ricordi s.r.l.-Milano for the English translation. Quotations used by permission of Ricordi.

3   Quotations from Herman and Apter's English translation of Puccini's *La bohème*. Copyright © 1997 by Casa Ricordi s.r.l.-Milano for the English translation (to be published). Quotations used by permission of Ricordi.

4   Quotations from Herman and Apter's English translation of Rossini's *L'occasione fa il ladro (A Thief by Chance [Opportunity Makes the Thief])*. Copyright © 2007 by Casa Ricordi s.r.l.-Milano for the English translation. Quotations used by permission of Ricordi.

5   Quotations from Herman and Apter's English translation of Verdi's *Ernani*. Copyright © 1994 by The University of Chicago and Casa Ricordi s.r.l.-Milano for the English translation. Quotations used by permission of Ricordi.

6   Quotations from Herman and Apter's English translation of Verdi's *Luisa Miller*. Copyright © 2004 by The University of Chicago and Casa Ricordi s.r.l.-Milano for the English translation. Quotations used by permission of Ricordi.

7   Quotations from Herman and Apter's English translation of Verdi's *Il trovatore*. Copyright © 2002 by The University of Chicago and Casa Ricordi s.r.l.-Milano for the English translation. Quotations used by permission of Ricordi.

Douglas R. Hofstadter

Quotations from *Le Ton beau de Marot*. Copyright © 1997 by Basic Books. Quotations used by permission of Douglas Hofstadter and Perseus Books Group.

Amanda Holden

For further information about the work of Amanda Holden, please contact her at <amandajulietholden@googlemail.com>.

1   Quotations from Holden's English translation of Donizetti's *Maria Stuarda (Mary Stuart)*. Performable English translation copyright © 1998 by Amanda Holden. Quotations used by permission of Amanda Holden.

2   Quotations from Holden's English translation of Mozart's *The Abduction from the Seraglio*. Performable English translation of the sung lyrics copyright © 1999, 2009 by Amanda Holden. Quotations used by permission of Amanda Holden.

3 Quotations from Holden's English translation of Smetana's *The Bartered Bride*. Performable English translation copyright © 2006 by Amanda Holden. Quotations used by permission of Amanda Holden.

4 Quotations from Holden's English translation of Mozart's *The Magic Flute*. Performable English translation copyright © 2007 by Amanda Holden. Quotations used by permission of Amanda Holden.

5 Quotations from Holden's English translation of Puccini's *La bohème*. Performable English translation copyright © 2009 by Amanda Holden. Quotations used by permission of Amanda Holden.

Tom Lehrer

Quotation from "The Hunting Song." Copyright © 1953 and 1954 by Tom Lehrer. Quotation used by permission of Tom Lehrer.

Joseph Machlis

Quotations from Machlis's English translation of Verdi's *La traviata*. Copyright © 1962 by Casa Ricordi s.r.l.-Milano for the English translation. Quotations used by permission of Ricordi.

Ruth and Thomas Martin

1 Quotations from THE MAGIC FLUTE by W. A. Mozart. English version by Ruth and Thomas Martin. Copyright © 1952 (Renewed) by G. Schirmer, Inc. (ASCAP). International Copyright Secured. All Rights Reserved. Used by Permission.

2 Quotations from LA TRAVIATA by Giuseppe Verdi. English version by Ruth and Thomas Martin. Copyright © 1946, 1961 (Renewed) by G. Schirmer, Inc. (ASCAP). International Copyright Secured. All Rights Reserved. Reprinted by Permission.

J. D. McClatchy

Quotations from *Seven Mozart Librettos: A Verse Translation*. Copyright © 2011 by W. W. Norton & Company. Quotations used by permission of W. W. Norton & Company.

Andrew Porter

Quotations from *The Ring of the Nibelung*, translated by Andrew Porter. Copyright © 1976 by W. W. Norton & Company. Quotations used by permission of W. W. Norton & Company.

Jeremy Sams

Quotations from Sams's English translation of Wagner's *Das Rheingold*. Copyright © 2002 Josef Weinberger Limited. Reproduced by permission of the copyright owner.

David Spencer

For further information about the work of David Spencer, please contact his agent: Patricia McLaughlin c/o Beacon Artists Agency / 1501 Broadway, Suite #1200 / New York, NY 10036; (212) 736–6630, <beaconagency@hotmail.com>.

(1) Quotations from Spencer's English translation of *La bohème:* New English Adaptation and Lyrics. Copyright © 1984, 2002 by David Spencer. Quotations used by permission of David Spencer.

(2) Quotations from "Collaborating with the Dead, or: How I Rewrote *La Bohème*," *Opera Monthly:* June 1990: 20–25. Copyright © 1990 by David Spencer. Quotations used by permission of David Spencer.

Hendrik van der Werf

Quotations from *The Extant Troubadour Melodies: Transcriptions and Essays for Performers and Scholars*, Rochester, New York: van der Werf. Copyright © 1984 by Hendrik van der Werf. Quotations of transcriptions of the music of Bernart de Ventadorn used by permission of Hendrik van der Werf.

George F. Whicher

Quotation from *The Goliard Poets*. Edited by George F. Whicher, translated by George F. Whicher, from THE GOLIARD POETS. Copyright ©1949 by George F. Whicher. Reprinted by permission of New Directions Publishing Corp.

James J. Wilhelm

Quotation from *Medieval Song: An Anthology of Hymns and Lyrics*. Copyright © 1971 by James. J. Wilhelm. Used by permission of Victor Boyer.

Acknowledgments

First, to those to whom this book is dedicated: our fathers, Joseph Herman and Marvin Apter, who led us to our love of music drama, and Michael Spierman, founder and artistic director of the Bronx Opera Company in New York City, who took a chance on us when we were totally unknown.

Next, to two other people who were likewise willing to give us a chance, and with whom we have had many productive discussions regarding translation problems and solutions: Philip Gossett, Robert W. Reneker, Distinguished Service Emeritus Professor of Music at the University of Chicago, senior general editor of the University of Chicago Press's and Ricordi's critical edition of the Works of Verdi, and general editor of Bärenreiter's edition of Works of Gioachino Rossini; and Gabriel Dotto, director of the Michigan State University Press, general editor of Ricordi's critical edition of the Operas of Puccini, and co-general editor (with Roger Parker) of Ricordi's critical edition of the Operas of Donizetti.

To our friend, the distinguished Swedish opera composer and translator Jonas Forssell, for writing the Foreword to this book.

To Mary Stewart Kiesgen, Nina Nash-Robertson, and Beth Macleod, colleagues of Ronnie Apter at Central Michigan University, whose direct and indirect help and support were invaluable.

To Harold Ax, David Randolph, and Garyth Nair, three great choral conductors who gave us the thrill of direct involvement with performance, and whose deaths leave a great gap in the world of music.

To the many many fellow translators who have encouraged and cooperated with us over the years and on this book in particular, especially Burton Raffel, Douglas Hofstadter, Amanda Holden, and David Spencer.

To the artistic and music directors on both sides of the Atlantic who were willing to commission new translations from us or use our existing ones.

To the publishers of our translations for the musical stage, Ricordi in Milan and Musica Russica in San Diego, and the many people in both places responsible for putting our work into print.

To Jeremy Munday, Andrew Wardell, and all the others at Bloomsbury Press, for their many helpful editorial comments and suggestions, and for accepting the daunting task of publishing a book with so many tables and musical examples.

And finally, to our sons Dan and Ry Herman, who had to grow up hearing their parents playing (banging?) on a piano and singing (screaming?) words at each other, and who offered us solutions to translation problems on many occasions.

Opera is theater isn't it? Theater should communicate, shouldn't it? What good is theater if it can't be understood?

(David Spencer [1954–], American translator, adapter, and lyricist, 1990: 20, remembering the words of a professor at Queens College, New York City)

[W]e immediately fell to translating the Italian Operas; and as there was no great Danger of hurting the Sense of those extraordinary Pieces, our Authors would often make Words of their own, that were entirely foreign to the Meaning of the Passages which they pretended to translate . . . By this Means the soft Notes that were adapted to Pity in the Italian, fell upon the Word Rage in the English; and the angry Sounds that were turn'd to Rage in the Original, were made to express Pity in the Translation. It oftentimes happen'd likewise, that the finest Notes in the Air fell upon the most insignificant Words in the Sentence. I have known the word *And* pursu'd through the whole Gamut, I have been entertain'd with many a melodious *The*, and have heard the most beautiful Graces Quavers and Divisions bestow'd upon *Then, For*, and *From*; to the eternal Honour of our English Particles.

At present, our Notions of Musick are so very uncertain, that we do not know what it is we like, only, in general, we are transported with anything that is not English: so if it be of a foreign Growth, let it be Italian, French, or High-Dutch, it is the same thing. In short, our English Musick is quite rooted out, and nothing yet planted in its stead.

(Joseph Addison [1672–1719], British essayist, poet, and statesman, in *The Spectator*, No. 18, March 21, 1711; quoted in Grout and Williams, 1988: 167–68)

1

Translation and music

Sung words, like all other texts, can be translated from a source language, frequently abbreviated SL, into a different target language, frequently abbreviated TL. Like other translations, translations of sung words can be literal or literary, with both designations referring to a range of possibilities. For example, literal translations, conveying meaning, can be word by word, phrase by phrase, or sentence by sentence, depending on the intended use of the translation:

> Some . . . are intended for study by singers and choir directors; others for audiences to read, either quickly in the concert room or slowly at home; yet others are meant for speaking before a performance, or for projection on screen. (Peter Low, 2013: 72)

In contrast to literal translations, concerned only with meaning, literary translations of sung lyrics attempt to reproduce formal elements of the original text, such as rhyme and meter, and to convey connotations and subtexts. They may or may not ask the audience to confront elements of a foreign culture—that is, they may foreignize or domesticate the text (see Chapter 3). Some, the principal concern of this book, are performable to the music composed for the source-language lyrics. Such performable translations have been called "equirhythmic(al)," "vocal," "synchronized," and "music-linked" (Golomb, 2005: 121) in addition to the perhaps more easily recognizable terms "performable," "singable," and "singing."

Translations, usually literal, projected onto screens above or at the sides of the stage are called "surtitles" or "supertitles," in contrast to the subtitles displayed at the bottom of movie and television screens.

Rear window captions, that is, captions projected onto the rear wall of the theater and viewed in mirrors, were originally developed as an aid to the hard-of-hearing. Translations displayed on individual screens in front of each seat are called electronic librettos or Met titles, because the Metropolitan Opera in New York was the first opera house in the United States to use them. Unlike surtitles, electronic librettos and rear window captions are viewable only by those who wish to view them, and so do not distract nonviewers. Electronic librettos can be programmed to offer a choice of target languages, and can also display the source text for those who know the original language but, for whatever reason, still cannot understand the words as sung.

Translations are rarely strictly literal or literary, but instead take on both literal and literary aspects.

Because singable translations are almost always designed to fit the original music, they face a constraint beyond those imposed on other translations. No translation is ever "perfect," but this constraint, discussed in detail in Chapters 2 and 11, perhaps renders singable translations even less "perfect." Burton Raffel (1928–), a noted translator and writer about translation, states five reasons why all translations must be imperfect:

1   No two languages having the same phonology, it is impossible to re-create the sounds of a work composed in one language in another language.

2   No two languages having the same syntactic structures, it is impossible to re-create the syntax of a work composed in one language in another language.

3   No two languages having the same vocabulary, it is impossible to re-create the vocabulary of a work composed in one language in another language.

4   No two languages having the same literary history, it is impossible to re-create the literary forms of one culture in the language and literary culture of another.

5   No two languages having the same prosody, it is impossible to re-create the prosody of a literary work composed in one language in another language. (1988: 12)

By prosody is meant the rhythm of syllables of a language (Hall, 1964: 406–7), always reflected to some extent in the musical setting of words. Therefore, a singable translation must somehow set words of a language with one prosody to music composed to fit the prosody of a different language.

If total re-creation in a translation is impossible, if "only the original is the original" (Raffel, 1988: 89), what then should translators do? They certainly should not cry *traduttore, traditore* (translator, traitor) and give up, because:

> The impossibility of exact re-creation does not preclude the very real possibility of approximation—and it is precisely on approximation that good translation . . . must be built. (Raffel, 1988: 13)

To the principle of approximation may be added the principle of compensation: adding such things as alliteration and humor, at points in the translation where they do not occur in the original, to compensate for losses in the translation at points where they do. This practice is sometimes called "non-local translation." John Dryden (1631–1700), one of the first to write systematically about translation into English, declared in 1685:

> [W]here I have enlarg'd them [that is, where Dryden has added thoughts or embellishments apparently not in the source texts], I desire the false Criticks wou'd not always think that those thoughts are wholly mine, but that either they are secretly in the Poet, or may be fairly deduc'd from him: or at least, if both those considerations should fail, that my own is of a piece with his, and that if he were living, and an *Englishman*, they are such, as he wou'd probably have written. (Dryden, 1685, "Preface to *Sylvae*," *Works*, 3: 3–4)

Approximations and additions can always be made in more than one way. Therefore, different translations, each with successes and failures, are always possible. Just as there is no such thing as a perfect translation, there is no such thing as a best translation, heated arguments of critics and theoreticians to the contrary notwithstanding.

1.1 A topic of increasing interest

Although the translation of sung lyrics has a long history, interest has increased during the past few years. Notable among university programs devoted to translation and music, and to the wider field of word–music interactions in general, is that at the University of Edinburgh, Scotland, directed by Professor Peter Dayan. An international project on "Translating Music" was launched in 2013, led by Lucile Desblache of the University of Roehampton in England, Helen Julia Minors of Kingston University in England, and Elena Di Giovanni of the University of Macerata in Italy. Two relevant organizations beyond academia are the Lyrica Society for Word–Music Relations (http://www.lyricasociety.org/), which sponsors conferences and conference sessions and publishes the journal *Ars Lyrica*; and the International Association for Word and Music Studies, which also sponsors conferences—most recently in November 2014 at Aarhus University, Denmark—and publishes the proceedings in the book series *Word and Music Studies*.

In addition to conferences sponsored by the organizations mentioned, there have been three recent international symposia: "Music, Poetry and Translation" at Barnard College in New York City in 2010; "Translation in Music: An International Interdisciplinary Symposium," at Cardiff University in Wales in 2014; and "From Translation to Semio-Translation: Origins, Evolution, and Metamorphoses," a World Congress of the International Association of Semiotic Studies (IASS) in Sofia, Bulgaria, also in 2014.

Important recent collections of articles addressing many aspects of translation and music include *Song and Significance: Virtues and Vices of Vocal Translation* (Gorlée, 2005a) and *Music, Text and Translation* (Minors, 2013). Articles in the first cover a wide range of topics: hymns, operas, musicals, popular songs, and folk songs never performed twice in exactly the same way. Articles in the second cover operas, songs, various types of translation, cultural issues, and projected captions.

In the past, the translations of sung lyrics most discussed were performable ones. Today, much attention is given to literal or quasi-literal projected captions. Good guides to the literature, at least up to 2008, are the general bibliography of "Translation and Music" (Franzon et al., 2008), and the annotated bibliography of "Opera Translation" (Matamala and Orero, 2008), both in the special issue of the journal *The Translator* devoted to "Translation and Music" (Susam-Sarajeva, 2008). That special issue also contains several articles and reviews of interest, about popular songs, folk songs, and musicals, plus Charlotte Bosseux's discussion of the musical episode of the television series *Buffy the Vampire Slayer*. More recently (2011), Bosseaux has prepared a good review of articles about both performable translations and projected captions.

Like the writings about them, singable translations also go back a long way, at least to the anonymous seventeenth-century English translation of the Italian libretto by Aurelio Aureli (1652–1708) for the 1655 opera *Erismena* by composer Francesco Cavalli (1602–76) (Clinkscale, 1992: II: 64). Despite this long history, there is still no consensus on the answer to the question: If there is no such thing as a perfect, or a best, singable translation, what then constitutes a good one?

An imprecise answer is easily given. A good singable translation must satisfy two criteria: it must work on stage, and it must still be closely enough related to the source so that it is not an entirely new piece.

Attempts at more precise answers, some of which are discussed throughout this book, have prompted many theoretical and practical writings in such fields as semiotics, that is, the study of signs and symbols viewed as elements of communicative behavior (see Jakobson, 1959; Gorlée, 1994, 1996, 1997a, 1997b, 2002, 2004a, 2004b, 2005b, 2005c; Kaindl, 1995, 2004, 2005; Desblache, 2004, 2007, 2008, 2009, 2013; and Bosseaux, 2011); word–music interrelationships (see Corse, 1987); and even art theory (see Langer, 1953).

Problems discussed by semioticians include but are not limited to questions of translatability and untranslatability; equivalence, fidelity, and infidelity; the function of a fallible translator; translation and re-translation; the fate of the source text; the destiny of the target text (that is, the audience or audiences for which the translation is intended); and additions to compensate for lost aspects of the original.

In 1959, semiotician Roman Jakobson (1896–1982) proposed three types of translation: "intralingual," or the rewording of verbal signs (a spoken or written text) within a single language; "interlingual" (the interpretation of verbal signs in one language by the verbal signs in another language); and "intersemiotic" (the interpretation of verbal signs by a nonverbal system) (Jakobson, 1959: 233). A singable translation requires a type of translation beyond the three proposed by Jakobson, because the task is to transfer one set of signs, the verbal, from an interacting pair of two sets of signs, the musical and the verbal, into another set of verbal signs which, in conjunction with the music, will create an interaction either equivalent to the original interaction or, if different, still somehow related and desirable.

Performances involve a third set of signs, the visual, encompassing scenery, props, costumes, makeup, and the physical bodies, movements, and facial expressions of the performers. On occasion, translators have to modify a translation to accommodate visual elements, especially when dubbing a movie or television show for which no visual element can be changed. When dubbing, a fourth set of signs becomes of concern: the voice qualities of the performers. Charlotte Bosseaux discusses voice quality using examples from the dubbed French versions of songs from the television show *Buffy the Vampire Slayer* (Bosseaux, 2008), mentioned above, and the movie *Gentleman Prefer Blondes* (Bosseaux, 2013). In the latter article, she explains why the use of an inappropriate voice greatly lessens the sexiness of the character performed by Marilyn Monroe.

Recently, there has been much interest in translation within and between modes, that is, the various sets of signs. Luis Pérez-González gives a full discussion of audio-visual translation in particular (2014) and multimodal translation in general (2015).

1.2 *Prima la musica?*

For most genres of music with sung lyrics, the words are usually written first and then set to music. Notable exceptions are folk or children's songs for which performers are expected to create new verses; contrafacta for which new lyrics are set to existing music (frequently to turn a religious piece into a secular one or vice versa); parodies, in which new lyrics to existing music are used for mockery; and, of course, translations. During certain eras, poets could not write opera librettos any way they wished, because the various types of operatic arias each had their own prescribed meters and verse forms (Trowell, 1992: II: 1195). Nonetheless, it was still the case of *prima le parole e poi la musica* (first the words and then the music) in order of creation.

However, many believe it is the opposite in order of importance: *prima la musica e poi le parole* (first the music and then the words). At least two operas, from the eighteenth and twentieth centuries, have as their main theme the relative importance of words and music: the directly named *Prima la musica e poi le parole* (1786), composed by Antonio Salieri (1750–1825) to a libretto by Giovanni Battista Casti (1724–1803); and *Capriccio* (1942), the final opera of Richard Strauss (1864–1949), composed to a libretto by Clemens Krauss (1893–1954) and the composer, based on the work of Stefan Zweig (1881–1942) and Joseph Gregor (1888–1960).

The battle between "logocentrism" and "musicocentrism" has raged for centuries, and is far from over (Gorlée, 2005b: 8).

Whatever the opinions of others, composers and lyricists have thought words to be important. In popular song and musical comedy, the librettist is always mentioned, sometimes second as with Richard Rodgers (1902–79) and Oscar Hammerstein (1895–1960), sometimes first as with William S. Gilbert (1836–1911) and Arthur Sullivan (1842–1900). Words are also important for opera, as any account of operatic history that pays attention to librettos makes plain (see, e.g., Patrick J. Smith, 1970/75, *The Tenth Muse: A Historical Study of the Opera Libretto*; Peter Kivy, 1988, *Osmin's Rage: Philosophical Reflections on Opera, Drama, and Text*; Arthur Groos and Roger Parker, 1988, *Reading Opera*; and the long article on the opera libretto by Brian Trowell, 1992, which includes an extensive bibliography). American composer Virgil Thomson (1896–1989) states flatly, "Opera writing, in my view, is a two-[person] job. It takes a poet and a composer . . ." (Thomson, 1982: 19). For more on how composers should and do treat words, see Thomson's 1989 book, *Music With Words: A Composer's View*.

Opera translator and director Donald Pippin (1926–) states the case for librettists:

I have . . . a profound and unanticipated respect for librettists. Often criticized, berated, scorned and parodied, they knew what they were doing.

They knew how to build a sturdy dramatic framework for the composer to flesh out, and collectively they created what we know as opera, the ultimate expression of passion in action. Often working from hit plays of the day, their job was to abridge, to mold in terms of musical design, to provide a precise and varied sequence of arias, duets, ensembles, finales; and above all, to get to the big scenes with a minimum of explanation. In short, the problems of a playwright, much exacerbated. Where the novelist can lavish two or three hundred pages of description and analysis, the playwright is reduced to a scene, the librettist to maybe one or two lines of recitative. (Pippin, 1998)

Whatever the actual relative merits of words and music, the prevailing opinion at any time is probably due more to fashion than anything else, especially for works of "high culture" such as operas and art songs. At the dawn of the operatic era early in the seventeenth century, when composers such as Claudio Monteverdi (1567–1643) and Francesco Cavalli (1602–76) ruled the operatic roost, operas were known by the names of their composers. However, according to Carrie Churnside, citing the research of Ellen Rosand:

Mid-century the situation reversed, with more than half of the libretti printed between 1637 and 1675 failing even to give the name of the composer. During this period . . . [composing music] was a "service profession." (Churnside, 2014: 63)

Today, composers again predominate: most people other than opera professionals are hard-pressed to name the librettists of even their favorite works. Indeed, for some theorists, words are little more than a pretext for composing music. According to Susanne K. Langer (1895–1985), "music swallows words . . . song is music . . . When a composer puts a poem to music, he annihilates the poem and makes a song" (1953: 152–53). David Burrows echoes this sentiment:

[T]here is no redemption by association for weak composers: noble words never saved a bad tune, whereas a good tune has often rescued ignoble words. (Burrows, 1990: 79)

Langer goes so far as to say that it may be better if the words are not very good:

A poem that has perfect form, in which everything is said and nothing merely adumbrated, a work completely developed and closed, does not readily lend itself to composition. It will not give up its literary form . . . On the other hand, some very fine lyrics make excellent texts, for instance Shakespeare's incidental songs, the robust, simple verses of Burns, most of Verlaine's poetry, and notably Heine's. (Langer, 1953: 154–55)

Joseph Kerman (1924–2014) gives an example from *Le nozze di Figaro* (1786) by Wolfgang Amadeus Mozart (1756–91) of the salvation of bad lyrics by good music:

With Beaumarchais [Pierre Beaumarchais (1732–99), the author of the play (1784) on which Mozart's opera is based], the reconciliation is nothing—worse than nothing, it suggests fatally that the intricate plot had beaten the author, and that clemency was the only way he saw to unravel it. As for Da Ponte [Lorenzo da Ponte (1749–1838), Mozart's librettist], here is his contribution:

Count:	Contessa perdono!	Forgive me, Countess!
Countess:	Più docile io sono e dico di sì.	I am more gentle And answer you "yes."
All:	Ah tutti contenti saremo così.	We all are delighted To have it end thus.

With this miserable material before him, Mozart built a revelation, and saw how it could be supported by other elements in Beaumarchais's scaffolding. (Kerman, 1988: 90–91)

The role of lyrics is indeed to offer scaffolding for music, and therefore requires analysis by criteria different from those used for stand-alone poems and plays. An opera libretto, if read separately from its music, may indeed seem melodramatic in plot, weak in characterization, mediocre in poetic style, and shallow in theme. It is the music that adds dramatic sweep, complex characterization, poetic beauty, and depth of meaning. Otherwise, the libretto ought to be a spoken play. Brian Trowell explains the confusion:

The commonest cause of difficulty, overriding and compounding all others, is an inability to see (or hear) beyond the words on the printed page. Even a writer possessed of the most acute literary and dramatic sensibility will misunderstand the function and effect of the libretto unless he or she is also endowed with sufficient musicality to respond to the mysterious new compound that results from the fusion of words with music. (Trowell, 1992: II: 1193)

The transformative power of music is such that the "mysterious new compound" can be very different from the words alone. Composers are not content to merely accompany words. As opera composer Gioacchino Rossini (1792–1868) said:

[I]f the composer follows the sense of the words step by step he will compose music that is inexpressive, impoverished, vulgar, made like a mosaic, inconsequent, and ridiculous. (quoted by Trowell, 1992: II: 1201)

Thus, the libretto of *La traviata* (1853) should not be compared to the script of *Hamlet* and found wanting. The totality of *La traviata*, words and music together, is what should be compared to it. As a scaffolding for the music of Giuseppe Verdi (1813–1901), *La traviata*'s libretto by Francesco Maria Piave (1810–76) is estimable.

The bad reputation of librettos is not only due to their being mistaken for spoken plays or spoken poetry. Opinion has also been shaped by bad translations (see Apter and Herman, 1995), corrupt scores, and short synopses. A notorious example of a corrupt piano-vocal score is the still widely available 1904 Schirmer edition (later reprinted by Kalmus) for the German opera *Der Freischütz* (1821) by composer Carl Maria von Weber (1786–1826) and librettist Johann Friedrich Kind (1768–1843), edited by and including a performable English translation by Natalia Macfarren (1827–1916) and Theodore Baker (1851–1934). The entire first scene of Act III is omitted, a dialogue scene necessary for dramatic continuity.

Disdain for opera librettos can be pervasive:

As far as content is concerned, there rarely seems to be a happy medium in opera. Texts tend to be either over-simplistic or repetitive or based on fiendishly complicated historical plots. In either case, jealous baritones generally scheme the murder of amorous tenors while (not always seemingly) feeble sopranos die of unrequited love singing top Cs. (Desblache, 2009: 72)

An extreme version of this opinion, dismissing the entire genre of opera altogether, is expressed by Lehman Engel (1910–82), a historian of the Broadway musical:

In opera, romance was written for two large bovines who (perhaps luckily) never managed to reach each other until death overtook one or the other. (Engel, 1972: 82)

However, Desblache also gives a more nuanced argument:

Operas performed today are primarily 18th and 19th century works. In many cases, the text used to support the music has aged, and libretti topics that seem irrelevant to our present lives have contributed to the decline of certain pieces of work, in spite of their musical qualities. (Desblache, 2004)

This argument is interesting, but should not be extended to mean that any work of art from a culture separated historically, geographically, or linguistically from that of its audience is irrelevant. Great works of art often transcend the limitations of their specific culture. Besides, audiences may be interested in the cultural differences. Available aids to comprehension include explanatory program notes for live performances, jacket notes for recordings, and footnotes in librettos and scores. Translators can also work some explanations directly into the performable text.

Joseph Kerman ably defends the combination of operatic words and music:

Of the many current . . . attitudes towards opera, two are most stultifying: the one held by musicians, that opera is a low form of music, and the one apparently held by everybody else, that opera is a low form of drama. These attitudes stem from the exclusively musical and the exclusively literary approaches to opera . . . Opera is excellently its own form. (Kerman, 1988: 16)

Kerman's statement may be expanded to all works for the musical stage: song is neither a low form of music nor a low form of poetry. That being so, it is the task of translators for the musical stage to translate the words while being mindful of their relationship to the music, in order to bring what "is excellently its own form" from one language and culture into another.

In this book, we attempt to explain just how translators actually do this. We explore topics applicable to translation in general, such as foreignization and domestication; adaptation, re-translation, and multiple translation; cultural and temporal differences and shifts; and censorship, and show how they affect translations for the musical stage. And we explore topics specific to translations for the musical stage, such as the constraints imposed by music and musical form; the extent to which words and music each delineate character; the mechanics of rhythm, rhyme, and repetition; sound and sense; limitations imposed by the human voice; and the frequent need to put the right word on the right musical note.

2

Singable translations

Singable translations were once prized. According to Arthur Jacobs (1922–96), composers in the nineteenth century

lent not only their sanction but their active participation to the process of translation, and were ready to provide such musical modification as was thought necessary. Wagner with the French-language version of *Tannhäuser* (1861, Paris), Gounod with the English-language *Faust* (1864, London) and Verdi with the French version of *Otello* (1894, Paris) afford well-known examples. (Jacobs, 1992: IV: 787)

Musicologist Philip Gossett states:

The idea that operas, for aesthetic reasons, should be sung in the languages in which they were originally written is relatively modern . . .

Performing operas . . . in translation has always had both a practical and a cultural function . . .

Certain operas were more widely known during the nineteenth century in translation than in the original tongue. (Gossett, 2006: 380–81)

In fact, during the first half of the nineteenth century, "to be translated was an opera's infallible mark of international success" (Jacobs, 1992: IV: 787). This sentiment persisted, though often as a minority view (see Preston, 2003, and Montgomery, 2006, for the situation in the United States; and Loos, 1992, for the situation in Germany). Opera translator Andrew Porter (1928–2015), in the Introduction to his translation of Wagner's 1876 tetralogy *Der Ring des Nibelung (The Ring of the Nibelung)*, asked, "Has there ever been a great composer who did not prefer his works to be performed in the language of the country?" (1976: xv). To which Colin Graham (1931–2007), artistic director of the Opera Theatre of Saint Louis, answered: "Not one composer ever lived who wanted his opera to be performed in a language foreign to his audience" (1986: ii). Not one? Rather, as Gilbert and Sullivan said, "hardly any": "You want to understand the words? Then read them" (composer and conductor Pierre Boulez [1925–], quoted by Brian Trowell, II: 1193).

In English-speaking countries, the situation prior to Word War II can only be described as peculiar (Peyser, 1922; Orr, 1941; Tunbridge, 2013). Operas originally in French, German, and Russian were routinely performed in Italian translation, especially in the United States (including at the Metropolitan Opera in New York City) and the United Kingdom. Novelist Edith Wharton (1862–1937), without too much exaggeration, wrote in *The Age of Innocence* (1920) that

> an unalterable and unquestioned law of the musical world required that the German text of French operas sung by Swedish artists should be translated into Italian for the clearer understanding of English-speaking audiences. (Wharton, 1920: 4)

However, the three reasons for performing opera in Italian had nothing to do with arguments for or against translated words. First was the desire to accommodate the world's celebrated opera singers, most of whom were, or claimed to be, Italian. Second was to recognize the fact that many great operas *had* been written in Italian and the last internationally recognized Italian opera composer, Giacomo Puccini (1858–1924), was still a vivid memory. Third was the opinion held by some that Italian, with its generally nondiphthongized vowels and lack of guttural consonants, is the most "musical" of languages. The preference for Italian was perhaps most ludicrously expressed in 1914 in the journal *Musical America* by Edoardo Ferrari-Fontana (1878–1936), a leading Italian tenor of his day. Said Ferrari-Fontana, speaking of Richard Wagner's *Tristan und Isolde* (1859): "Wagner himself would have rejoiced if he could have heard his music free of Teutonic gutturals" (*Musical America*, February 7, 1914).

Similarly, the current absence of singable translations from many of the world's important stages probably has more to do with the exigencies of opera's and art song's international star system than with arguments about translated words. Since the end of World War II, the number of operatic superstars has decreased while the number of opera houses bidding for their services has increased. Also, contemporary superstars come from varied linguistic backgrounds, and, thanks to air travel, perform everywhere.

From the 1950s on,

> sought after singers such as Maria Callas [1923–77] could fly to New York or London, give a couple of performances and return home. Such a schedule made it difficult if not impossible to relearn an opera in a second language. Indeed, it quickly became apparent that the draw of a superstar was far more important than the ability to understand the libretto. (Anonymous, Introduction to Andrew Porter's translation of Mozart's *The Abduction from the Seraglio*, 1986: ii)

Still, there are opera companies throughout the English-speaking world that routinely perform in English, relying on performable translations for works not originally in English. Most are small companies not usually employing superstars (though some have launched them). Two major companies are the English National Opera, a London Company with origins dating back to 1889; and the Opera Theatre of Saint Louis, founded in 1976, the productions of which include many world and American premieres. The New York City Opera, founded in 1943, was another major performer of translations. However, it gradually stopped performing them, and almost never did so by the time it went bankrupt and ceased operations in 2013.

The subject of translation invariably comes up when opera companies strive to increase the size of their audiences because "[b]y far the most crucial and contentious aspect of opera accessibility today concerns the language in which the opera is sung" (Desblache, 2013: 11). However, the English-speaking world has a 300-year history of performing operas and art songs almost exclusively in foreign languages, a history that has driven away both performers and audience members who relish words. As Samuel Johnson (1709–84) famously stated, to such people opera is "an exotick and irrational entertainment, which has been always combated, and always has prevailed" (Johnson, 1779: I: 451).

Conversely, some who do not care at all about words enjoy opera only for the sense impressions it makes. For them, opera is a succession of vocal fireworks on syllables that may as well be "la la la," preferably accompanied by spectacular costumes and scenery. Their credo is, "I don't care what language I don't understand opera in."

Rudolf Bing (1902–97), former general manager of the Metropolitan Opera in New York, purportedly believed that singers should share in this ignorance. A reported conversation, perhaps apocryphal, in the 1950s between him and stage director Margaret Webster (1905–72), had Webster pressing

> "*Mister* Bing", as she called him, about inadequate rehearsal time, technical backwardness and the deficiencies of singers as actors. She told him that

she "couldn't do a thing" with Richard Tucker [1913–74], who took over the role of Don Carlo from Jussi Bjoerling [1911–60]. "It does help when the singers know what the words mean", she sensibly noted. "I entirely disagree", Bing countered. "Where would we be if singers knew the meaning of their words! They might then even start thinking about them— can you imagine a greater disaster [?]." (*Opera News*, February 1999)

Unlike Rudolf Bing, James Levine (1943–), the current music director of the Metropolitan Opera, does believe that singers should know what the words mean, but only from literal prose translations. In the Introduction to a book including literal translations, he dismisses singable translations, stating that

these [literal prose] English versions are intended to convey as precisely as possible the meaning and nuances of the originals . . . [They] enhanced the understanding of singers in the Met productions—and thus, also enhanced the impact of their performances—for they had worked from scores lacking any English, even a singing version. (Levine, 1991: x)

However, most literal translations do not show word-note matches or supply background cultural material, which diminishes their value to performers. Prose translations that do show word-note matches are those of translators Nico Castel, Anton Belov, and numerous others, published by Leyerle Publications. The Leyerle translations follow most of the helpful suggestions Brian Mossop (2013) makes regarding translations for choral singers: they provide word-by-word and phrase-by-phrase translations, as well as pronunciation guides. As for background material, it is sometimes included with translations but more often included in critical editions, such as the 1996 critical edition of the 1869 version of *Борис Годунов (Boris Godunov)* by Модест Мусоргский (Modest Musorgskiy) (1839–81), edited by Евгений Левашев (Yevgeniy Levashev).

Complex literal translations such as those published by Leyerle, together with background material such as that supplied by Levashev, may perform the functions envisioned by Levine. However, no literal translation can supply performers and audience with the fully nuanced experience of a good singable translation.

2.1 Musical and verbal constraints

Some argue that, whatever the merits of translation in general, translating sung lyrics for performance is bad. Rudolph Bing's argument above may be specious, but James Levine's is not: in order to fit the music, a singable translation must sacrifice some literality, some meaning. Levine and many others also have another reason, one they assume to be so obvious that they rarely state it: a work for the musical stage consists of words and music, and to change either, according to them, is to betray the work. They believe that it is especially important to not change the music, and argue that the sounds of the words are part of the music. Those who make this argument neglect two important facts: (1) a work for the musical stage consists not only of words and music, but of the interaction between the two; therefore, for an audience that does not understand the words, this aspect is lost and the work is automatically changed; (2) a work for the musical stage usually consists of more than words and music, and these other features, such as sets and costumes, are often ones never envisioned by the work's creators.

All translation is a process of gain and loss, and it is not the translator's task to preserve any particular aspect of the original but, as Ezra Pound (1885–1972) said, to somehow "show where the treasure lies" (*Literary Essays*, 1968: 200). That is, the translation should communicate to the target-language audience that the original work is worth its attention by revealing at least something of the special excellence of the original. This does not necessarily mean preserving the sounds of the words at all times, though it could mean creating word–music sounds that re-create the overall beauty and pleasure of the original, while also, if possible, re-creating some of the original's word–music interactions.

Another argument against singable translations into English, mentioned in the preceding section, is that Italian is *the* language of music, or at least of serious music, while English, with its many consonants and diphthongized vowels, is "unmusical":

[T]here is a widespread misapprehension that any language other than English is better suited to singing. This attitude has usually been the result of careless translations or bad composers who refuse to take into proper account the rich sounds and special cadences our language has. (Engel, 1972: 113)

Not only does this misapprehension inveigh against *any* singable work in English, but it disparages works in languages such as German, Czech, and Russian. As for English, composers who do "take into proper account the rich sounds and special cadences [of] our language" go as far back as Thomas Campion (1567–1620) and Henry Purcell (1659–95). However, despite this long history, setting English to music still has a way to go. According to American composer Virgil Thomson (1896–1989):

[T]o make the writing of English operas seem a worthy way of life, that I think is the preoccupation today of forward-looking composers in both

England and America . . . opera composed in English is still unfinished
business. (Thomson, 1989: x)

Even someone who prefers the sound of Italian to that of English can still enjoy
sung English for other reasons. For a given sense unit, Italian usually employs
more syllables than does English. While this ratio is often seen as an obstacle
that forces translators to pad lines, Donald Pippin sees it as an opportunity:

[I]n terms of pure, musical sound, Italian undeniably has the advantage;
but for sense, I prefer English. Let me give you an example: "La primavera
arriverà". Translated: Spring will come. Bear in mind: the translator has to
keep to the same number of syllables as the original. Typically: Italian nine;
English three. This means that the English version has to say something
about spring: budding flowers, gentle breezes, young love, hope, promise,
what you will. In short, this is the translator's golden opportunity to expand,
to probe, to clarify, to bring into focus something that in the original is often
vague, generalized, abstract. (Pippin, 1998)

Yet another argument against singable English translations is that the
problems entailed are insurmountable. As Eugene Nida (1914–2011) and Peter
Low, as well as other theorists, have pointed out, insofar as opera is drama
and song is mini-drama and/or poetry set to music, the problems entailed in
creating singable translations include all those entailed in translating spoken
plays and nonsung poetry. However, the presence of music changes the
nature of both drama and poetry. The action must be compressed and the
meditative moments enlarged. The poetry must have rhythms and sounds
that can be musically set and sung. Further, once the libretto is set to music,
that music is deemed largely unchangeable. But the music was composed
to fit the prosody of the source language. Nonetheless, the translated text,
despite its inherently different prosody, must be both comprehensible to the
target audience when sung and easily singable by performers.

Simply fitting target-prosody text to source-prosody music can present an
enormous problem:

The translator of poetry without musical accompaniment is relatively
free in comparison with one who must translate a song—poetry set to
music. Under such circumstances the translator must concern himself
with a number of severe restrictions: (1) a fixed length for each phrase,
with precisely the right number of syllables, (2) the observation of
syllabic prominence (the accented vowels or long syllables must match
correspondingly emphasized notes in the music), (3) rhyme, where
required, and (4) vowels with appropriate quality for certain emphatic or
greatly lengthened notes. (Nida, 1964: 177)

By "syllabic prominence," Nida means "prosody," which in this book will be divided into two syllabic properties: stress (accent) and burden. By "burden," closely related to the "quantity" of classical Greek metrics, is meant the "weight" of a syllable that determines both the minimum time required to sing it and the relative time it requires in comparison with the syllables beside it.

Peter Low (2005: 192) describes the process of translating sung words in a somewhat different way, as a pentathlon with five criteria: singability, sense, naturalness, rhythm, and rhyme. By "naturalness," Low means such things as "register and word order" (195). The success of a translation, Low states, then depends on the total score in all five "events," with a perfect score not required in any individual "event."

Other criteria, in addition to those listed by Nida and Low, include the need to sometimes place a word or idea on specific musical notes and, especially for an extended dramatic work such as an opera, the need to preserve both plot details and the way individual characters speak. Translators must also decide on the overall translation "style," a somewhat amorphous term we use to encompass such things as overall language register—high, middle, low—and time period, and the use or non-use of dialect.

After working out a set of principles for a particular translation, translators may still have to make decisions as to what aspect of the original is most important at any point in the translation: sense, sound, a rhyme, a joke, a literary allusion, a repetition—it is impossible to know in advance what may arise. Some translation theories give priority to certain aspects of the original, especially to rhyme scheme, meter, sound, repetition, and the position of certain words (such as names), and claim that one or more should be maintained throughout a translation. Those who have commissioned translations from us have sometimes requested that one or more of these aspects be preserved. (Preserving the position of words with important meanings is discussed in the next chapter.) However, the requirement that an aspect *always* be preserved is rarely explicitly stated by a translation theorist. Rather, these requirements constitute "translation norms" (Toury, 1980, 1995), unwritten rules that everyone at a given time in a given culture simply "knows." It will be shown in examples throughout this book that any attempt to unswervingly maintain even one of these aspects creates a straitjacket from which a good translation is unlikely to emerge.

Even the immutability of the music is not sacrosanct. Six musical changes are usually deemed small enough to be permissible if done sparingly and with concern for aesthetic effect (see Figure 2.1). The last two of these, which change only the verbal underlay, are usually considered to have less of an aesthetic effect than the first four, which are actual changes to the music. Composers themselves utilize any or even all six of the alterations when repeating words and phrases or when setting strophic songs.

FIGURE 2.1 *Allowable changes to the music.*

Consider the highly dissimilar prosodies of Czech and English. Czech has more unstressed syllables than English and more unstressed syllables with relatively heavy burdens. Czech is also trochaic, that is, the first syllables of words and phrases are almost always accented, and therefore almost always set on downbeats. The first syllables of phrases in largely iambic English are almost always unaccented and therefore set on upbeats. Unless some minimal changes to the music are allowed, the mis-match will almost certainly preclude meeting Low's criterion of naturalness. But the changes should be minimal, lest the overall rhythm of the Czech music be altered. Just what is "minimal" must be decided by every translator at every point of a musical score.

As an example of the process by which a Czech phrase is turned into English, consider the two-word phrase "*basa bručí*" (see Figure 2.2, which, for simplicity, shows only the soprano vocal line). Timothy Cheek translates "*basa bručí*" literally as "bass drones" (2010: 139). Like all Slavic languages, Czech has no "a" or "the," both of which would require an added pickup note in English. To avoid this, the singular "bass" must be made plural: "basses." Also, to fill up the last of the four notes, the one-syllable verb, "drones," must be replaced by a two-syllable verb, such as the gerund "droning." We could have stopped there, but believed that the phrase "basses droning" suffers from three defects: there is no finite verb, "droning" is not easy to understand ("bass" and "drone" are rarely used together in English), and "droning" is not an easy word to rhyme. Whether or not a phrase needs a finite verb depends on the rest of the sentence; in this case, we thought a finite verb to be required. And so we inserted "are" to make the progressive tense: "are droning." However, "are" uses up the second syllable of "basses," requiring a change of instrument to one that remains one syllable in the plural, such as "flutes." Flutes, of course, do not drone, and, as already mentioned, we wanted to replace "droning" anyway, by a word both more easily understandable and more easily rhymed. And so, "*basa bručí*" became "flutes are playing." Despite the altered meaning, we considered the words acceptable in context because, during this measure, two flutes (and a piccolo) *are* playing. Curiously, the only instruments droning, in the sense of playing sustained notes, are not the low (bass) instruments, but the oboes (Smetana, 1866–70, *Prodaná nevěsta*, m. 1549).

FIGURE 2.2 *Prodaná nevěsta* (The Bartered Bride), *I.5, m. 1549.*
Source: Herman and Apter (2003).

Fortunately, music not only presents problems for translators, but also opportunities. Two aural systems, the musical and the verbal, pattern sense when words are sung. Both words and music function on two levels, as meaning and as music. The words have sounds and the music can take on meaning by context or allusion, even in works not employing leitmotifs such as those used by Richard Wagner (1813–83). For example, Jacques Offenbach (1819–80) wrote a song for elves for his 1864 opera *Les fées du Rhin* (*The Fairies of the Rhine*). He re-used the music for the Barcarolle in *Les Contes d'Hoffmann* (*The Tales of Hoffmann*) (1881) where, in context, the rocking melody and the accompanying harp arpeggios signal that the singers are riding on the water in a gondola (see Lamb, 1992). This fact is not indicated by the words, which are about a "beautiful night" (see Figure 2.3 for the first four sung measures).

FIGURE 2.3 The Barcarolle from *The Tales of Hoffmann*.

Source: Offenbach, *Hoffmann*, Act IV.

Music can supply not only meaning, but also emotional resonance and dramatic color. By rising to a long, high note, Handel's melody for "The people that walked in darkness" (*Messiah*, 1741) causes the word "light" to shimmer (see Figure 2.4).

FIGURE 2.4 Messiah, *No. 11, mm. 12–14 and mm. 28–30.*

Finally, music can lessen prosodic differences. In arias, the rhythm of the spoken source language is usually at least partially distorted by the composer so as to conform to the rhythm of the music. A corresponding (though almost never identical) distortion of the target language can often bring it into synchrony with the musical phrase without loss of Low's criterion of naturalness. In speechlike recitative, on the other hand, the composer usually follows the rhythm of the spoken source language very closely, and the performer is expected to treat the written rhythm freely, to bring it even more into conformity with that of the source language. That freedom also benefits translators, because the singer is usually just as free to bend the rhythm to that of the target language.

2.2 Other factors

Some say that, no matter how good singable translations may be, they still are useless, because other factors are likely to destroy the comprehension and enjoyment of performances.

First is the training of singers. Singers act with their singing voices, which they are well trained to do, but must also engage in stage movement and physical expressiveness, and sometimes even spoken dialogue, which they are often not well trained to do. Theatrical producer and director Tyrone Guthrie (1900–1971) is reputed to have given sung drama the back-handed compliment: "If singers could act, there would be no [spoken] theater" (quoted by Joan Thorne, 2000: 20).

Acting deficiencies in singers are not always their fault nor that of their teachers. Because the training of a classical singing voice is time and labor intensive, singers have little time to devote to the art of acting. Also, they reasonably devote very little time to learning how to speak dialogue because they are rarely called upon to do so. Furthermore, because of the constraints imposed on them by the physical act of singing, singers are not as free as speaking actors to make facial expressions, assume body positions, and make body movements.

However, the expressiveness of sung music and the slow motion often imposed on body movements by music tempi can often compensate for acting deficiencies.

Sadly, in English-speaking countries, the pronunciation of sung words is often poor. English-speaking classical singing teachers, unlike their counterparts in other countries, sometimes train their pupils to scant clear diction in favor of a smooth vocal line. Lehman Engel has ranted:

The money wasted on fraudulent singing teachers [who tell singers to mispronounce English] could set the U.S. economy straight. (Engel, 1972: 214)

The most important thing that translators can do to help rectify this situation is to write good translations worth singing (and acting) well and, when necessary, good dialogue worth speaking (and acting) well. As Arthur Graham, a performer himself, has pointed out for art song:

The singer needs words that may be sung with sincerity, and part of the singer's sincerity is in the assumption that the text is worth hearing. A respected translation gives pleasure to the performer, as well as to the audience, and inspires artistic interpretation.

(A. Graham, 1989: 35)

Translators can also surreptitiously help singers to act. When we translated the baroque opera *Eraclea* (1700), with music by Alessandro Scarlatti (1660–1725) and libretto by Silvio Stampiglia (1664–1725), we substituted spoken unrhymed verse for many of the originally sung Italian recitatives, since the music for them had been lost. We feared that the singers, never having been trained to declaim verse, might lapse into a singsong recitation, so, as a performance aid, we printed the verse as if it were prose, and the singers did indeed declaim it correctly.

Unfortunately, the acoustics of opera houses can render ineffective all the efforts of singers to pronounce and project words. Many opera houses, especially in the United States, are gigantic barns in which no words can be understood from many of the seats. The large size of opera houses is partly due to economics—big houses sell more seats and bring in more money—and partly due to the peculiar 300-year history of opera in the English-speaking world having been almost always sung in languages other than English. But there is one fortunate unintended consequence of the fact that mainly smaller companies sing translations: when a translation is performed in a smaller house, it is much more readily understood.

2.3 Multiple audiences to satisfy

The translation of a novel has only three audiences: the publisher, the critics, and the readers. Works for the stage require a collaborative effort involving the participation of many groups and individuals with overlapping but not identical requirements. As shown in the discussion in Chapter 6 of Kurt Weill and Bertolt Brecht's *Die Dreigroschenoper (The Threepenny Opera)*, a purportedly single translation became three different translations, one for print, one for recording, and one for performance on stage.

For translations being considered for publication, the first audience is the publisher's editorial review board, which may have practical considerations unconcerned with art. Ricordi of Milan, Italy, for instance, requires that the notes remain as they are in the original score, with no notes added or deleted or tied. This is because the same music template is used for the publication of translations into several different languages. Ricordi also desires a translation leaning toward the literal, though it accepts a few additions and deletions. Rhyme is another of their requirements, although they do not demand that the rhyme scheme be exactly the same as in the source text.

If a translation is being commissioned for a production, it must satisfy the requirements of the artistic director of the producing company. Usually this involves discussions with the artistic director and possibly also with the conductor and stage director concerning the overall approach. At whatever point in the process the translation goes to the conductor and stage director, a few changes may have to be made, either because of an individual's taste or because of the requirements of a specific production. Once, a stage director asked us to insert the word "rape" into a dialogue, and, when he left the production, his replacement asked us to take it out! As for staging requirements, at one point in Carl Maria von Weber's one-act German *Singspiel Abu Hassan* (1811), with a libretto by Franz Carl Hiemer (1768–1822), Abu Hassan tells his wife to hide by getting into bed. He says, *"Hurtig, hurtig! Leg' dich nieder!"* ("Quickly, quickly! Lie down!"). Our performable translation is "In position! On the bed!," where "bed" rhymes with a word in a previous phrase. However, in one production there was no bed, so we provided the alternative: "In position! Hide your head" (see Figure 2.5).

Abu Hassan

FIGURE 2.5 Abu Hassan, *No. 9, mm. 48–49.*

Source: Herman and Apter (1980).

Sometimes alternate lyrics must be given for an entire musical number. For example, we changed the rhyme scheme completely in our translation of the concluding Vaudeville of Mozart *Die Entführung aus dem Serail* (*The Abduction from the Seraglio*) (1782), libretto adapted by Gottlieb Stephanie the Younger (1741–1800) from an earlier libretto by Christoph Friedrich Bretzner (1748–1807). Since some directors and conductors objected, we wrote an alternate version adhering more closely to the rhyme scheme of the original. Table 2.1 shows the two versions of the first stanza, in which Belmonte is thanking the Pasha for granting the four protagonists their freedom.

A translation must also satisfy the performers. Usually, explaining the reason for a translation choice can induce performers to accept what the translators write. This includes asking performers to sing difficult lines or to sound ugly on purpose. When they ask for reasonable adjustments or point out bad phonetic choices, translators should accommodate them. For example, in the Act I finale of the libretto by Emanuel Schikaneder (1751–1812) to Mozart's *Die Zauberflöte* (*The Magic Flute*) (1791), the character Sarastro has the word *doch* ("but, however, yet, still, nevertheless"). Mozart sets this twice on a low F (No. 8, mm. 422–23). We translated the word as "but." However, when a bass performing the role objected, believing that "but" both made him sound like a frog and could be mis-heard by the audience as "butt," we offered him "yet" as an alternative.

TABLE 2.1 *Die Entführung aus dem Serail*, No. 21a, mm. 1–14

Original German lyrics	Literal English translation

Nie werd' ich deine Huld verkennen,
   mein Dank bleibt ewig dir geweiht;
   an jedem Ort, zu jeder Zeit
werd' ich dich groß und edel nennen.
Wer so viel Huld vergessen kann,
den seh' man mit Verachtung an.
	Never will I underrate your kindness,
	my thanks always remain dedicated to you;
	in every place, in every time
	I will call you great and noble.
	Whoever can forget so much kindness
	is regarded with scorn.

Singable English translation (original rhyme scheme)	**Singable English translation (altered rhyme scheme)**

A noble heart takes satisfaction
   in giving goodness rightful praise.
   For the remainder of my days
I will recount your selfless action.
Such generosity of mind
should be acclaimed by all mankind.
(Herman and Apter, 1979a)
	I'll pay you tribute with my praises,
	and all the world will be amazed
	that you have nobly set us free.
	   Now I will be forever in your debt.
	   It is ignoble to forget
	an act of magnanimity.
	(Herman and Apter, 1979a)

Sometimes, translators should agree to provide alternate lyrics even if they can see no good reason for a change. In the Quintet in Act I of *The Magic Flute*, the three women tell Tamino and Papageno that they will be guided on their way by three boys:

Drei Knäbchen, jung, schön, hold, und weise
umschweben euch auf eurer Reise.

(*Die Zauberflöte*, No. 5, mm. 217–21)

(Three little boys, young, fair, gentle, and wise
will hover around you on your journey.)

These three boys are mysterious creatures, and their exact nature is usually left undetermined. We wished to call them "mages," which, though a somewhat archaic word, would let the audience know their mysteriousness, their magic powers, and their wisdom. (Merlin of Arthurian legend is a mage.) We also changed "boys" to "children" to allow for the very real possibility that girls might sing the roles. And so we wrote for our singable translation:

Three children will appear beside you.
They are the mages sent to guide you.

However, the singers claimed that they did not know the word "mage," that the audience would not know it either, and they refused to sing it. And so we changed our lines to:

Three children will appear beside you
with provident advice to guide you.

(Herman and Apter, 1982b)

In general, while translators should be willing to make changes, they should never allow publishers, directors, conductors, or performers to make changes on their own. Untrained sensibilities often come up with disharmonious interpolations, such as "ah, love" for a phrase heavily accented on "ah," resulting in a phrase sounding like "olive." Also, performers should not be allowed to insert words or phrases, much less whole arias, from other translations. In addition to usually being a breach of copyright, the result is almost always a clash of styles and conceptions that causes every translation involved to seem terrible.

In addition to all the parties previously mentioned, the translation must satisfy the paying audience. These people desire comprehensible lyrics that retain the characterizations and drama; they wish to laugh at the humorous parts and feel compassion at the sad parts, all conveyed by words which, with intended exceptions, can be beautifully sung. In short, the audience asks for a good show, which, for a translated work, begins, though most assuredly does not end, with a good translation.

2.4 A good example

The best way to show that good singable translations are possible is to give an example of a good one.

"Silent night, holy night," a translation of the German Christmas carol "*Stille Nacht, heilige Nacht*," has become so standard in English that many English speakers are unaware of its German origin. Begun as a set of six German verses by Joseph Mohr (1792–1848) in 1816, the carol was set to music by Franz Xaver Gruber (1787–1863) at Mohr's request and first performed in 1818. Some of the verses were translated into English by the Episcopal Priest John Freeman Young (1820–85) in 1863 and some anonymously, the whole translation appearing in the Sunday School Hymnal of Charles Lewis Hutchins (1838–1920) in 1871. The standard English version consists of three verses, translations of Mohr's verses 1, 6, and 2 in that order, and the music is slightly changed from Gruber's original. German verses 1, 6, and 2, a literal English translation, and the standard singable English translation are shown in Table 2.2. All six German verses, together with the original music, were found on May 10, 2014 on web page <www.stillenacht.at/en/text_and_music.asp>.

TABLE 2.2 *"Stille Nacht"*

Original German text	Literal English translation
Stille Nacht, heilige Nacht,	Silent night, holy night,
Alles schläft, einsam wacht	all are sleeping, awake is
Nur das traute hochheilige Paar.	only the companionable most holy couple.
Holder Knab' im lockigen Haar,	Lovely boy with curly hair,
Schlaf in himmlischer Ruh!	sleep in heavenly peace!
Schlaf in himmlischer Ruh!	Sleep in heavenly peace!
Stille Nacht, heilige Nacht,	Silent night, holy night,
Hirten erst kundgemacht	first proclaimed to the shepherds
Durch der Engel Halleluja,	by the angels' hallelujah,
Tönt es laut von fern und nah:	which rings out loudly near and far.
Christ, der Retter ist da!	Christ the Savior is here!
Christ, der Retter ist da!	Christ the Savior is here!
Stille Nacht, heilige Nacht,	Silent night, holy night,
Gottes Sohn, o wie lacht	Son of God, oh how love
Lieb' aus deinem göttlichen Mund,	smiles from Thy divine mouth,
Da uns schlägt die rettende Stund',	because the hour of salvation strikes for us,
Christ, in deiner Geburt!	Christ, in Thy birth!
Christ, in deiner Geburt!	Christ, in Thy birth!

Singable English translation
Silent night, holy night,
All is calm, all is bright
'Round yon virgin Mother and Child.
Holy infant so tender and mild,
Sleep in heavenly peace!
Sleep in heavenly peace!
Silent night, holy night,
Shepherds quake at the sight.
Glories stream from heaven afar,
Heav'nly hosts sing Alleluia;
Christ the Savior is born!
Christ the Savior is born!
Silent night, holy night,
Son of God, love's pure light.
Radiant beams from Thy holy face,
With the dawn of redeeming grace,
Jesus, Lord, at Thy birth,
Jesus, Lord, at Thy birth.

The English version utilizes allowable changes to the music discussed above. For example, in the second measure of the song, one English syllable, "ho-," is spread over two notes setting the two German syllables *hei-li-* (see Figure 2.6). This change in the verbal underlay is hardly noticed because, in the first measure, the German as well as the English has a single syllable spread over two notes (*Stil-* and Si-).

Stille Nacht, heilige Nacht

FIGURE 2.6 "Stille Nacht," *mm.* 1–2.

2.5 Singable translations versus projected captions

Some say that projected captions, in the form of surtitles, electronic librettos, or rear window captions, have made singable translations obsolete.

Captions are certainly useful in helping an audience understand what is happening on stage. They have the advantage over translated librettos read prior to a performance in that, if carefully done and carefully timed, they occur simultaneously with the performance and give the audience some idea of the interplay of the verbal and musical (and visual) elements of the work being performed. Three good articles on the craft of creating captions, with particular attention to surtitling, are those by Judi Palmer, Jacqueline Page, and Kenneth Chalmers in *Music, Text and Translation* (Minors, 2013).

Lucile Desblache writes about the specific benefits of surtitling:

The advent of surtitling, with its relatively unobtrusive ways of conveying the semantic message of operatic works, made it possible to watch and hear operas in their original language while conveying the libretto's message. In most cases, this method of transfer works extremely well and surtitles allow the audience to understand the gist of the plot. (Desblache, 2009: 73)

Desblache has also remarked on the popularity of surtitles:

[S]urtitles are overwhelmingly requested by the public. All surveys show their popularity. They are popular even when there is no language transfer issue, i.e., when the text is sung in the native tongue of the country. (Desblache, 2007: 167)

Desblache calls surtitles "relatively unobtrusive," but not everyone is of that opinion. James Levine, music director of the Metropolitan Opera, refuses to have them, and only allowed captions at all after the advent of electronic librettos, which can be turned on or off by individual viewers. And translator and stage director David Pountney (1947–) has declared:

> Surtitles are . . . a celluloid condom inserted between the audience and the immediate gratification of understanding. (Pountney, quoted by Desblache, 2007: 164)

Even good projected captions can distract from the onstage performance. Poor ones can be mis-timed or not in accord with the details of a particular production. Projected too soon, the text undercuts the singers' performance; too late, and the point of a joke may be lost; too inappropriate, and the serious becomes laughable and the humorous dull. As can happen when the captions are rented, a character in a motorcycle jacket may declaim, "Bring me my horse!" Also, captions tend to be less poetic than the original libretto and therefore, according to Kenneth Chalmers (2013), can upset not merely the poetic structure but even the musical structure as perceived by the audience.

Above all, projected captions cannot do justice to the fact that opera is drama and song is mini-drama. The audience deserves more than "the gist of the plot." Only a full *performable* translation can re-create the original work's subtleties of plot, nuances of character, and, above all, the interplay of words and music.

There is yet one more thing that performable translations can do that captions cannot: serve as models for future original English librettos. As Philip Gossett has remarked:

> Performing operas from other traditions in translation has always had both a practical and a cultural function. Practically, of course, it answered some of the objections raised in debates over the introduction of Italian operas into London during the first half of the eighteenth century: many critics perceived as absurd an entertainment performed in a language the audience did not understand. But translation, and the process of adaptation that often accompanied it, also helped works conceived in other traditions be absorbed into a national sphere and, ultimately, integrated stylistically into national traditions. (2006: 381)

In fact, it could be argued that one of the reasons why the traditions of the Italian Giuseppe Verdi (1813–1901) and the German Richard Wagner

(1813–83) have taken so long to be absorbed into English culture—the works of George Gershwin (1898–1937) and Benjamin Britten (1913–76) to the contrary notwithstanding—why only now there are a significant number of opera companies in the English-speaking world willing to tackle new (and old) works in English, is just the historical lack of performances in English translation. Also, just as a few good and great original works are usually found amid a sea of mediocre ones, so it requires the creation, and performance testing, of many translations to produce a few good and great ones. Without a significant number of worthy prior models, both original librettists and translators must forever start from scratch. Lehman Engel exaggerated, but not by much, when he said that contemporary English librettists can look back only on "translations that [are] invariably artless, awkward as poetry and as English, and remote from any naturalistic kind of expression!" (1972: 95).

3

Foreignization and domestication

eter Low's criterion of "naturalness" (2005: 192), discussed in the previous
chapter, is closely related to what others call "domestication," the opposite
of which is "foreignization." The terms are contemporary, first used by translator
and translation theorist Lawrence Venuti in a discussion of translations into English
in the United States and the United Kingdom (Venuti, 1993). However, both terms
describe long-held translation theories and approaches. John Dryden's comments
(see Chapter 1) allude to them, and the Victorian writer Matthew Arnold (1822–88)
discusses them extensively, coming down strongly on the side of domestication
(1860–61: I: 97–98, 100, 119). Others, such as Friedrich Schleiermacher
(1768–1834) and Francis W. Newman (1805–97), favor foreignization.

A domesticating translation is "smooth," written in a natural-sounding
target language. It is what the author, "if he were living, and an *Englishman*,
. . . wou'd probably have written" (Dryden, 1685, "Preface to *Sylvae*,"
Works, 3: 3–4). Friedrich Schleiermacher, in his influential essay *"Über die
verschiedenen Methoden des Übersetzens"* ("On the Different Methods of
Translating") (1813), rejects such domestication:

> In fact one might say that the goal of translating as if the source-language
> author had originally written in the target language is not only unattainable,
> but intrinsically null and void. (Translated by Douglas Robinson, in Robinson,
> 1997: 234)

A foreignizing translation emphasizes the foreign cultural elements of the
source text, with or (more often) without further explanation, so as to encourage

the intended audience to grapple with unaccustomed ideas. Schleiermacher, as paraphrased by Douglas Robinson, defined "foreignization" (though of course without actually using the term) as

> bringing the reader to the author, or training the target-language readership to accept, even to crave, translations steeped in the foreign flavour of their originals. (Robinson, 1997: 225).

Foreignization can range from extreme to slight. It can be spatial (referring to names, places, ideas, events, or customs from another part of the world), temporal (referring to names, places, ideas, events, or customs from a different era), or linguistic (calling attention to the fact that the translation is a translation), and is often a mixture of all three. If the foreignization is linguistic, the translation, as well as not being "smooth," is no longer "transparent" and the translators become "visible."

The decision to foreignize can be apolitical, such as ours to use seventeenth-century English for our translation of the French operetta *Le médecin malgré lui* (*The Doctor in Spite of Himself*) (see Chapter 7). Or it can be an ethical choice, a decision not to expropriate a literary work by domesticating it, or perhaps not to translate it at all if even a foreignizing translation cannot sufficiently avoid expropriation. This moral dilemma is particularly relevant if the literary work is from a subservient culture, such as that of a colony or former colony, and the translation is into a dominant culture, such as that of the colonizer. An example of such expropriation is the treatment of Czech operas by the majority German-speaking population of the Austro-Hungarian Empire. The loose 1893 German adaptation by Max Kalbeck (1850–1921) of *Prodaná nevěsta* (*The Bartered Bride*) (1866–70), a Czech comic opera composed by Bedřich Smetana (1824–84), was arrogantly advertised to the rest of the world as the "definitive" version. This lie (there is no other word for it) succeeded to the extent that there are still many information sources, including online sources, that refer to the opera by its German title, *Die verkaufte Braut*, rather than by its actual Czech title even when not specifically discussing German translations, and, as discussed in the next chapter, several English "translations" are of Max Kalbeck's adaptation rather than of the actual opera.

For some time now, following Arnold and Dryden, domestication has been the fashion for the translation of most literary genres. But Schleiermacher, as indicated above, favored foreignization, as did Francis W. Newman, who, in *Homeric Translation in Theory and Practice* (1861), took issue directly with Arnold. More recently, Vladimir Nabokov (1899–1977) ranted:

> I constantly find in reviews of verse translations the following kind of thing that sends me into spasms of helpless fury: "Mr. (or Miss) So-and-

so's translation reads smoothly". In other words, the reviewer of the "translation", who neither has, nor would be able to have, without special study, any knowledge whatsoever of the original, praises as "readable" an imitation only because the drudge or the rhymster has substituted easy platitudes for the breathtaking intricacies of the text. "Readable", indeed! A schoolboy's boner is less of a mockery in regard to the ancient masterpiece than its commercial interpretation or poetization. "Rhyme" rhymes with "crime", when Homer or *Hamlet* are rhymed. The term "free translation" smacks of knavery and tyranny. It is when the translator sets out to render the "spirit"—not the textual sense—that he begins to traduce his author. The clumsiest literal translation is a thousand times more useful than the prettiest paraphrase. (1955: 71)

Lawrence Venuti maintains, in *The Translator's Invisibility: A History of Translation* (1995/2008), that the translator's quest for invisibility has led to overly domesticated translations, and that there should be both more foreignness and more texts or parts of texts that call attention to themselves as translations. While he regards some domestication as inevitable, he sees transparency as an illusion:

By producing the illusion of transparency, a fluent translation masquerades as true semantic equivalence when it in fact inscribes the foreign text with a partial interpretation, partial to English-language values, reducing if not simply excluding the very difference that translation is called on to convey. (1995/2008: 20–21)

In short, Venuti claims that translation is an inherently contradictory process: insofar as it domesticates a foreign text, which it must at least to some extent in order to change the source language into the target language, it negates its very purpose, which is to somehow make the source text accessible, complete and unchanged, to the target audience. Therefore, he says, translators should reduce domestication to the minimum and increase foreignization to the maximum extent possible. Venuti further maintains that foreignizing, nontransparent, visible translations are needed for translators to begin receiving recognition for their work:

The translator's invisibility is thus a weird self-annihilation, a way of conceiving and practicing translation that undoubtedly reinforces its marginal status in Anglo-American culture . . . The typical mention of the translator in a review takes the form of a brief aside in which, more often than not, the transparency of the translation is gauged. This, however, is an infrequent occurrence [because the translator is often not mentioned at all and] . . . the fact that the text under review is a translation may be overlooked. (1995/2008: 8)

Contrary to the current fashion for most literary genres, singable translations still incorporate some foreignization. Indeed, the very presence of source-culture music exerts a foreignizing influence whenever a singable translation is performed. Also, foreignizing strictures are sometimes imposed on singable translations, strictures such as requirements to retain foreign proper nouns and rhyme schemes or to match source-language sounds.

A well-conceived foreignizing translation can usually overcome any reluctance on the part of the audience to encounter something strange. On the other hand, if foreignizing devices are applied blindly and injudiciously, the resulting translations are incomprehensible or silly. When this happens, the reader or audience may believe that the original authors or the translators or both do not know how to write singable lyrics. Because this has happened all too often, foreignizing singable translations have *not* reduced the translators' "marginal status in Anglo-American culture." As indicated by Venuti above, translators may not be mentioned at all in reviews of performances, except perhaps to be severely criticized. In our own experience, a highly favorable review of a production of our English translation of Mozart's *The Magic Flute* failed to even mention that it was sung in an English translation, much less name us as the translators; a different translator's handling of Puccini's *La bohème* was severely panned by critics when, in our opinion, the defects in the production were due entirely to the inadequacy of one of the lead performers.

3.1 Foreign words

The most obvious way to foreignize a translation is to leave in or add a few phrases in the source language.

La fille de Madame Angot (*Madame Angot's Daughter*) (1872) is a French comic operetta with music by Charles Lecocq (1832–1918) and a libretto by the team of Clairville (1811–79), Siraudin (1813–83), and Koning (1842–94), drawing on characters created by the playwright A. F. E. Maillot (1747–1814) at the turn of the nineteenth century. To situate the action in France, we put some optional French words into the spoken dialogue of our English translation, to be used or not by the stage director and performers. For example, when a character says *"Oui, mesdames"* ("Yes, ladies"), we give both the French and English as options, though, of course, the rest of the character's statement continues in English. A few lines later, when another character speaks of the cost of an item, we state the amount in *livres* rather than dollars.

A source text itself may include a few foreign words, that is, words not in the source language, to achieve some effect. If their comprehensibility or lack thereof are about the same for both source-language and target-language speakers, they should probably not be translated, because both audiences, source-language and target-language, will experience the same effect. However, if the foreign words are likely to be comprehensible to source-language speakers but incomprehensible to target-language speakers, they should probably be translated. Since translation directly into the target language eliminates the original foreignizing effect, the words can be translated into a language other than the target language if the result is comprehensible to the target-language audience. As an example, consider a phrase in the Czech opera *Prodaná nevěsta* (literally, *The Sold Bride*, usually rendered into English as *The Bartered Bride*) (1866–70) by composer Bedřich Smetana (1824–84) and lyricist Karel Sabina (1813–77). The phrase, uttered by the Principal Comedian in Act III, Scene 2, is "*kumstus kumstórum.*" The speaker has Czechified the German word "*Künstler*" ("artist"). Despite the fact that such borrowings from German were frowned upon by the Czech intelligentsia, the speaker has attempted to elevate himself and his lowly troupe to the realm of high art by further expanding the borrowing into a higfalutin Latinized phrase. Our translation, "*artistus artistorum,*" changes the Latinized Czechified German into Latinized French.

Some librettos are written entirely in a "foreign" language, that is, a language not likely to be understood by any audience. Two works that come to mind are *Oedipus Rex* (1927, revised 1948) by Igor Stravinsky (1882–1971), with a Latin libretto taken from a translation of the ancient Greek play, and *Satyagraha* (1979) by Philip Glass (1937–), with a Sanskrit libretto taken from the *Bhagavad Gita*. Stravinsky may have thought *Oedipus Rex* to be so familiar a work that it needed no translation. Performances of *Satyagraha* are usually accompanied by supertitles in the language of the audience. Whatever the reasons for the languages of the librettos, neither composer is likely to welcome (or have welcomed) performable translations.

Sometimes, even a work with no foreign words can benefit from a translation that includes a few that are foreign. At the end of Act II of Giuseppe Verdi's *La traviata* (1853), some men at a party pretend to be Spanish bullfighters. Their first line in the original Italian is "*Di Madride noi siam matadori*" ("We are matadors from Madrid") (No. 7, mm. 131–33). To accentuate the pretense, we translated this into Spanish: "*Buenas noches, señoras y señores*" ("Good evening, ladies and gentlemen"), and then continued our translation in English.

Without a supporting context or an obvious reason for them, foreign words are usually inappropriate. In an English-language production of *La traviata*, the word "*andiam*" ("let's go") was left in Italian. The sudden switch out of English was not an instance of Italian foreignization; it was merely odd.

3.2 Wardour Street

A second way to foreignize is to write in a foreignizing diction, an English that is not quite English. One such form of English is the pseudo-archaic diction known as "Wardour-Street," so-named by William Morris (1834–96), a British artist, writer, and translator, after the antique and theatrical costume shops located on that London street. Wardour Street is an amalgam of obsolete words from many different periods, mingled with contemporary language to create a diction no one ever actually spoke. Not too long ago, translators into English routinely foreignized certain works by employing this diction, in order to indicate that the events described happened "long ago and far away."

Some literary events do happen "long ago and far away" and for them Wardour Street can be a good choice. Consider the famous 1869 rendition by Dante Gabriel Rossetti (1828–82) of the medieval French *Ballade des dames du temps jadis* (The Ballad of Dead Ladies) by François Villon (1431–63?). Rossetti's translation of the second stanza is:

> Where's Héloise, the learned nun,
>   For whose sake Abeillard, I ween,
> Lost manhood and put priesthood on?
>   (From Love he won such dule and teen!)
>   And where, I pray you, is the Queen
> Who willed that Buridan should steer
>   Sewed in a sack's mouth down the Seine? . . .
> But where are the snows of yester-year?
>   (Rossetti, 1961: 100–101; Rossetti's ellipses)

According to the *Oxford English Dictionary*, "ween" and "teen" went out of common use in the seventeenth century, "dule" by the end of the sixteenth century, and "yester-year" was coined by Rossetti himself.

In the poem, "Buridan" refers to Jean Buridan (1300–1358), an Aristotelian philosopher, logician, and scientific theorist. The Queen is Jeanne of Burgundy (1292–1329), widow of Philip V, called *le Long*, that is, "tall" (1292/3–1322), who, according to legend, ordered people who displeased her to be dropped into the Seine River from a tower. These are medieval persons from the century before Villon, but the whole collection of dead women (and men) in the poem is much more widely scattered over time. In the first stanza, for example, Villon mentions Flora and Thaïs, ancient Roman and Greek courtesans, respectively, as well as the mythological Echo. Thus, Rossetti's language conveys the hazy time sense of the original.

Victorians and Edwardians used Wardour Street for telling myths, legends, and fairy tales, and for translating such material. Howard Pyle employed it for re-telling the legend of Robin Hood (1883), as did Henry Gilbert (1912). Unfortunately, Victorian and Edwardian translators of poems from the past used Wardour Street so indiscriminately that it came to be disparaged as "translatorese."

Frederick Jameson (1839–1916) used it to translate Richard Wagner's myth-based *Der Ring des Nibelungen* (*The Ring of the Nibelung*) (1876), despite the fact that Wagner was Jameson's contemporary. An excerpt from his translation is shown in Table 3.1, part of a song the Rhine daughters sing to Alberich in *Das Rheingold* (*The Rheingold*) (1869), the first part of the *Ring*.

TABLE 3.1 *Das Rheingold*, Scene 1, pp. 39–40.

Original German text	Literal English translation
Schäme dich, Albe!	Shame on you, elf!
schilt nicht dort unten!	do not scold down there!
höre was wir dich heissen.	hear what we tell you.
Warum, du Banger,	Why, you fearful one,
bandest du nicht	did you not hold on to
das Mädchen, das du minn'st?	the girl you woo?

Wardour-Street translation by Frederick Jameson
Shame on thee, imp!
why chid'st thou down yonder?
hear the words that we sing thee!
Say wherefore, faint-heart,
didst thou not hold
the maiden thou dost love?
(Jameson, 1896: 25–26)

Whatever mythologizing effect Jameson's translation may have had for Victorians, the comprehension of modern audiences is likely to stop at "chid'st" in the first line.

3.3 Homophony

Another foreignizing practice is to make the translation homophonic, that is, to keep the sounds of translated words as close as possible to those of the source-language words. The sounds of the original words are part of the poetry, say advocates of this practice, and should therefore be reproduced as closely as possible (see Hilson, 2013). Advocates of homophony for singable translations argue that the sounds of the sung words are part of the musical impression.

Extreme examples of homophonic translations of nonsung poetry are Louis and Celia Zukofsky's versions of poems by the ancient Roman Catullus. Here are the first two lines of Poem 26:

> Furi, villula vestra non ad Austri
> flatus opposita est neque ad Favoni
> > (Mynors, 1958: 19; syllable-opening *u* regularized to *v*)

> (Furius, your cottage is not exposed
> to the blowing South Wind nor to the West Wind)

For their second line, the Zukofskys (1969) say that Furius has no "flaw to oppose a taste naked to Favonius." Most would agree that such extreme homophony is absurd. Those who wish to hear the sounds of a source poem without comprehension are free to read it aloud (or have it read aloud to them) in the source language.

While excess is to be avoided, a moderate degree of homophonic translation is advisable in a singable translation, since a singer's voice quality is influenced by the sounds of words in conjunction with pitch. Later in this book, we will discuss how and when to imitate foreign sounds. However, again we warn that sudden, unintegrated foreignization sounds silly. A line in Mozart's *Die Zauberflöte* (*The Magic Flute*) (1791), "*Nur stille! stille stille! stille! bald dringen wir in Tempel ein!*" (No. 21, mm. 744–58) ("Just [be] quiet! quiet! quiet! quiet! soon we will break into the temple!"), was translated into English by Ruth and Thomas Martin as "Now stilly, stilly, stilly, stilly, as we approach the temple door" (1941/51: 159).

3.4 Important words

Another foreignizing stricture would keep important meanings on the same musical notes as in the original. Proponents argue that, since all words can be considered to be intimately tied to the musical notes on which they are set, important words should not be moved from their original musical positions—regardless of what this does to English grammar.

This stricture is often applied full strength to translations of Wagner's *Der Ring des Nibelungen* (*The Ring of the Nibelung*) (1876) because Wagner's use of leitmotifs often makes the notes on which words are set part of their very meaning, not just of their emotional or musical effect.

Andrew Porter (1928–2015) points out the losses and gains this entails. He says that he strove

> [t]o keep important words—such as *Liebe, Leid, Ring, Rhein*—and especially the proper names exactly where Wagner placed them. Their sounds and rhythms often have a motivic significance; they coincide with particular harmonies . . . [Therefore, instead of writing] "You who inspired me to feel this love", [I wrote] "You who this love in my heart inspired", which reads less well but makes far better musical sense. For the same reason, Brünnhilde's "One thing I did know, that you still loved the Wälsung", . . . was changed to " . . . that the Wälsung you loved." (1976: xv–xvi)

Other translators have treated word positions in the *Ring* as Porter does. Table 3.2 gives an excerpt from *Das Rheingold* (*The Rhinegold*) (1869), the first part of the *Ring*, sung by the character Mime, together with the Edwardian translation of Margaret Armour (1860–1943). Whatever its other virtues or faults, Armour's translation is comprehensible and, in this short excerpt, preserves the musical positions of eight important words: "evil," "arts," "Fashioned," "Alberich," "mighty," "magic," "Trembling," and "marvel."

TABLE 3.2 *Das Rheingold*, Scene 3, p. 173

Original German text	Literal English translation
Mit arger List	With crafty cunning
schuf sich Alberich	Alberich shaped
aus Rheines Gold	from the Rhine's gold
einen gelben Reif:	a yellow ring:
seinem starken Zauber	at its mighty magic
zittern wir staunend . . .	we tremble in wonder . . .
Edwardian translation by Margaret Armour	
By evil arts	
Fashioned Alberich	
A yellow ring,	
From the Rhinegold forged,	
At whose mighty magic	
Trembling we marvel . . .	
(Armour, 1911: 41)	

Today, for works not employing musical leitmotifs (and even, to some extent, for works which do), most commissioners of singable translations do not require that the positions of important words be preserved, with one notable exception: names. When we were asked to translate Verdi's *Ernani* (1844), we were enjoined to keep names on their original notes when possible. Our editors, looking at our translation of "*Sorta è la notte, e Silva non ritorna!*" ("Night has fallen, and Silva has not returned!") (see Figure 3.1), asked that our performable translation, "Darkness has fallen, and still no sign of Silva," be changed to "Darkness has fallen, and Silva still is absent." Their suggestion does fit the music and, unlike our line, preserves the position of the name. However, we sang our translation and theirs, arguing that Verdi would prefer the one that sounded better, and our editors, with whom we enjoyed working and who made many helpful suggestions, let our translation stand.

FIGURE 3.1 Ernani, *No. 3, mm. 12–15.*
Source: Herman and Apter (1994).

When the English forms of proper nouns are much better known to English speakers than the forms used in the source text, it is probably better to use the English forms. This, of course, is a domesticating gesture, and precludes maintaining the musical positions of the words if the English forms have a different number of syllables or a different accent pattern than those in the source text. Some examples are Russian "*Москва*" ("*Moskva*") with the accent on the second syllable versus English "Moscow" with the accent on the first syllable; and Italian "*Inghilterra*" versus English "England." Even the names of persons can have a different number of syllables if the names are inflected. For example, Jeník is the male protagonist of the Czech opera *Prodaná nevěsta* (*The Bartered Bride*) (1866–70). "Jeník" is the two-syllable nominative form, and the only form likely to be used in English. However, the Czech text also uses inflected forms such as the four-syllable "Jeníkovi."

Sometimes translators change names for historical accuracy.

Consider *Maria Stuarda* (*Mary Stuart*) (1835), an Italian opera with music composed by Gaetano Donizetti (1797–1848) to a libretto by Giuseppe Bardari (1817–61). The historical English names were all Italianized according to Italian custom of the time. Our decision to restore the characters' historical names in our translation also required changing the musical notes on which the names are set. A good example occurs near the beginning of Act I, when the chorus and the

Earl of Shrewsbury ask Queen Elizabeth to show Mary mercy. The seventeen-syllable, mostly iambic Italian line, including the Italianized name "Elisabetta," is "*Il bel cor d'Elisabetta segua i moti di pietà*" ("Let the good heart of Elizabeth follow the promptings of pity"). Our singable translation is shown in Figure 3.2.

Earl of Shrewsbury

FIGURE 3.2 Maria Stuarda, No. 1, *mm. 236–39*
"Elisabetta" becomes "Elizabeth."
Translation by Mark Herman and Ronnie Apter
Source: Herman and Apter (1997).

In her 1998 translation, Amanda Holden sometimes used a different strategy: when changing names, rather than re-setting them, she simply eliminated them when that could be done without harming the libretto. An excerpt from her translation is shown in Figure 3.3.

Earl of Shrewsbury

FIGURE 3.3 Maria Stuarda, No. 1, *mm. 236–39,*
"Elisabetta" is eliminated
Translation by Amanda Holden
Source: Holden (1998).

If a foreign name appears very frequently in a libretto, it may be impractical or undesirable to use a common English equivalent, even if one exists. One such name occurs in *Carmen* (1875) by Georges Bizet (1838–75). The name of the title character in the French libretto is foreign in that Bizet usually accents it on the second syllable, whereas the corresponding English name is accented on the first syllable. The corresponding name in Spanish, the native language of the character if not of the opera in which she appears, is also accented on the first syllable. However, Carmen is often addressed by name alone, or by name with very few additional words, leaving few or no musical notes on which to move the name so that it would be properly accented in English. Domesticating the name would therefore require removing it, which would prevent, among other things, José's cry "*Ah! Car-MEN! ma Car-MEN*" (No. 27, mm. 205–7) at the end of the opera.

If source-language names have meaningful resonances, or actual meanings, it may be desirable to domesticate them into the target language. In Smetana and Züngel's Czech opera *Dvě vdovy* (*Two Widows*) (1874/77), the name "Mumlal" resonates with the meanings "mutterer" and "grumbler." "Grumple" would retain some of the same resonances in English, and translators must decide whether or not to call him that. In Wagner's *Ring*, many of the names have meaningful resonances: the first parts of the names "Woglinde," "Wellgunde," and "Flosshilde" resonate with "wave," "wave/billow," and "flow/fin," respectively.

Sometimes it is desirable to change a name because, while it has a source-language meaning, it has *no* common target-language equivalent. In *The Beggar's Opera* (1728) by John Gay (1685–1732), the police chief's name is Lockit. Bertolt Brecht (1898–1956) changed it to Tiger Brown in *Die Dreigroschenoper* (*The Threepenny Opera*) (1928) "because the pun in 'Lockit' wouldn't speak to a German audience even in translation" (Mordden, 2012: 105).

It is also sometimes desirable to leave names in their foreign forms even if they do have target-language equivalents, or even exact translations. For example, the Russian city *Нижний Новгород* (*Nízhniy Nóvgorod*, the former name of *Горький* [*Gór'kiy*]) would not usually be called "Lower Newtown," although that is the English translation of the Russian name.

3.5 Rhyme

Many Victorian and Edwardian translators obeyed a stricture that held that the original poetic form should be exactly reproduced, no matter what else was lost (see Apter, 1984; 86–87). This stricture was applied to translated art songs and libretti even if the musical setting ignored the poetic form. When imposed upon a translation from a rhyme-rich language such as Italian into a rhyme-poor language such as English, this stricture can be foreignizing indeed. And it ignores the fact that there may be no way to reproduce the meter at all. Syllable-count meters are possible in languages such as French which, when spoken, pronounce all syllables with approximately the same burden. English does not. Syllable-count verse does not sound metrical in English—listen to some syllable-count poems by Marianne Moore (2003), who did not expect them to sound metrical. Neither writing an English line with the same number of syllables as in the source nor using English poetic feet that roughly reproduce the syllable count of the source reproduces the original meter.

Ways to alter the rhymes (and sometimes even the meter) to accommodate English while still fitting the music are discussed later in this book. Here we will only give an example of the harm that a slavish reproduction of rhyme can cause.

Consider a few lines from Verdi's *Il trovatore* (*The Troubadour*) (1853) (Salvadore Cammarano, 1801–52, librettist) as translated by the Victorian Natalia Macfarren (1827–1916) (see Table 3.3).

TABLE 3.3 *Il trovatore*, No. 3, mm. 166–81

Original Italian text	Literal English translation
Di geloso amor sprezzato arde in me tremendo il foco! Il tuo sangue, o sciagurato, ad estinguerlo fia poco!	The terrible fire of my spurned, jealous love burns in me! Your blood, wretch, would be too little to extinguish it!

Singable English translation by Natalia Macfarren
Raging flames in my breast are stirring, From my vengeance now naught can save thee, Death hath mark'd thee with shaft unerring, Traitor, dost thou dare to brave me? (Macfarren, 1898: 41)

In order to end-rhyme (or off-rhyme) *abab* as in the original, Macfarren inverts English word order from the normal "flames are stirring in my breast," "naught can save thee from my vengeance," and "unerring shaft." The three inversions and the use of the archaic second-person singular (a la Wardour Street) violate Peter Low's criterion of naturalness (2005: 195). In addition, Macfarren's foreignization is too generalized. There is no attempt to make the words seem Italian (the location of the opera's creation) or Spanish (the location of the opera's setting) or from the fifteenth century (the time in which the opera is set). Macfarren's diction simply sets the story "long ago and far away" and dissipates the force of the Italian words.

3.6 Repetition

Another proposed foreignizing stricture is that repetitions in the translation should exactly reproduce repetitions in the original. The reasoning behind this is that, just as musical repetitions are part of the music, so are verbal repetitions. However, exact repetition may be impossible. In the trio of the final scene of *Il trovatore*, the gypsy Azucena repeats the ten-syllable phrase "*in sonno placido io dormirò*" ("*in peaceful slumber I will sleep*"). Our ten-syllable singable translation is "and I will peacefully lie down to sleep." In some repeats, Verdi omits "*io*" ("I"). However, "*io*" is in the position of the English word "lie," and an exact syllable-for-syllable repeat would be the nonsensical "and I will peacefully down to sleep." Instead, we eliminated the syllable and still fit the music by changing the phrase to the nine-syllable "and I will sleep, will peacefully sleep."

Even if exact reproduction of repetition is possible, it may be undesirable because it precludes other, more desirable, elements, including other foreignizing elements.

In the four-line refrain of the "Political Song" near the end of Act I of Lecocq's *La fille de Madame Angot (Madame Angot's Daughter)* (1872), the first line is variable while the other three lines are repeated exactly each time the refrain is sung. There are also internal repeats in the second and third lines. Table 3.4 gives the French lyrics, a literal English translation, and a singable translation of our devising which follows the French repeats exactly. The three people mentioned are Paul François Jean Nicolas, vicomte de Barras (1755–1829), the executive leader of the French Directory regime of 1795–99; Anne Françoise Élisabeth Lange (1772–1816), an actress at the Comédie-Française and the Théâtre Feydeau; and the fictional financier Larivaudière. In *La fille de Madame Angot*, Lange is the mistress of both Barras and Larivaudière but, in reality, it is unlikely that Barras was one of Lange's numerous lovers.

TABLE 3.4 *La fille de Madame Angot*, The Refrain of the "Political Song"

Original French lyrics	Literal English translation
Refrain 1:	**Refrain 1:**
Barras est roi, Lange est sa reine,	Barras is king, Lange is his queen,
c'n'était pas la peine, c'n'était pas la peine,	it wasn't worth the trouble, it wasn't worth the trouble,
non pas la pein' assurément	certainly not worth the trouble
de changer la gouvernement!	to change the government!
Refrain 2:	**Refrain 2:**
Voilà comme cela se mène;	That is how it is;
c'n'était pas la peine, *etc.*	it wasn't worth the trouble, *etc.*

TABLE 3.4 *Continued*

Refrain 3:	Refrain 3:
Il chiffonne la souveraine,	He [Larivaudière] rumples the queen,
c'n'était pas la peine, *etc.*	it wasn't worth the trouble, *etc.*

Singable Translation which follows the French Repeats

Refrain 1:
Lange and Barras! It wasn't worth it,
it just wasn't worth it, it just wasn't worth it,
just wasn't worth the pain we spent
to overthrow the government!

Refrain 2:
Nothing has changed and so we curse it,
it just wasn't worth it, etc.

Refrain 3:
What have we done? We can't reverse it,
it just wasn't worth it, etc.

In the French lyrics, the phrase *"c'n'était pas la peine"* is pithy and interesting, and also demonstrates the elisions characteristic of nineteenth-century Parisian market slang (about which more below). What the translation needs is something equally pithy and, if possible, foreignizing: it should signal France as the setting. The English version in Table 3.4 is neither pithy nor interesting nor particularly French, and also not particularly easy to sing. If allowed to use a different pattern of repetition, we can create a much more singable translation. We can also signal the French setting by including the common English translation of the famous French expression *"plus ça change, plus c'est la même chose"* ("the more things change the more they stay the same"). Our three refrains, each repeating only the last two lines, and also rhyming *abcb* rather than the original *aabb*, run:

Refrain 1:
Viva Barras and mistress Lange,
the king and queen in all but name!
Did monarchy fall to prove the more
things change the more they stay the same?

Refrain 2:
Viva Barras, Larivaudière,
and all the rest who are to blame!
Did monarchy fall *etc.*

Refrain 3:

Viva Larivaudière and Lange,
who never think to blush for shame!
Did monarchy fall *etc.*

(Herman and Apter, 1989)

We also change the music slightly by tying together some notes to reduce the number of English syllables, and by shifting the break after the second *"peine"* in French back a syllable, to a position before the word "Did" in English. The music for the first refrain is shown in Figure 3.4.

Allegro non troppo

Bar-ras est   roi, Lange est___   sa   rei-ne, c'n'é-tait pas la
Vi - va Bar - ras and mis - tress Lange, the king___ and

pei-ne, c'n'é-tait pas la   pei - ne, non pas la pein' as - su - ré-
queen in all___ but name! Did mo-nar-chy fall to prove the

ment   de   chang - er   le   gou - ver - ne - ment!
more things change the   more they stay   the same?

FIGURE 3.4 La fille de Madame Angot.
First refrain of the "Political Song".
Source: Herman and Apter (1989).

3.7 Nonsense words

Nonsense words are composed of syllables used just for sound or comic effect. Most translations leave them as they are in the source language. This has a foreignizing effect, because nonwords almost always incorporate the allowable sounds and sound combinations of a specific language. "Bibbidi-Bobbidi-Boo," the title of a 1948 song by Al Hoffman, Mack David, and Jerry Livingston, first heard in the 1950 Walt Disney film *Cinderella*, and "Supercalifragilisticexpialidocious," the title of a song by Richard M. and Robert Sherman written for the 1964 Walt Disney film *Mary Poppins*, are unmistakably *English*, as is "Wadoo, zim bam boddle-oo," part of the refrain of "It Ain't Necessarily So" (George and Ira Gershwin, *Porgy and Bess*, 1935).

When most or all of a source is composed of nonsense words, it makes no sense to leave them untranslated. A famous example of a much-translated nonsense poem is Lewis Carroll's "Jabberwocky" (Carroll, 1871: 153), the first line of which is, "Twas brillig, and the slithy toves." Two well-known translations are Robert Scott's German (1872), "*Der Jammerwoch: Es brillig war. Die schlichte Toven,*" and Frank L. Warren's French (1931), "*Le Jaseroque: Il brilgue: les tôves lubricilleux.*" These and other translations into languages ranging from Afrikaans to Welsh can be found at <http://www.waxdog.com/jabberwocky/translate.html> (accessed September 29, 2014).

Few works for the musical stage are written like "Jabberwocky." One that is, *La figlia del mago* (*The Sorcerer's Daughter*) (1981, revised 1991), by composer Lorenzo Ferrero (1951–-) and librettist Marco Ravasini (dates not available), is discussed in Chapter 7. However, several works for the musical stage include just a few nonsense words. In that case, translating the nonsense is usually optional.

In *Das Rheingold* (1869), the first part of Richard Wagner's *Der Ring des Nibelungen* (*The Ring of the Nibelung*) (1876), non-words are the first sounds uttered by singers following the long 136-measure orchestral introduction. (This introduction is minimalist in that it consists entirely of inversions and decorations of the E-flat major chord.) What Woglinde, one of the Rhine daughters, sings is:

Weia! Waga!
Woge, du Welle,
walle zur Wiege!
wagala weia!
wallala, weiala weia!

The literal meaning of the second and third lines is "Billow, you wave, surge to the cradle!" Lines 1, 4, and 5 consist of nonsense words, suggesting the rocking motion of the waves of the Rhine River. Also, the words alliterate on the "v" sound (spelled "w" in German) and have assonance: "*weia, waga, woge, Wiege, wagala*" and "*Welle, walle, wallala, weiala.*"

Most translators do not attempt to create equivalents in English. In our own domesticating translation, we do. Suggested by the German word "*Wiege*" (cradle), our new nonsense words suggest a lullaby:

Lula leia,
billowing water,
swirling in waves of
shimmering wonder,
lulala, lalala leia!
        (Herman and Apter, 1983b)

3.8 Slang

Slang is notoriously difficult to translate, and many translators do not try. Slang usually marks a time as well as a place, and can enter and leave a language so quickly that a translation employing it can seem out of date almost as soon as it is completed. For example, "groady to the max" ("grotesque or repellent in the extreme") entered English in the 1960s and is now virtually gone. But not all slang is short-lived; according to the *OED*, "ain't" has been in the language since 1778.

The omission of slang smoothes and domesticates a translation. However, omission may also falsify a translation if slang is a substantial component of the source text.

Charles Lecocq's *La fille de Madame Angot* (*Madame Angot's Daughter*) (1872) includes a substantial amount of slang. This French comic operetta, once popular worldwide, preceded and greatly influenced the subsequent operettas of Gilbert and Sullivan. The libretto forcefully demonstrates that one response to disaster is laughter. The original Madame Angot, with her upper-class wealth (and pretensions) and fishwife manners, was created after the disastrous French Revolution; the operetta about her daughter, set in the time period immediately following the Revolution, was created after the disastrous Siege of the Paris Commune. During the 1871 Siege, which occurred a few months after France lost the Franco-Prussian War, the French Army of Versailles killed at least 20,000 fellow Frenchmen.

Two forms of slang are utilized in *La fille de Madame Angot*. One is the affected "deboned" diction used by the fashionable set, such as the *incroyable* and conspirator Trénitz. In this diction, more specifically called a sociolect since it is consciously used by a segment of society to set itself apart, many of the consonants found in standard French are eliminated. This is especially true for *r*, and so *"bonjour," "toujour,"* and *"gloire"* are pronounced *"bonjou," "toujou,"* and *"gloie."* These words are directly "translatable" into English by dropping *r*'s and a final *g*, to yield, in context, "evenin," "evah," and "glowy." Depending on one's point of view, such a translation is foreignizing, since it includes words not in standard English, or domesticating, since it brings a foreign aspect of the original into a form readily comprehensible to English speakers. In fact, such a translation is both; translations often cannot be slotted into neat categories.

The other form of slang used in *La fille de Madame Angot* is that of the Parisian market, a form of slang *not* readily translatable into English. Table 3.5 gives an insult duet between Clairette (Mme Angot's daughter) and Mlle Lange.

TABLE 3.5 *La fille de Madame Angot*, No. 10, mm. 85–127

Original French lyrics	Literal English translation
MLLE LANGE:	**MLLE LANGE:**
Je ne t'en veux pas, petite,	I do not hold it against you, little one,
mais dans ce bien heureux temps,	but in that very happy time,
je t'aurais répondu vite,	I would quickly have answered you
sur le ton de tes parents:	in the style of your parents:
[les poings sur les hanches]	*[with her hands on her hips]*
Eh, dis donc, Mamzelle Suzon,	Hey, listen, Mamzelle Susie,
si tu parles sur ce ton,	if you speak in that style,
ah! nom d'un nom, ah! nom d'un nom,	oh! good grief, oh! good grief,
je te crèpe le chignon!	[idiom] I'll have a fight with you!
	[literally] I'll backcomb your hair bun!
CLAIRETTE:	**CLAIRETTE:**
Et moi, je t'aurais répondu:	As for me, I would have answered you:
[même jeu]	*[same gesture]*
Tiens, voyez donc c'te vertu	Hold on, take a good look at this virtuous woman
qu'a les bras et les jamb's nus,	who bares her arms and legs,
est'c' que çà n'srait pas Vénus,	it couldn't be Venus, could it?
est'c' que çà n'srait pas Vénus	it couldn't be Venus, could it?
qui viendrait d'sortir des eaux	who would come up from the waters
pour effrayer les pierrots.	to scare clowns.

Soon after its debut, *La fille de Madame Angot* was translated by Henry J. Byron (1835–84), a prolific British dramatist, a friend of and some time collaborator with W. S. Gilbert, and an editor, journalist, director, theater manager, novelist and actor. Here is his singable translation of the lyrics in Table 3.5:

MLLE LANGE:
   Dear Clairette, I'm now quite alter'd,
      but in days gone long ago
   to reply I'd not have falter'd
      in the style of Ma'me Angot:
   Well, come on, Mamzell' Suzon,
   if me you sing verses on,
   my life upon, my life upon,
   I'll demolish your chignon!

CLAIRETTE:
   And I, to say this I would dare:
   Let us see this virtue rare,
   all must sure my horror share,

here behold, 'tis Venus fair,
here behold, 'tis Venus fair,
  Venus rising from the sea,
  none more classical could be!
    (Byron, no date listed)

Byron was unable to refer literally to bare arms and legs on the stage of his time, but his classical allusion would bring up the image of a nude Venus to those familiar with paintings of her rising from the sea. "Ma'am" and "mamzelle," which might seem foreignizing to Americans, are British English pronunciations. However, Byron does foreignize with "Suzon" and "chignon."

We felt we needed some sort of slang to follow the story line, which in part depends on the revelation that Clairette is adept at market slang. However, as already mentioned, most actual slang words are both evanescent and culture bound, often signaling a particular group. Therefore, any specific English-language slang would not be "transparent." It would not set the action in Paris in 1797, but in an English-speaking time and place: perhaps early twentieth-century working-class Brooklyn or mid-nineteenth-century Cockney London. But any slang we used would still have to be domesticated enough to be comprehensible. We decided on a sort of Wardour Street of slang, mingling terms and phrases originating from several groups and eras: "swell," 1810; "lip," 1821; "get a load of," theater slang, 1929; "drip," 1930s; "listen up," army use, 1970s (*OED*):

MLLE LANGE:
Though I do not hold a grudge, dear,
  in that bygone time of bliss,
in the manner of your parents,
I'd have scolded you like this:
  [with her hands on her hips]
Listen up, ya little drip,
if ya give me any lip,
I'm gonna grab a hunk o' hair
and I swear I'll let 'er rip!

CLAIRETTE:
I would have answered you as well:
  [with her hands on her hips]
Get a load o' this mam'zel,
ain't she lookin' awful swell,
Venus poppin' from the shell,
showin' what she has to sell.
  I seen better merchandise:
  twice as good at half the price.
    (Herman and Apter, 1989)

3.9 Jokes

Some humor is necessarily lost in translation. Some jokes are not translatable, or at least not translatable locally, that is, at the same point in the translation as they are in the source. Some jokes, even if translatable, will not be understood by the audience, or will be missed by the translators. Some jokes involving *double entendre* will be eliminated because the translators, for one reason or another, decide that only one of the meanings should be conveyed. And some jokes will be omitted because the text including them, such as a piece of spoken dialogue, is cut.

Since a translation of a comical work should be comical, we advocate adding context-appropriate jokes to compensate for those that have been lost, though such a domesticating gesture is frowned upon by those in favor of fully foreignized translations.

3.9.1 Jokes in a foreign language

In rare instances, the point of a joke is that it is in a foreign language, that is, a language other than the language of the source text, and so it should remain foreign. In the French operetta *Le médecin malgré lui* (*The Doctor in Spite of Himself*) (Gounod 1858), Sganarelle launches into a torrent of nonsense Latin in order to befuddle the other characters. He conjugates first-year Latin verbs, declines first-year Latin nouns and adjectives, throws in pieces of Latin prayers, tosses in medical terms at random, and even claims to speak a word or two of Greek and Hebrew (No. 8, mm. 237–55). To someone who does not know any Latin, the stream of what would be perceived as nonsense syllables is mildly funny; to someone who has studied Latin, the words are hilarious.

3.9.2 Missed jokes

When the target culture is very different from the source culture, the audience, and even the translators, may miss some jokes.

Ziad Rahbani (1956–) is a Lebanese playwright. The literal English translation of a verbal exchange in one of his plays is:

> And what if Zalim [a horse] does not win?
> Then Jarbu'a [a strange name for a horse, meaning "female rat"] will.
> May God [new meaningless verb derived from "Jarbu'a"] your neck!
> (Elzeer, 2010: 199–200)

This is funny to the Lebanese because it distorts a set expression in the Levantine dialect of Arabic, "May God break your neck!," and because the

Lebanese consider it funny for a meaningless word in one statement to be derived from a meaningful word in a previous statement.

One does not have go as far afield from English as Arabic to find jokes that may be missed. Among the lyrics of *Carmina Burana* (with the accent on *CAR)* is "*Veni, veni, venias*" (Hilka, Schumann, and Bischoff, 1930–71: No. 174; Orff, 1936: No. 20), a sexually explicit poem relying on the double meaning of the Latin verb "*venire*": "to arrive" and "to have an orgasm." The English word "come" has the same two meanings. Included in "*Veni, veni, venias*" are the words "*hyria*" and "*hyrie,*" which some translators assume are nonsense words. They are not. They are textual variants of "*hyrca*" and "*hyrce,*" which are in fact the words found in Orff's choral cantata (in some editions, both are "*hyrca*"). These in turn are variant spellings of the vocative case for "*hircus*" and "*hirca,*" the Latin words for male and female goats, animals traditionally considered to be hyper-sexed. Considering Orff's setting for double chorus in which the two choruses call these words back and forth to each other, our translation has one chorus calling "billy" and the other calling "nanny."

3.9.3 Double entendre

Conveying *double entendre* in situ is often difficult. The meaning spread of a single word in the source may be parceled out among several words in the target language. Not matching *double entendre* loses wit, but matching it often requires a highly subtle form of domestication: verbal humor usually cannot be conveyed via foreignization.

In *Die Entführung aus dem Serail* (*The Abduction from the Seraglio*) (1782), shortly after the opening of Act III, when protagonist Belmonte and his servant Pedrillo are starting to carry out their planned escape from the Pasha's seraglio, there is a dialogue in which Pedrillo tells Belmonte what to do to avoid arousing the watchmen's suspicions:

> Singen Sie indessen eins. Ich hab' das so alle Abende getan; und wenn Sie da auch jemand gewahr wird oder Ihnen begegnet—den alle Stunden macht hier eine Janitscharenwache die Runde—, so hat's nichts zu bedeuten, sie sind das von mir schon gewohnt . . .
>
> (Sing in the meantime. I have done so every evening; and when you also become aware of someone there, or they encounter you—because a Janissary watch makes the rounds here every hour—, so it [your singing] will mean nothing [to them], because they are already used to that from me . . .)

In addition to the surface meaning of the words, second tenor Pedrillo has just told first tenor Belmonte exactly what he thinks of the latter's singing ability.

Many translators followed the fad of making deep cuts to the dialogue, among them Edward J. Dent (1952), Ruth and Thomas Martin (1944/62), and Elkhanah Pulitzer (2003). They thereby lost the joke. However, several translators do leave the dialogue in:

In the meantime sing something. I used to do that every evening. And if anyone meets you or notices you—the Janissaries make the rounds every hour—they won't think anything of it. (John Bloch, 1957: 59)

Sing something while I'm gone. I sing every night, so if the Janissaries hear you they won't think much of it. (Herman and Apter, 1979a: 147)

In the meantime, sing a little something. I used to do that every evening. So if you encounter anyone or someone spots you—the Janissaries make their rounds every hour—they won't think anything of it. (J. D. McClatchy [prose dialogue from a nonsingable verse translation], 2011: 235)

Most of our work while translating those lines involved struggling to come up with "much" instead of "anything."

Just before the above interchange, Pedrillo, contemplating escape from captivity, becomes very nervous. He says he feels *"als wenn ich's größte Schelmstück vorhätte."* This has two meanings. The first is "as if I [the character Pedrillo] were performing a very bad deed" and the second is "as if I [the tenor portraying Pedrillo] were performing in a very bad theater piece."

Once again Edward J. Dent (1952), Ruth and Thomas Martin (1944/62), and Elkhanah Pulitzer (2003) automatically lose the joke by omitting the dialogue. Here are the versions of the other translators:

My heart is going as wildly as if I were going to commit a terrible crime. (John Bloch, 1957: 59)

It's as if I were engaged in some foul play. (Herman and Apter, 1979a: 147).

My heart is squeezed as tightly as if I were committing a terrible crime. (J. D. McClatchy [prose dialogue from a nonsingable verse translation], 2011: 235)

Bloch and McClatchy just translate the surface meaning. After coming up with "foul play," a pretty good cognate for "Schelmstück," we found ourselves stymied by the fact that "engaged in foul play" and "engaged in a foul play" each has only one of the required meanings. Only when one of us shouted, "Some! Some foul play!" did the two meanings come together.

Double entendre can also occur during sung texts. In Alessandro Scarlatti's baroque opera *Eraclea*, an elderly tutor pursues a young girl who is really a boy in disguise, and laments the loss of sexual prowess with age. The joke depends on the double meaning of the Italian verb "*venire*," the same double meaning discussed above for Latin "*venire*" and English "to come." This particular joke made us nervous, but, to our delight, our commissioners urged us to include it (see Table 3.6).

TABLE 3.6 *Eraclea*, No. 16, mm. 1–21

Original Italian lyrics	Literal English translation
Io tengo, tengo,	I hold on, I hold on,
io tengo, tengo,	I hold on, I hold on,
ma, ma più non posso,	but, but more I cannot do,
ma più non posso.	but more I cannot do.
Già me ne vengo,	Already I have arrived/come,
già me ne vengo,	already I have arrived/come,
Alfeo s'è mosso,	Alfeo has been moved/aroused,
s'è mosso,	has been moved/aroused,
s'è mosso,	has been moved/aroused,
Alfeo s'è mosso,	Alfeo has been moved/aroused,
s'è mosso.	has been moved/aroused.

Singable English translation
With every road blocked,
I cannot hold on.
Ah, I am an old don
and go off half-cocked.
I disregard her.
It's getting harder.
I cannot leave her;
my fever
is growing.
She has me coming
and going.
(Herman and Apter, 1992b)

Although we held to the intent of the original, we domesticated the translation by substituting English detail for Italian repetition, which also allowed us to pile on even more double meanings.

Another *double entendre* in both Italian and English is "*comune*" (common), meaning both "usual" and "mediocre." Using this word, the servant Martino easily disparages his master Parmenione in Rossini's *L'occasione fa il ladro* (*A Thief by Chance*) (1812) (see Table 3.7).

TABLE 3.7 *L'occasione fa il ladro*, No. 7, mm. 53–65

Original Italian lyrics	Literal English translation
insomma	in sum
è un di quegli esseri	he is one of those people
comuni in società,	common in society,
è un di quegli esseri	he is one of those people
comuni in società,	common in society,
comuni in società,	common in society,
comuni in società.	common in society.

Singable English translation
In essence,
he's a common type
in our society,
a very common type
in our society,
as common as can
be in our society.
(Herman and Apter, 2007)

3.9.4 Added jokes

Footnotes can sometimes be worked into a performable translation to explain a historical or cultural allusion, but a joke explained is a joke no more. We believe it is better to let untranslatable jokes go and, as John Dryden said, add new ones that

> may be fairly deduc'd from [the original author]: or at least . . . [be] of a piece with his. (Dryden, 1685, "Preface to *Sylvae*," *Works*, 3: 3–4)

Added jokes are a form of domestication, justified by the fact that failure to compensate for inevitable losses makes translation a process of diminution, truly a second-rate imitation.

We added a joke, a *double entendre*, to our translation of "The Ballad of Madame Angot" in *La fille de madame Angot (Madame Angot's Daughter* (1872) (see Table 3.8). The joke depends on the second meaning of "char" in British slang: to act as a charwoman, a house cleaner, a job often given to widows.

TABLE 3.8 *La fille de Madame Angot*, No. 2, mm. 4b–20b

Original French lyrics	Literal English translation

En ballon elle monte,
    la voilà dans les airs,
et plus tard elle affronte,
    les mers et les déserts.
Au Malabar captive,
    la croyant veuve hélas!
on veut la bruler vive,
    c'est la mode là-bas.
	She goes up in a balloon,
	here she is in the air,
	and later she confronts
	seas and deserts.
	On Malabar captive,
	they believe her a widow alas!
	they want to burn her alive,
	it is the fashion over there.

Singable English translation

She sailed across the ocean,
    she went up in balloons,
she thumbed her nose at pirates,
    and thundered at typhoons.
The natives tried to burn her
    in Hindu Malabar.
The took her for a widow,
    but she refused to char.
(Herman and Apter, 1989)

Whatever the theoretical arguments, and whichever overall strategy is chosen, working translators know that decisions regarding foreignization and domestication often depend on the specific words, phrases, or concepts to be translated, and that such decisions depend on the particular work being translated, the specific source and target languages, the audience for which the translation is made, and the abilities and proclivities of the translators.

4

Adaptation and re-translation

4.1 Adaptation

When does a translation deviate so far from the source that it becomes an adaptation? Recent discussions may be found in the article by John Milton ("Between the Cat and the Devil," 2009) and the book edited by Lawrence Raw (*Translation, Adaptation and Transformation*, 2012). But writers have been struggling with this question for some time. John Dryden, probably the first influential English translation theorist, wrote in 1680:

> All Translation, I suppose, may be reduced to these three heads:
>
> First, that of Metaphrase, or turning an Authour word by word, and Line by Line, from one Language into another . . . The second way is that of Paraphrase, or Translation with Latitude, where the Authour is kept in view by the Translator, so as never to be lost, but his words are not so strictly follow'd as his sense, and that too is admitted to be amplyfied, but not alter'd . . . The Third way is that of Imitation, where the Translator (if now he has not lost that Name) assumes the liberty not only to vary from the words and sense, but to forsake them both as he sees occasion; and taking only some general hints from the Original, to run division on the groundwork, as he pleases. (Dryden, 1680, Preface to *Ovid's Epistles*, *Works*: I: 114–15)

Today, Dryden's metaphrase would probably be called a literal translation, his paraphrase a literary translation, and his imitation something between an adaptation, that is, a work rooted in another work, and a spin-off, a work merely suggested by another work. An example of the latter is a set of singable lyrics entirely different from those in the source language, possibly retaining no more of the original than the title. As Peter Low describes it:

> [S]ome people ignore sense altogether: they take a foreign song-tune and devise for it a set of TL [target-language] words which match the music very well but bear no semantic relations with the ST [source text]. While this may at times be good and appropriate, it is not translating, because none of the original verbal meaning is transmitted. Such practices have no place in discussions of translation. (Low, 2005: 194)

We agree.

Some writers are uncomfortable calling any version a translation if it can stand on its own as a literary work. They believe that the changes necessary to transfer a work from a source to a target language are always great enough to require that the result be called an adaptation, and that this is especially true if the words have to fit pre-existing music. Other writers believe that works that stand on their own can occupy a position somewhere between translation proper and adaptation. To designate this intermediate position, Johan Franzon has suggested "creative transposition" (2005: 264), a term first used by Roman Jakobson (1959: 238) for the translation of poetry, and J. P. Sullivan has suggested "creative translation" (1964: 17–20). As examples of creative transposition, Franzon (2005: 263–64) cites several versions of *Die Dreigroschenoper* (*The Threepenny Opera*) (1928) by playwright/librettist Bertolt Brecht (1898–1956) and composer Kurt Weill (1900–1950), each specifying a different number of cannon on Pirate Jenny's ship.

However blurry the boundaries, we believe that it is useful to distinguish between translating and adapting. We define translating as not changing anything major in the original. Moreover, in our opinion, altering the number of cannon on Pirate Jenny's ship does not constitute a major change. Therefore, we consider all the target texts mentioned by Franzon to be translations. A version with more radical changes, say one in which Mack the Knife is not reprieved from hanging, would be, in our nomenclature, an adaptation.

(As a sidelight to this discussion, Desblache [2008: 106–7] points out that works for the musical stage, such as operas, are often adaptations of existing works in languages other than those used for the operas. The many adaptations of Shakespeare's plays into non-English operas are prime examples of this.)

Some adaptations arise from the very nature of the original works; for example, works left incomplete at their composers' deaths, or works that have survived only in an incomplete form. Any translation (or production) that of necessity completes such a work is probably best called an adaptation. A work in this category is the opera *Князь Игорь* (*Knyaz' Igor'* [*Prince Igor*]) by the Russian composer Александр Бородин (Alexander Borodin) (1833–87).

Adaptations can also come about when a work for the musical stage exists in more than one version. Multiple versions are more common than many people imagine. Philip Gossett (2006) gives a full discussion of what is involved when choosing which version of a nineteenth-century Italian opera to perform. When several versions exist, a translation (or production) of any one would not necessarily be an adaptation. However, if stage directors decide that there are parts of more than one version that they cannot bear to discard, they will create their own adaptation including parts from several versions. For example, directors often combine the two versions of the opera *Борис Годунов* (*Boris Godunov*) (1869; 1872) by the Russian composer Модест Мусоргский (Modest Musorgskiy) (1839–81).

There are other reasons for adaptation: for instance, the translators' desire to change something the target audience may not tolerate, such as a villain like Mack the Knife not getting his righteous punishment. While we know of no version in which Mack the Knife is hanged, there is a Victorian musical adaptation of *Le médecin malgré lui* (*The Doctor in Spite of Himself*), a 1666 prose farce by Molière (1622–73). In the Victorian version, contrary to Molière's, the protagonist Sganarelle is stripped of his bogus "doctorhood" at the end.

While contemporary audiences will not bat an eye at "immoral" endings such as those in *Die Dreigroschenoper* and *Le médecin malgré lui*, they often cannot stomach real or perceived sexism and racism. Many versions of Mozart's *Die Zauberflöte* (*The Magic Flute*) veer toward adaptation by muting sexist and racist lyrics, including the famous 1975 film version by Ingmar Bergman (1918–2007), performed in Swedish translation with English subtitles. In addition, Bergman's film turns the character Sarastro into Pamina's father, illustrating another reason for adaptation: the desire to change the original into something deemed more relevant. In this case the war between Sarastro and the Queen of the Night is changed from a dynastic battle into a family dispute.

The first translation of a major work often serves as an introduction to the work in the target culture. In an effort to bridge cultural differences, or to explain unfamiliar theories of the author, this first translation may lean toward adaptation. André Lefevere (1945–96) discusses (1982) three different translations from German into English of *Mutter Courage und ihre Kinder* (*Mother Courage and Her Children*) (1939, first performed 1941), by playwright/lyricist Bertolt Brecht with music composed by Paul Dessau (1894–1979). According to Lefevere, each translation (published in 1941, 1967, and 1972, respectively) distorted what Brecht actually wrote to a lesser extent than the translation preceding it. This, says Lefevere, had little to do with the competency of the translators and much to do with the fact that, between 1941 and 1972, Brecht's reputation among English speakers was transformed, in no small part because of the first two translations, from that of an unknown German playwright to that of a theatrical icon. By 1972, Brecht no longer needed adaptation to make him culturally acceptable.

Adaptations seeking to provide "relevancy" move the work into the target culture and/or update it to a contemporary, or at least more recent, time period. Motivations for this can be commercial, artistic, or both. Famous (or infamous) examples of such adaptations are the versions of the three Mozart/Da Ponte operas by American stage director Peter Sellars (1957–) who, in 1989, set *Le nozze di Figaro* (*The Marriage of Figaro*) (1786) in New York City's Trump Tower, *Don Giovanni* (1787) in New York City's Spanish Harlem, and *Così fan tutte* (*The Way They're Made*) (1790) in a diner on Cape Cod, Massachusetts. All three were performed in the original Italian. More recently, adaptations of Mozart operas performed in English versions include Kenneth Branagh's 2006 film of *The Magic Flute*, set during World War I; Donald Pippin's 2012 version of *The Abduction from the Seraglio*, in which Pasha Selim was once a student at Columbia University in New York, though he still has eighteenth-century views on women; Bari Biern's 2013 *Abduction* set in the nineteenth-century American Wild West, in which the hero Belmont must rescue his beloved, the famous British actress, Lillie Langtry, from the clutches of her obsessed admirer, Judge Roy Bean; and Vid Guerrerio's 2013 version of *The Marriage of Figaro*, in which Figaro and Susanna are undocumented immigrant workers on an estate in Beverly Hills. In 2010, Oregon Opera Theater presented an English version by Katie Taylor of Wagner's *Das Rheingold* (1869), adapted into an episode of the television series "Baywatch." The performances were preceded by a demonstration of Wagner's leitmotifs, which were given such names as "knuckle sandwich," "safety," "love theme," and "pissed off."

Donald Pippin (1926–), though a translator and director of a few updated versions himself, disparages such adaptations:

> One of the current trends in the opera world, it would seem, demands that the director prove his creativity by changing the locale and period of the opera in question to something wildly different from what the misguided composer intended. Thus *Aida* moves to Cambodia, *Così fan Tutte* to South Carolina, *Norma* to God knows where.
>
> This is a practice for which Pocket Opera [the company of which Donald Pippin is artistic director] has little tolerance, and one to which we have yielded only once, despite the relative ease with which we leap from one continent to another. (Pippin, 1984)

These sentiments are widely echoed by operatic purists.

Pippin suggests yet another cause of adaptation:

> But I soon found out it's a superfluous ability [to know other languages]. My primary concern is to make [English] words that fit the music, and for

that you sometimes have to go quite far afield from the literal translation. Whether or not you know the original language, in the end you basically have to discard it and find your own words. (Pippin, 2002)

Indeed, translators have to find their own words, but they still have to start somewhere. If they do not know the source language, they could start from an intermediate translation into a language they do know. If so, some argue that the result is likely to be an adaptation: even if the intermediate translation is not very different from the source, and the final translation not very different from the intermediate, the combined difference, in their opinion, is still likely to make the final version an adaptation.

Translation of a translation, while likely to produce an adaptation, may still not do so. Translation of an adaptation is certain to. A famous example is *Prodaná nevěsta* (1866–70), a Czech comic opera composed by Bedřich Smetana (1824–84) to a libretto by Karel Sabina (1813–77). The title literally means *The Sold Bride* but is usually rendered more euphoniously into English as *The Bartered Bride*. In 1893, for a production in Vienna, *Prodaná nevěsta* was adapted by Max Kalbeck (1850–1921) into *Die verkaufte Braut*. Kalbeck cavalierly and drastically changed a work not only "quintessentially Czech" (Tyrrell, 1992: I: 334), but which had achieved popularity in large part precisely because it was "quintessentially Czech." Among other things, Kalbeck Germanized the characters' Czech names: the hero Jeník became Hans, and his half-brother Vašek became Wenzel. Names are important, because, if the names are German, the characters become only vaguely Czech. However, the name changes are minor in comparison with Kalbeck's wholesale re-writing of parts of the libretto. Table 4.1 shows the first stanza of the opening chorus: the original Czech, a literal translation of the Czech, Kalbeck's re-written German version, and a literal translation of Kalbeck's version.

Our own performable translation is

When God gives you health, enjoy it.
When God gives you health, enjoy it.
What is wrong with happiness, happiness?
What is wrong with happiness, happiness?
What is wrong with happiness, happiness?
(Herman and Apter, 2003)

Three other easily available singable American translations are those by Marian Farquhar (1879–1965), included in the English-only Schirmer edition of 1956; Paul Csonka (1905–95) and Ariane Theslöf (no dates available), published in the Kalmus edition of 1968, which also includes Kalbeck's German text; and Donald Pippin, available on the Pocket Opera website.

TABLE 4.1 *Prodaná nevěsta*, Opening Chorus, 1st Stanza

Original Czech lyrics	Literal English translation of the Czech lyrics
Proč bychom se netěšili,	Why should we not make merry,
proč bychom se netěšili,	why should we not make merry
když nám pán Bůh zdraví dá, zdraví dá,	when to us the Lord God gives health, gives health,
když nám pán Bůh zdraví dá, zdraví dá,	when to us the Lord God gives health, gives health,
když nám pán Bůh zdraví dá, zdraví dá?	when to us the Lord God gives health, gives health?

German adaptation by Max Kalbeck (1893)	Literal English translation of Kalbeck's adaptation
Seht am Strauch die Knospen springen!	See the buds appear on the bush!
Hört die muntern Vögel singen!	Hear the cheerful birds sing!
Glanz und Jubel weit und breit, weit und breit!	Radiance and rejoicing far and wide, far and wide!
O du schöne Frühlingszeit, Frühlingszeit,	Oh, you beautiful springtime, springtime,
o du schöne Frühlingszeit, Frühlingszeit!	oh, you beautiful springtime, springtime!

(Marian Farquhar was a champion tennis player, posthumously inducted into the International Tennis Hall of Fame in 2006, and Ariane Theslöf was Paul Csonka's fifth wife!) In all three versions, the introductory chorus, following Kalbeck, is about spring; there are no references to health or to God as the giver of health. To omit the reference to God is to omit a major aspect of the character of these rural Czechs: their reflexive piety.

It is interesting to look at some British translations of the same stanza, those by Rosa Newmarch (1857–1940), Joan Cross (1900–93) and Eric Crozier (1914–94), Tony Harrison (1937–), and Amanda Holden (1948–). Two of the translators, Rosa Newmarch and Amanda Holden, do translate the Czech. However, Newmarch's translation (1934) was replaced in the Boosey and Hawkes English-only edition by the translation of Cross and Crozier (1945/78), which, while apparently not influenced by the adaptation of Kalbeck to the same extent as the American translations, once again eliminated God and health. The version by Tony Harrison, known to many Americans because it has been performed by the Metropolitan Opera in New York, similarly eliminates both God and health.

The two British translations eliminating God and health also veer toward adaptation in another way. Cross and Crozier say that the rural Czechs have "earned a holiday," which shifts the focus to workers' rights and away from fate and God's gifts. Tony Harrison goes further: not only have the characters "earned this holiday" but, just as Kalbeck turned the rural Czechs into Germans, Harrison turns them into members of the British working class. Harrison's translation of the opening stanza is:

> Still got strength to face the worst with,
> well-brewed beer to beat a thirst with,
> we've all earned this holiday, holiday,
> we've all earned this holiday, holiday,
> we've all earned this holiday, holiday!
> (Harrison, 1978: 1)

Harrison invents a special idiom, dropping expected articles, pronouns, and helper verbs—note the absence of the expected first word "We've" from his first line above. Not only is this idiom consonant with his overall working-class characterization, but it is also his way of coping with Czech trochees, that is, words and phrases accented on the first syllable. Harrison's adaptation proceeds more or less consistently throughout. A telling detail occurs later in the opening chorus, where Sabina's libretto says that women do housework, men go out drinking, and couples bicker. This is handled in various ways by the various translators, but only Harrison converts petty bickering into "Women all cheat you! Husbands all beat you!" (Harrison, 1978: 1).

Prodaná nevěsta is not unique in having multiple translations, but it is unusual in having so many published English versions that are adaptations.

Yet another reason for adaptation is the need to remedy perceived defects in the original, especially structural defects that reduce stageworthiness. This is the reason for our own adaptations of the French comic operetta *Le médecin malgré lui* (*The Doctor in Spite of Himself*) (1858) and Verdi's early comic opera *Un giorno di regno* (*A Day in the Reign*) (1840).

Le médecin malgré lui, composed by Charles Gounod (1818–93) to a libretto by Paul Barbier (1825–1901) and Michel Carré (1821–72), was adapted from the 1666 prose farce of the same name by Molière (1622–73). Gounod's adaptation is just one of many transformations that Molière's play has undergone over the course of three and a half centuries. Most famous among English versions is the 1732 play by Henry Fielding (1707–54), *The Mock Doctor; or, the Dumb Lady Cur'd*, which played at the Theatre Royal in Drury Lane, London.

The most significant structural flaw in *Le médecin malgré lui* is that it runs out of music at the end. In an operetta, spoken dialogue moves the plot along, but is usually perceived by the audience as a bridge between musical numbers. Therefore, any long stretch of dialogue, no matter how witty, tends to drag. At the end of *Le médecin*, dialogue alone conveys the elopement of the lovers Lucinde and Léandre, the capture of the protagonist Sganarelle, the arrival of Sganarelle's wife Martine, the lovers' return, the consent of Lucinde's father Géronte to the lovers' marriage, and Sganarelle's release. Finally, there is music: a chorus from the end of Act I is repeated.

We are not the first to have noticed the missing music. In 1923, the French composer Erik Satie (1866–1925) wrote music to bridge the gap (and to turn the spoken dialogue into recitatives). *Le médecin* was performed with the additional Satie music, in the original French, at Yale University in 2004.

There is a second structural problem in *Le médecin*, rooted in theatrical practicalities. As the operetta is written, Lucinde, potentially a lead soprano, scarcely opens her mouth. Perhaps the part was originally written for a good comic actress rather than for a good singer. Whatever the reason, the lack of a prominent aria for the soprano is a problem: lead sopranos demand an aria.

Fortunately, both structural problems could be solved simultaneously by inserting a soprano aria, No. 5 from Act II of Gounod's 1864 opera *Mireille*. The music of this aria, with entirely new English lyrics unrelated to the French text in *Mireille* but relevant to *Le médecin*, both gave Lucinde her aria and broke up the overly long final dialogue.

Some new dialogue was required as a lead-in to the extra aria for Lucinde, and, while writing it, we took the opportunity to solve a third structural problem, the servant Valère's mysterious disappearance from Gounod's (and

Molière's) third act. To give Valère something to do in Act III, we let him be the one to discover the elopement of Lucinde and Léandre.

The structural flaw in *Un giorno di regno* (*A Day in the Reign*) stems from the fact that a character, the Marquise, has two scenes in which she recognizes her disguised lover, the Chevalier Belfleur, the second scene taking place as if the first one had never occurred. This odd state of affairs may have arisen in an attempt to give the soprano performing the Marquise a conventionally placed entrance aria. Whatever the reason, today the two recognition scenes are dramatically unacceptable. Therefore, we eliminated the first scene, moved its music to a position later in the opera, and revised the lyrics to make them suitable for their new position.

4.2 Re-translation

In this book, "re-translation" is defined as the creation of a new target text when one or more target texts already exist. The term is not used for the translation of a translation, a so-called translation chain. Nor is it used to mean "multiple translation," a related term concerning the re-creation of different aspects of the original by means of different translations. Multiple translation is discussed in Chapter 9.

A recent book on re-translation is *Retranslation: Translation, Literature and Reinterpretation* (2014) by Sharon Deane-Cox, and Anthony Pym discusses it in *Method in Translation History* (1998: 82).

Why re-translate? The glib answer is that all the existing translations are bad, or, even if not so bad, the re-translators believe that they can do better. Barbara Folkart writes:

> Many translations are inferior to the originals . . . For one thing, translations are not always held to the highest standards of artistic creation for their day. (Folkart, 2007: 135)

Bad existing translations are not the only reason to re-translate. Re-translation may be required because translations, even those that are adequate when created, become dated. They cannot escape the literary conventions and cultural assumptions prevailing at their creation. Rather, using a term coined by Gideon Toury (1980, 1995), they adhere to "translation norms," and these change over time. While not exactly rigid prescriptions, these norms are the hidden rules followed by the majority of translators. An example is the Victorian requirement that translations preserve the rhyme schemes of the original.

Rarely, a very good translation nearly contemporaneous with the original work endures, such as the anonymous English translation, probably first performed in 1674, of Francesco Cavalli's 1655 Italian opera *Erismena*. It may even happen that a very good translation made long after the date of its source endures, such as the German versions of Shakespeare's plays by August Wilhelm von Schlegel (1767–1845), but this is an occurrence rarer still. Target languages change; readers and/or the audience will tolerate originals in archaic language but usually not translations (though, as discussed in Chapter 7, sometimes archaic language is a possible translation choice).

Another possible reason for re-translation is that all or most of the existing translations of a given work are adaptations. An example is Smetana's *Prodaná nevěsta*, discussed in the previous section. The songs of the Belgian singer-songwriter Jacques Brel (1929–78) also fall into this category. His songs were popularized in the musical revue *Jacques Brel Is Alive and Well and Living in Paris*, which debuted in 1968 and has been performed around the world. However, many of the English lyrics in that show are loose adaptations of the French originals. Arnold Johnston has been re-translating, re-recording, and re-staging Brel's work with considerable success, and has recently obtained exclusive rights to translate Brel's work into English from Brel's widow. Some reviews of Johnston's translations are available at <http://www.wmich.edu/wmu/news/2005/06/007.html> (accessed November 19, 2014). Interestingly, more literal translations sometimes preserve other qualities of the original, which one would expect to be lost in the attempt to preserve meaning. On the website mentioned, Michael Phillips, theater critic for the *Chicago Tribune*, is quoted as saying that "In many instances, translator Arnold Johnston's lyrics to Brel's melodies scan better than the English-language versions heard in 'Alive and Well.'"

A new adaptation may be needed because the existing ones fail to fully correct the structural defects of the original work.

Finally, re-translation may also be motivated by practical considerations. There may be no singable translations (or adaptations) suitable for a particular production; or an existing suitable translation entails prohibitive royalty costs; or an existing translation would be suitable if a few words were changed or added, such as obscenities the translator was obligated for some reason to omit, but the copyright holder of the translation will not allow changes.

Regarding the last, the performance history of Bertolt Brecht and Kurt Weill's *Die Dreigroschenoper* (*The Threepenny Opera*) in the United States is instructive. Although there are still arguments over exactly who did or did not allow what, one undisputable fact is that the performable English translation by Marc Blitzstein (1905–64), one of the towering achievements of the English-speaking and singing stage, as well as of the translator's art and craft, has never been published in its entirety. A book of vocal selections (Blitzstein, 1984) and an original-cast recording (Blitzstein, 1954) of the 1954 New York Off-Broadway production are the only items easily available.

Die Dreigroschenoper was adapted by Brecht and Weill from the German translation by Elisabeth Hauptmann (1897–1973) of the English ballad opera *The Beggar's Opera* (1728) by John Gay (1685–1732). (There is good evidence that Elisabeth Hauptmann was also an uncredited co-author with Brecht.) *Die Dreigroschenoper* opened in Germany in 1928, and had been translated into eighteen languages by the time Brecht and Weill were forced to flee Germany and the Nazis in 1933. The first American production, also in 1933, performed in a now-lost English translation by Gifford Cochran and Jerrold Krimsky, was poorly received. The next American production, performed in the version by Marc Blitzstein, was a hit, running in New York from 1954 to 1961. The next major American production—small companies were also beginning to perform the work—ran for nine months in New York in 1976–77 and was performed in an English translation by Ralph Manheim (1907–92) and John Willett (1917–2002), who promised their commissioners that they would be faithful to Brecht's original German, especially in not following Blitzstein's softening of obscenities. There have also been other English translations, most notably by Eric Bentley (1916–), made before the Blitzstein translation, and by Michael Feingold (included in the 2000 critical edition) and Jeremy Sams (1957–), both made since the Manheim and Willett translation.

All the re-translations discussed so far have been actual translations. But some so-called re-translations are anything but. They are merely mash-ups of several existing translations. Several years ago, the director/"translator" of an off-Broadway production of a play by Anton Chekhov (1860–1904) created such a "translation," and later, in an interview, bragged that he knew not one word of Russian.

Even more egregious are translations that are stolen outright, sometimes with a few words changed, sometimes left as is, in order to avoid paying performance royalties or to get some sort of credit (such as an academic publication credit).

While stealing is both unethical and illegal, it is not necessarily unethical for some words of a prior translation to appear in a later one. As Andrew Porter says in the Introduction to his translation of Wagner's *Der Ring des Nibelungen*:

> In fact, one soon discovers that all *Ring* translators . . . have leant on the work of their predecessors. This is reasonable and right; in any case, the ways of translating a short sentence in tempo are not limitless. (Porter, 1976: xiii)

Of particular interest in this regard is the word *"entsagt,"* the third-person present tense form of *"entsagen,"* which is what Alberich must do with respect to "love" if he wishes to forge the gold into a ring (Wagner, 1969: 63). Langenscheidt's Encyclopaedic Muret-Sanders German-English Dictionary gives the possible meanings of *"entsagen"* as "to give up, forswear, forgo, renounce, abstain, deny." Of all these meanings, "forswear" is especially good because it includes "swear," which foul-mouthed Alberich certainly does. This is how Frederick Jameson translates the word (1896: 43), as do Stewart Robb (1960:14) and William Mann (1960: 26). For some reason, in Mann's book, *"entsagt"* has been replaced by *"versagt,"* a word overlapping in meaning with *"entsagt"* but lacking the meaning "forswear." Nonetheless, Mann still chose "forswear." Jeremy Sams does not give the original, so it is impossible to know which German word he worked from, but he translates similarly: "forswore" (2002: 8). Andrew Porter, whose original reads *"versagt,"* translates differently: "renounce" (1976: 15).

Ethical or not, the partial reliance on previous translations has produced some cynical comments. As quoted by Gary Racz (2013):

> I strongly favor regarding translation . . . as a cumulative undertaking, and therefore borrowing—or stealing—whenever you see that your own best solution to a problem is clearly inferior to someone else's. (Donald Frame, 1989: 82)

> [I am] a jackal who comes along after the kill to nose over the uneaten hunks [and] keeps everything he likes. (William Gass, 1999: 76)

Most of our own translations for the musical stage are re-translations. However, it is our practice not to look at the translations of others until we are well beyond the first drafts of our own, in order to ensure that our own ideas are not influenced by conscious or subconscious memories of the ideas of others.

One of our re-translations is that of Giuseppe Verdi's *Il trovatore (The Troubadour)* (1853), composed to an Italian libretto by Salvadore Cammarano (1801–52), completed by Leone Emanuele Bardare (1820–74) after Cammarano's death, based on the Spanish play *El trovador* (1836) by Antonio García Gutiérrez (1813–84). In addition to providing a good performable text, we hoped, by our re-translation, to stimulate a critical re-evaluation of the opera itself. No one reads a text more closely and more critically than do translators, making every translation perforce a critical analysis of the source. Ezra Pound maintained that it is one of the best types of critical analysis (see Apter, 1984/87: 7–8 and Chapter 9 of this book).

Il trovatore opened at the Teatro Apollo in Rome and was an instant success, becoming and remaining, until about 1950, the most performed opera in the world. It remains highly popular to this day. Nonetheless, it is frequently touted as the quintessentially silly Italian opera, parodied by everyone from Gilbert and Sullivan to the Marx Brothers. David Osborne, who, unlike some others, gives a correct synopsis, calls the plot "preposterous" (2004: 502). So, have critics for more than 150 years been wrong and the public right? The short answer is yes!

There are at least three generally held misconceptions about *Il trovatore*. The first is that there are witches in the story. While witches are superstitiously talked about, no witches appear in the opera either onstage or offstage. The second is that the protagonist Manrico is in fact the Count de Luna's younger brother. That may or may not be so. The only one who could know, the gypsy Azucena, is delusional, her words untrustworthy. Directors can stage the work as if Manrico is the brother, as if he is not the brother, or as if it is impossible to know. The third misconception is that some parts of the plot make no sense, such as Manrico's riding off to battle with his men at the end of Act III and then suddenly being in prison at the beginning of Act IV. This makes perfect sense: Manrico has been captured in battle by de Luna during events that occurred offstage between the two acts. Clear stage direction (and translation) makes this obvious.

What is it about *Il trovatore* that audiences love? According to musicologist Roger Parker:

> if one trait can be singled out that best accounts for the opera's success, it is probably the sheer musical energy apparent in all the numbers. Time and again we find a relentless rhythmic propulsion in the accompaniment, and a tendency for the melodic lines to be forced into a restrictive compass, freeing themselves rarely but with consequent explosive power. (Parker, 1992: IV: 827)

Energy, propulsion, explosive power! All of which can be quashed by a bad translation!

Table 3.3 in Chapter 3 showed how Natalia Macfarren's obsessive adherence to the original rhyme scheme blunted the force of some of *Il trovatore*'s lines. Her translation can also blunt the forward movement of the opera. While it may seem absurd to be concerned in 2015 about a translation published in 1898, Macfarren's remains the translation from which many learn what the opera is about. The Schirmer edition including it is still in print and widely distributed in the United States.

Near the end of Act III, just as Manrico is about to marry his beloved Leonora, he learns that de Luna has captured Azucena (his adoptive and perhaps even biological mother) and is about to burn her at the stake. Manrico rushes out in an attempt to rescue Azucena, an attempt that proves to be spectacularly unsuccessful (which is why the beginning of Act IV finds both him and Azucena in prison). As Manrico is about to rush out, Verdi propels the music forward in a famous tenor aria by setting the tempo in a moderately fast 3/4 time at 100 beats per minute, and by means of a rhythmic figure in the accompaniment (see Figure 4.1). This rhythmic figure, which Verdi used many times in his operas, has been described as "vulgar" by many, and may even be so when played loudly by the orchestra (the score including the Macfarren translation marks it *mezzoforte*). However, Verdi's original dynamic marking is *piano*.

FIGURE 4.1 Il trovatore, *No. 11, mm. 138–39.*

Table 4.2 shows the second stanza of the Italian lyrics, together with a literal English translation, Macfarren's singable translation, and our own singable translation.

In her need to rhyme exactly as in the original, Macfarren inserts irrelevant or twisted thoughts: "I, who implor'd thee." "Implor'd thee" to what? In the source text, Manrico acknowledges Leonora's suffering; he does not worry about his own heart. By rhyming *abcb* rather than *abab*, we can adhere closely to what Manrico actually says.

Unsurprisingly, both adaptation and re-translation are centuries-old traditions, because no translation can ever be suitable for all times, or even for all purposes at a given time. Performances on the musical stage are always a collaboration between the composer, the librettist, the performers, the director, the conductor, the set designer, and the costumer. A translation for the production of an opera, say, set at the time of the action could be very different from a translation for a production set at the time of the work's creation, and again different for a production with a contemporary setting. Works with structural flaws may become stageworthy with a little tinkering. Incomplete works or works with missing parts may need the gaps filled in. The musical stage, like the stage in general, lives only in performance and, with or without a change in the script, no two performances are ever the same.

TABLE 4.2 *Il trovatore*, No. 11, mm. 155–76.

Original Italian lyrics	Literal English translation
Era già figlio prima d'amarti; non può frenarmi il tuo martir! Madre infelice, corro a salvarti, o teco almeno corro a morir!	I was her son before I loved you [Leonora]; Your suffering will not hold me back! Unhappy mother, I run to save you, or at least run to die with you!
Singable Translation by Natalia Macfarren (1898)	Singable Translation by Herman and Apter (2002)
She was my mother ere I ador'd thee, I'll not desert her, though my heart break. Farewell, belov'd one, I, who implor'd thee, my wretched mother cannot forsake!	Though you may suffer, I cannot stay here; she is my mother, you are my bride. Unhappy mother, I swear to save you or to die with you there at your side!

5

Dealing with difference

We live in an era of rapid cultural change. People find it difficult to adapt to such change, and it is no surprise that cultural change is a theme in some works for the musical stage: for instance, the Bock/Harnick/Stein musical *Fiddler on the Roof* (1964), based on stories by *Sholem Aleichem* (1859–1916), in which the characters' initial devotion to "tradition" is shattered by the necessity of survival; and Verdi's *Ernani* (1844), based on the play *Hernani, ou l'Honneur Castillan* (*Hernani, or Castillian Honor*) (1830) by Victor Hugo (1802–85), whose title character is destroyed in part by his inability to adapt to a society in which the judicial power of the state has replaced personal vengeance.

However, most works for the musical stage are not about cultural change. They are firmly rooted in a specific culture, usually including at least some elements alien to other cultures. Some believe that music itself, as a "universal" language, can bridge cultural differences at least partially. Mezzo-soprano Joyce DiDonato (1969–) has remarked:

> When everything is working as it should in opera, it's the nearest thing I know to understanding how others might think and feel, even if they are totally different from me. (DiDonato, 2014: 5)

It is true that, much of the time, translators do not try to deal with cultural differences. They simply translate what is said, relying on the music and a "willing suspension of disbelief," together with the overall context, to sufficiently explain everything necessary to enjoy a work. However, cultural differences sometimes pose translation problems not solvable by straightforward translation. As Annie Brisset asks:

How should the cockney dialogue in *Pygmalion* be translated? What French-language dialect equivalent should be used to render the [L]unfardo of Buenos Aires [a dialect arising in the late 19th and early 20th centuries among the lower classes of Buenos Aires, since spread into general use] in translations of Robert Arlt's novels? . . . What is the French equivalent of the English of the American South in Faulkner's novels? . . . Should the translator re-create the feeling of the time period of the text for the contemporary reader? Or, conversely, should the archaic form of the language be modernized to make the text more accessible to the contemporary reader? . . . Should Cicero's style be rendered by the style of a well-known politician of modern times? (Brisset, 1996: 344)

Additional questions arise: How should material purposefully incomprehensible to its original audience be translated? How should words in the original text foreign to the source language be translated? Is there any way to indicate that these foreign words signify a past or present colonial influence?

The answer to the last question is often "no." There is no way to translate into English words such as "*tchesterfield,*" found in a novel written in Québécois, in which the many loan words from English denote a form of linguistic oppression. Calling a sofa a chesterfield in an English text loses the point. Calling it a *canapé* draws attention to the language of the source text, but still makes no suggestion of linguistic oppression. Moreover, it might leave many readers wondering why anyone would sit on an appetizer. To explain linguistic oppression in such an instance, translators must rely on extralinguistic, paratextual means such as footnotes or program notes.

5.1 Conventions

5.1.1 Musical conventions

Translators of performable lyrics, by the very nature of their task, cannot change the musical conventions inherent in a work. For many works for the musical stage, this means that translators must deal with music that signals the time and place of a work's creation rather than the time and place of its dramatic setting. This is the way many composers compose, because they are most comfortable with their own musical idiom, because they wish to be comprehensible to their audience, or because, as in early nineteenth-century Italy, it is the only approach acceptable. Such music is usually "transparent" to its first audience, who see no musical obstacle to the dramatic presentation of a different time and place. However, the music may very well be a problem for audiences of a different time and place. Stage directors and production designers, but not translators, may sometimes "solve" this problem by costuming or setting a work in the time and place of a work's creation rather than those of its setting.

Of course, there *are* works for the musical stage that strongly evoke times or places other than those of their creation. Among them is the opera *Carmen* (1875), with music by Georges Bizet (1838–75) and libretto by Henri Meilhac (1830–97) and Ludovic Halévy (1834–1908). Bizet, though French, wrote music that signals Spain (or at least it does so for non-Spaniards; Spaniards sometimes complain that it is not authentic). *Carmen*'s Overture, for instance, opens with a bullfight march and Act I includes at least two numbers having a Spanish or Spanish-influenced form: Carmen's famous Habanera (No. 5) and the Seguidilla (No. 10). In similar fashion, Kander, Ebb, and Masteroff's *Cabaret* (1966) musically signals pre-Nazi Germany. The opening staccato vamp of the first musical number is reminiscent of the Weimar music of Kurt Weill, and the Nazi anthem "Tomorrow Belongs To Me" (Act I, No. 10) is reminiscent of the Silcher/Heine German song *"Die Lorelei."*

Other works make smaller gestures toward the time and place of the dramatic setting. Verdi signals Paris by opening *La traviata* (1853) with music for the rapid galop known today as the can-can, although most of the opera's music is clearly Italian. Rodgers and Hammerstein's *The King and I* (1951) employs the "March of the Siamese Children" to make an "inflection" (as Rodgers is said to have called it) toward Siam.

But many works for the musical stage lack even the gestures of Verdi and Rodgers. The Broadway musical *Camelot* (1960), with music by Frederick Loewe (1901–88) and libretto by Alan Jay Lerner (1918–86), is set in medieval England, but its music always signals mid-twentieth-century America.

Music signaling the "wrong" time and place can create problems for translators.

Consider *Maria Stuarda (Mary Stuart)* (1835), an Italian opera by composer Gaetano Donizetti (1797–1848) and librettist Giuseppe Bardari (1817–61). Although set in sixteenth-century England at the Court of Queen Elizabeth, *Maria Stuarda* does not make the slightest musical gesture toward that time and place. Figure 5.1 shows part of an orchestral interlude in the first number. The notes run up and down scales in parallel thirds (treble clef, mm. 131–32), an Italian folk-song motif that firmly anchors the opera in nineteenth-century Italy. In consequence, before the action even begins, a non-Italian audience is signaled to expect a nineteenth-century Italian setting.

FIGURE 5.1 Maria Stuarda, *No. 1, mm. 130–33.*

A domesticating translation of *Maria Stuarda* into contemporary English creates a double set of semiotic clashes: with the time and place signaled by the music and with the time of the dramatic events signaled by contemporary English. Translators can choose to eliminate the second clash by translating into Elizabethan English (although that could create other problems, and we know of no translators who have done this for *Maria Stuarda*). The clash created by the music can only be eliminated by the audience's "willing suspension of disbelief" or a change of dramatic setting by the stage director or production designer.

5.1.2 Dramatic conventions

Dramatic conventions, though still difficult to alter, are somewhat more open to translatorial intervention than are purely musical conventions.

A dramatic and musical convention for mid-nineteenth-century French operettas required every act to end with a chorus. Conforming to this rule is *Le médecin malgré lui (The Doctor in Spite of Himself)* (1858) by Charles Gounod, based on the 1666 prose farce by Molière (1622–73). The operetta generally follows Molière's plot line, except at the end of Act I, where an obligatory chorus is inserted. In this chorus (No. 5), woodcutters and their wives sing of their honest labor and rustic pleasures, good words and music with no counterpart in Molière's original and totally out of place after a slapstick trio, which dramatically and musically is the logical end of the act. Although we did not change its position or alter the lyrics in our translation, we did suggest in notes that the chorus be eliminated or repositioned. The notes also suggested a cut in post-trio dialogue and the addition of a new stage direction to make either change work.

A purely dramatic convention, though one with musical implications, required the name of every character on an Italian stage to be Italian, regardless of the character's actual nationality. This convention remained in effect through the middle of the nineteenth century. The names could be Italianized versions of the original names, such as Elisabetta and Maria Stuarda for Elizabeth and Mary Stuart in Donizetti's *Maria Stuarda* (1835); or completely different, such as Violetta and Alfredo for Marguerite and Armand, the former being the names in Verdi's *La traviata* (1853), the latter being the names in the French novel (1848) and play (1852) *La Dame aux camélias (The Lady of the Camellias)* by Alexandre Dumas *fils* (1824–95) on which the libretto of *La traviata* is based.

When translating changed names, translators must decide whether or not to leave them changed. Should the main characters in *La traviata* be Violetta and Alfredo? Or be Anglicized to Violet and Alfred? Or be restored to Marguerite and Armand? Natalia Macfarren (1898) and Ruth and Thomas Martin (1946/61) Anglicized Alfredo to Alfred but left Violetta alone. We, and also Joseph Machlis (1962), chose to leave the names as in Italian. We believed English-speaking opera-goers to be so familiar with the Italian names that they have become, in effect, the "real" names.

Not changing names can also have consequences for translators. In *La traviata*, Paris is mentioned several times, as is Provence, the region of southern France where Alfredo grew up. A person named Alfredo from Provence and Paris? We tried to mute the connection to France by eliminating the French place names. Since the libretto makes a sharp distinction between Paris itself (the "city") and its suburbs (the "country"), we felt justified in changing "Paris" to "the city." This has the added advantage that "the city" has the same number of syllables and the same stress pattern as "*Parigi*," the Italian word for "Paris," so we were spared the misery of trying to fit "Paris" into an unaccommodating musical phrase. Similarly, since Provence is invoked mainly as a place of sunshine and warmth, we felt justified in calling it "the South." This did require shifting it in the musical phrase to notes that would accommodate it.

Since, unlike the names in *La traviata*, the names of the French characters in Verdi's *Un giorno di regno* (1840) are not well known to English speakers, we felt free to change them from Italian to French. Edoardo became Édouard; his beloved Giulietta was once more Juliette, their names in the French play on which the libretto of *Un giorno di regno* is based. Thus was eliminated one small element of the semiotic clash arising from the mixture of Italian music, French setting, and English translation. However, in a domesticating gesture, we also chose to use the spoken form of French names, the form in which they are more familiar to English speakers. Thus, in our English translation, "Juliette" is pronounced "Ju-LIET" as in spoken French, and not "Ju-LIET-tuh" as in sung French.

The problem of names is minor compared to the problem posed by a dramatic convention of Baroque opera: the sheer length of a work. Complete Baroque operas often run about four hours. In their own day, roughly 1650 to 1750, performances were lengthened even more to five or six hours by interpolated unrelated scenes and acts called *intermedi*—ballets, acrobatics, farces, or magic shows. The audience behaved rather like contemporary crowds at a baseball game, talking with friends, eating and drinking, paying more or less attention to the performance, and cheering especially athletic vocal feats. Knowing that the audience would not be paying too much attention, creators of Baroque operas used and reused a few simple plots. There was minimal plot development and much repetition of information. Modern audiences, accustomed to paying attention and sitting still, would be bored stiff—literally.

The obvious solution is to eliminate *intermedi* and make cuts in the opera proper. Unfortunately, in our experience, the obvious solution does not work very well. Critical theory of the Baroque era placed high value on balanced construction, and works such as Alessandro Scarlatti's *Eraclea* (1700) conform to this esthetic. In the plot, three love affairs allow the display of different reactions to the emotions of love. A mature trio of lovers struggles to balance the conflicting claims of love and duty. A quartet of teen-agers plays at love and jealousy, switching with ease from one "eternal" love to another. Finally, in a farcical subplot, a pompous elderly tutor finds himself helplessly in lust with a young servant girl—who is really a boy in disguise. All this is played out while adhering to another convention of the period: the allotment of one unmixed emotion per aria. The existence of mixed emotions was known, but it was felt that examination of an emotion in its "pure" state would give better, clearer information. (This notion derives from the ancient Greek theory that there is a pure "type" of all things, including emotions, despite the fact that all the things humans can see are impure, contaminated by "accidents".) In conformity with this belief, Baroque operas examined falling in love in one series of arias; jealousy in another; the claims of honor in yet another. While each character displayed only one unmixed emotion at a time, the audience, over the course of the opera, was presented with a range of possible feelings.

If cuts are made, structural problems arise: a stage of love does not get fully examined here; a matching incident is lopped off there. The result is an imbalance hard to pinpoint. When a cut version of our translation of *Eraclea* was produced, the opera still seemed too long to most of the audience, possibly because its structure had been destroyed. We do not know whether a remedy exists, but we propose, as an experiment, an attempt to replicate the Baroque experience: a full-length performance, perhaps even complete with *intermedi*, but in a dinner-theater setting, house lights up, refreshments served at buffet tables the whole time, with the audience free to move about and talk quietly.

5.2 Common knowledge

The expression "every schoolboy knows that" is not used much any more. A common body of knowledge among "educated" people no longer exists.

Many in the United States, for example, though possessing college degrees, have never heard of Mozart or Verdi or Rodgers and Hammerstein. Therefore it is often unrealistic to assume that twenty-first-century audiences know the cultural assumptions inherent in artistic works or understand allusions to previous works. Despite this, a direct translation of the libretto often suffices to explain everything needed by the performers and the audience.

Common customs and attitudes in past works for the musical stage, alien to our own time yet not needing further explanation, include the deference due royalty, mocked in Verdi's *Un giorno di regno* (1840), and the absolute right of parents and guardians to determine whom their children or wards may marry. The latter is a prominent feature of no less than twelve works we have translated for the musical stage. Tellingly, only one is a twentieth-century work: *La figlia del mago (The Sorcerer's Daughter)* (1981/91) with music by Lorenzo Ferrero (1951–) and libretto by Marco Ravasini (dates unavailable), a fairy tale created to introduce children to the conventions of Italian opera. Contemporary Western women (and men), including royalty, generally marry whomever they wish. When Tex Ritter (1905–74) sang "Oh to be torn twixt love and duty" (music by Dimitri Tiomkin [1894–1979], words by Ned Washington [1901–76]) on the soundtrack of the 1952 film *High Noon*, the choice was one to be made by the protagonist himself, not by any other party.

Some customs do need further explanation from translators: for instance, the fact that certain land-holding widows in mid-nineteenth-century Bohemia (now the Czech Republic) could vote, although women in general were disenfranchised. It is necessary to know this in order to understand some of the motivations and events in *Dvě vdovy (Two Widows)* (1874/77), a Czech opera with music by Bedřich Smetana (1824–84) and libretto by Emanuel Züngel (1840–95). The character Karolina, one of the "Two Widows," does say "I vote" (Act I, Scene 2), but we believe that more explanation is needed and so we provide it in footnotes to the printed text and in program notes.

Allusions can be to "real life," but more often are to previous or contemporary artistic works and conventions. Allusions to or even direct quotations from other works are used to borrow ideas, words, or musical phrases; to pay homage to another work (or to its creators); and to make fun of another work or the conventions utilized in its creation.

Like cultural assumptions, many allusions require no effort on the part of translators beyond translation. It is interesting but not really necessary to know that the orchestral *"Notturno"* ("Nocturne") opening Act II of *La figlia del mago* (*The Sorcerer's Daughter*) is based on a tone row taken from a work by Anton Webern (1883–1945).

It is somewhat more important to know the allusions in the songs of Johannes Brahms (1833–97) but, as with some explanations of customs, translators can inform the performers in footnotes to a printed edition, and performers can inform the audience by announcements from the stage (see Schmalfeldt, 2014, for a discussion of Brahms's allusion to a song by Robert Schumann [1810–56] and for a bibliography of material on Brahms's allusions).

Allusions are of concern for translators working out of English as well as for those working into English. For instance, the operettas of Gilbert and Sullivan provide a trove of allusions, parodies, and direct quotations from other works. Indeed, when the first two bars of "When a merry maiden marries" in the G&S operetta *The Gondoliers* (1889) was said to be too much like the first two bars of the ballad "Love's Old Sweet Song" (1884), Sullivan famously replied, "We had only eight notes between us." Some G&S allusions are explicit. In *The Mikado* (1885), the title character sings a song in Act II in which the words "By Bach, interwoven / With Spohr and Beethoven" are accompanied by a quotation of the main theme from Bach's *Great Fantasia and Fugue in G minor*, BWV 542. More obscure, at least for a twenty-first-century audience, is the beginning of a song (No. 5) in *H.M.S. Pinafore* (1878), "Sorry her lot," whose first words are remarkably similar to those beginning an aria in Mozart's *Die Entführung aus dem Serail* (*The Abduction from the Seraglio*) (1782) (No. 10b), "*Traurigkeit ward mir zum Lose*" ("Sorrow became my lot").

Sometimes the translators themselves add an allusion. In *Dvě vdovy* (*Two Widows*), the three main characters are educated mid-nineteenth-century Czechs. It is reasonable to assume that they are familiar with the operas of Mozart, which were extremely popular in Bohemia. Therefore, for an exchange in Act I, Scene 6 between the characters Karolina and Ladislav:

> **Karolina:** Stáří vaše, na den stanoveno?
> **Ladislav:** Narozen jsem před třiceti lety!
>
> (**Karolina:** Your age on the day in question?
> **Ladislav:** I was born thirty years ago!)

our performable translation reads

> **Karolina:** State your age on the day in question.
> **Ladislav:** Thirty years and twenty-seven minutes.
> (Herman and Apter, 1984)

This is an allusion to the famous exchange in Mozart's *Die Zauberflöte* (*The Magic Flute*) (1791), Act II, Scene 15:

> **Papageno:** Sag du mir, wie alt bist du denn?
> **Weib:** Wie alt?
> **Papageno:** Ja!
> **Weib:** 18 Jahr und 2 Minuten.

(Papageno: Tell me, how old are you then?
Woman: How old?
Papageno: Yes!
Woman: 18 years and 2 minutes.)

An opera whose allusions to operatic conventions create much of its comedy is *L'occasione fa il ladro ossia Il cambio della valigia* (*Opportunity Makes the Thief [or, A Thief by Chance] or Baggage Astray*) (1812), an Italian farce with music by Gioacchino Rossini (1792–1868) and a libretto by Luigi Prividali (1771–1844), adapted from the play *Le prétendu par hasard, ou l'occasion fait le larron* (*Engaged by Chance, or Opportunity Makes the Thief*) (1810) by Eugène Scribe (1791–1861). This opera mocks, parodies, and plays with several operatic conventions in force at the time of its creation: overly complex plots, identity switching, the cowardly scheming nature of servants, falling in love with a portrait, and falling in love at first sight. The convention of the arranged marriage is one of the motivators of the dramatic action.

It is easy to retain much of the parody in *L'occasione* by translating fairly literally. We did not elucidate the allusions, believing (or perhaps hoping) that an audience familiar with opera would be able to identify them. When *L'occasione* premiered, identity switching would have brought to mind the identity switches in Mozart's *Così fan tutte* (*The Way They're Made*) (1790). In *Così*, two men disguised as strangers woo and win each other's fiancées. *L'occasione* ups the ante, parodying not only *Così*'s switches, but also the scandal they caused. It was thought reprehensible that, in *Così*, young unmarried women were each being led on by the wrong fiancé. In *L'occasione*, both the men and the women switch identities, with the result that the lovers are always decorously paired. We could have explained the connection between the two operas by letting a character in *L'occasione* make a statement referring to *Così*. We did not. Instead we relied on the double switches and resulting confusion to make the parodic point.

We also did not make any special effort to pair the act of falling in love with a portrait in *L'occasione* with the "Portrait Aria" in Mozart's *Die Zauberflöte* (*The Magic Flute*) (1791). Neither did we pair the parody of falling in love at first sight with any particular opera. *L'occasione*'s protagonist Parmenione does it twice, once with a portrait and later with a woman who is not the one depicted in the portrait. (*Die Zauberflöte*, by the way, is perfectly capable of mocking itself. Tamino falls in love at first sight with a portrait. Pamina ups the ante by immediately falling in love upon first *hearing* that Tamino is in love with her.)

However, we did draw attention to *L'occasione*'s adherence to the convention of the clever, cowardly, scheming servant. This dramatic convention goes at least as far back as the classic dramas of the Greeks and Romans. *L'occasione fa il ladro* signals that it is making fun of the convention, as opposed to merely utilizing it, with a moment of meta-drama during which the performer almost steps out of character to comment. Grilled about the identity of his master Parmenione, the servant Martino says (Recitative before No. 7, mm. 4–7):

> La verità! Ma come mai, signore, pretenderla si può da un servitore?
> (The truth! But how, sir, can that be asked of a servant?)

This bit of meta-drama gave us license, we believe, to point Martino's slyness. While refusing to reveal his master's identity, he slips in a devastating word-picture, which, of course, is a lie. Or is it? We point his slyness by emphasizing the two different English meanings of "common" (see Table 3.7 in Chapter 3).

Another convention to which our translation draws attention is *L'occasione*'s mockery of overly complex plots, a staple of opera since soon after its inception. By the mid-seventeenth century, complex plots were being parodied in comic operas such as *Erismena* (or *L'Erismena)* (1655), with music by Francesco Cavalli (1602–76) and libretto by Aurelio Aureli (fl 1652–1708). *Erismena* presents the audience with the following Argomento, a series of events occurring before the opera begins:

> [W]hile on a visit to Armenia, Prince Erimante of Media fell in love with Arminda, sister of King Artamene. Before they could marry, Erimante was summoned home to succeed his father as king. Arminda died giving birth to their child, Erismena. When Erimante learnt of Arminda's death he vowed to live a celibate life, but he abandoned this noble intention when he fell in love with his Iberian slave, Aldimira. Erismena, ignorant of her father's identity, grew up outside the Armenian court. Yet she seemed to have had some connection with it because she met Prince Idraspe of Iberia, who on a visit to Armenia seduced her. Although his original intentions were honourable, he left in search of new conquests. Reaching Media, he assumed the name of Erineo, attained a position at court and fell in love with Aldimira, now King Erimante's favourite. When Erismena discovered that Idraspe had gone to Media, she disguised herself in men's clothes and joined the Armenian army. (Clinkscale, 1992: II: 63–64)

We hope you got all that, because the opera is about to start.

The plot of *L'occasione fa il ladro* is similarly complicated. Some of its complications have already been mentioned, including double identity switching (with one woman pretending to be another woman pretending to be a servant) and double falling in love at first sight. All ends happily, with the planning of a double wedding.

Once again, the creators of *L'occasione fa il ladro* reveal via meta-drama that they are mocking a convention, rather than merely utilizing it. The final lines of a quintet in the middle of the opera are shown in Table 5.1. Since modern

TABLE 5.1 *L'occasione fa il ladro*, No. 4, mm. 324–92.

Italian lyrics	Literal English translation
Di tanto equivoco, di tal disordine nel cupo, orrible, confuso vortice, urta, precipita, s'avvolge, rotola, perduto il cerebro per aria va: ma si dissimuli, che senza strepito già tutto in seguito si scoprirà.	Because of such misunderstanding, of such disorder in a dark, horrible, confused whirlpool, he knocks about, plunges headlong, embroils himself, spins; brain lost, through the air he goes: but he is deceived, because without any hubbub, of course all later on will be laid bare.

	Singable English translation
	Oh how confusedly implausibilities of great perplexity resist analyses! Insane complexities increase relentlessly in whirling vortices of growing force! But soon reality will end the masquerade and everything will be made clear, of course. (Herman and Apter, 2007)

audiences often experience meta-drama, we believed we had to accentuate the wink in the lyrics by exaggerating somewhat; otherwise Prividali's "of course all later on will be laid bare" might not be noticed. Therefore, until nearly the end, we pile multi-syllabic words on top of each other to intensify the confusion signified in the Italian by the hectic tempo. We then add the word "masquerade" and emphasize "of course" by moving the phrase to the end of the line and the end of the quintet.

There is another quasi-meta-dramatic moment near the end of *L'occasione* when Uncle Eusebio, although almost all has been explained, complains, "*Io sbalordito resto*" ("I remain bewildered") (No. 9, mm. 31–33). After the giddy whirl of the plot, his line may give comfort to those members of the audience who share his bewilderment.

And also to confused critics. Richard Osborne, in the entry on *L'occasione* in the *Grove Dictionary of Opera* (1992: III: 644), incorrectly states that the portrait with which Parmenione first falls in love is a portrait of one of the onstage characters. It is not; it is a portrait of a woman who never appears in the opera at all.

5.3 Historicity

History is not what you thought.
It is what you can remember.
(Sellar and Yeatman, 1931: vii)

Americans remember George Washington (1732–99), who lived over 200 years ago. Britons remember Henry V (1386–1422), who lived six centuries ago. But who remembers Eyre Massey Shaw (1830–1908), who was still alive little more than a century ago?

In Act II of Gilbert & Sullivan's *Iolanthe* (1882) the Fairy Queen sings:

Oh, Captain Shaw!
  Type of true love kept under!
  Could thy Brigade
  With cold cascade
Quench my great love, I wonder!

Captain Shaw was Chief of the London Fire Brigade, and just happened to be sitting in the front row on opening night so that the Fairy Queen could ask him personally whether or not his company's fire hoses could extinguish her burning passion (Green, 1961: 301). Undoubtedly, audience members who were there and knew what was happening were delighted.

When confronted with a historical reference like the one to Captain Shaw, translators into non-English languages (and stage directors for English-language productions) have the following options:

1   Do nothing. The audience has to make do with the incomprehensible reference.

2   Provide an explanation for the audience in program notes.

3   Provide footnotes for the performers in the printed text. If the performers know what they are talking about, the context and the performances may be able to communicate sufficient understanding to the audience.

4   Somehow work an explanation directly into the performable text.

5   Rewrite the lyrics, substituting a character or event that the audience knows for the character or event it does not know.

6   Eliminate the reference.

Lecocq's *La fille de Madame Angot (Madame Angot's Daughter)* (1872) is chockful of historical references. This French comic operetta preceded and greatly influenced the Gilbert and Sullivan operettas that followed. It was created in 1872 and set in France in 1797, during the period of the Directory (1795–99), a government which, while still Revolutionary, put an end to the Reign of Terror of 1793–94. The title character is fictional, but several other important characters are historical persons, including the onstage Mademoiselle Lange (1772–1816), an actress, and the offstage Paul Barras (1755–1829), the leader of the five-person Directory. In addition to these two, the work drops the names of no fewer than seven other offstage historical persons, ranging from the military commander Pierre Augereau (1757–1816) to the composer François-Joseph Gossec (1734–1829). Months are given their Revolutionary names, for example, Thermidor, the Julian calendar's mid-July through mid-August. Two battles are called French victories: one actual victory, Montenotte, where Napoleon first defeated the Austrians in 1796; and one terrible defeat, Aboukir, the site of the destruction of the French fleet by the British Navy under Nelson in 1798. The British name for Aboukir is The Battle of the Nile.

The librettists apparently did not care whether or not their historical references were correct. History is what you remember! There is no need to refer to half-forgotten schoolbooks to get the facts right. A mishmash of events is all that is needed to create an aura of the period. It is of little importance that the conspiracy recounted in the plot sets the operetta in September 1797, but the characters allude to events of 1798.

We too try to preserve the aura of historicity without too great a concern for exact detail. We leave the name-dropping in situ—a foreignizing gesture—and provide footnotes so that the actors can tell whether the names are real or fictitious. The stage director of the first production cut some of these references. We domesticate the reference to Aboukir. In context, the exact battle is immaterial so long as it is an easily recognizable French defeat. We cannot just say "Battle of the Nile" because Americans would not recognize it, and so we substitute "Agincourt," the famous French loss to the English in 1415.

Historicity is a more complicated issue for Donizetti's *Maria Stuarda* (1835). This opera recounts the events leading up to the execution of Mary Stuart, Queen of Scots (1542–87), on the orders of Queen Elizabeth I (1533–1603). These events can reasonably be expected to be known by at least some members of an English-speaking audience. However, several of the events in the opera are not historically true. Some were believed to be true at the time of the work's creation, and some were deliberately falsified. All events, true or not, were slanted by the work's creators.

In the received British Protestant view of history, Mary is a villain. In Donizetti's opera, told from the Italian Catholic viewpoint, she is very much a victim.

The facts (together with a few speculations) are these: In 1566, Mary's private secretary, David Rizzio (1533–66), was murdered. Historians speculate that one of the murderers was Mary's second husband, Henry Stuart, Lord Darnley (1545–67). His motivation was jealousy. In 1567, Darnley himself was murdered, and rumors spread that Mary was involved in the murder, supposedly motivated by the wish to avenge Rizzio's death and to continue an adulterous affair with James Hepburn, Earl of Bothwell (1534–78), who in fact became her third husband within a few months. Fleeing the rumors and in fear of her life at the hands of parties supporting Scotland's Protestant Reformation, Catholic Mary sought refuge in England. England, like Scotland, was Protestant, but there were a large number of Catholic English subjects, both openly and in secret. As the great grand-daughter of Henry VII (1457–1509), Mary had a claim to the English throne. When she refused to repudiate this claim, Elizabeth put her under house arrest. Then, in 1570, Pope Pius V (1504–72, declared a saint in 1712) issued the papal bull *Regnans in Excelsis*, excommunicating Elizabeth, denouncing her as "the servant of wickedness," stripping her of the title "Queen of England," and absolving her Catholic subjects of any allegiance to her (Plowden, 1999: 171). This essentially sealed Mary's fate, because now her very existence, as the presumptive "rightful" Catholic heir to the throne of England, was a threat to Elizabeth's crown and life. Matters came to a head when Mary was tried, convicted, and sentenced to death for complicity in the so-called Babington plot of 1586. Elizabeth delayed signing the death warrant, fearing the consequences of executing an anointed ruler. She finally signed it, and Mary was beheaded in February 1587.

So, was Mary a murderer or a martyr? The play *Maria Stuart* (1800) by Friedrich von Schiller (1759–1805), upon which the libretto for the opera is based, takes the position (V.7, lines 3697, 3729–30), believed by historians at the time, that Mary was complicit in the murder of Darnley but innocent of conspiring against Elizabeth. Modern historians believe the opposite in both cases. Current thinking is that Mary was innocent of complicity in the plot to murder Darnley, and that the so-called casket letters produced at her trial were forgeries designed to traduce her reputation. On the other hand, modern historians do believe that Mary was a party to the attempt to assassinate Elizabeth, though they also believe that the "plot" was largely an entrapment scheme (Fraser 1969: chapter 24).

At least one modern historian, Jenny Wormald, complains that the entire question of Mary's guilt or innocence has been a distraction from more important historical matters (1988; revised 2001: 18). But it is just the possibility of a crime of passion, especially if absurd or lurid like the murders of Rizzio and Darnley, that attracts the most attention, that becomes the stuff of romance, Hollywood films (never accused of too much historical accuracy), and opera.

A 1997 production of *Maria Stuarda*, sung in Italian in the Netherlands, included bald-headed women in red (possibly as personifications of the classical Roman image of Fortune) strolling around Westminster Palace; what may have been a cocaine-sniffing scene; and a dancer, at times representing Mary and at times representing Elizabeth, worked like a marionette by George Talbot, the Earl of Shrewsbury (1528–90). As staged, this was not a historical drama.

Translators of this opera must decide whether or not it *is* a historical drama, and, if so, on which version of history they will rely. The main driver of the plot, a love triangle between Elizabeth, Mary, and Robert Dudley, Earl of Leicester (1532–88), and a pivotal event, a meeting between Elizabeth and Mary, are both fictitious. Nevertheless, both we and Amanda Holden decided that there is enough real history in *Maria Stuarda* to consider it a historical drama.

Holden, a British translator whose British audience is likely to revere Queen Elizabeth I, domesticates the history in that she makes Elizabeth a stronger and wiser monarch than does the libretto. We leave Elizabeth's character alone, but, feeling that the political reasons for executing Mary deserve some space, insert them where possible.

Consider the first words of Queen Elizabeth when she enters at the beginning of Act I. The King of France has asked for her hand in marriage, and she tells her assembled Court, in a literal English translation:

Yes, the King of France desires, together with my heart, the English throne. Doubtful still am I [whether] to accept the exalted invitation, but, if the well-being of my faithful Britons causes me to set out to the altar of Hymen, this right hand shall rule the destinies of both France and England.

This is both good politics and historically fairly accurate. She will only marry if it is both good for her people and if she, rather than the French King, will rule both countries.

Then, to herself, she sings the real reason for her hesitation: her love for Leicester. The original Italian lyrics, a literal translation, and the singable translations of both us and Amanda Holden are shown in Table 5.2.

TABLE 5.2 *Maria Stuarda*, Act I, No. 1, mm. 133–1450

Original Italian text	Literal English translation

(da sé)
Ah quando all' ara scorgemi
    un casto amor del Cielo,
quando m'invita a prendere
    d'Imene il roseo velo,
un altro core involami
    la cara, la cara libertà!
E mentre vedo sorgere
fra noi fatal barriera,
fra noi fatal barriera,
ad altro amor sorridere
    quest' anima non sa,
    quest' anima, no, non sa.
	(to herself)
	Ah, when a pure love [sanctioned] by Heaven
	leads me to the altar,
	when it invites me to take up
	the rosy veil of Hymen,
	another heart has stolen from me
	my dear, my dear liberty!
	And when I see, rising
	between us, the fatal barrier,
	between us, the fatal barrier,
	my soul cannot smile
	on another love,
	my soul cannot, no, cannot.

Singable translation by Herman and Apter (1997)	**Singable translation by Amanda Holden (1998)**

(to herself)
Though licit love is offered me,
    love approved by Heaven,
bidding me don the marriage veil
    and yield my self-possession,
another, another has stolen,
stolen my cherished, cherished liberty!
I see a fatal barrier
rise up to separate us,
rise up, rise up to separate us.
My soul cannot smile upon a love
    that cleaves my heart from me,
    my heart from me, my heart from me.
	(aside)
	If ever the will of heaven be
	    I must be led to the altar;
	if when I whisper my marriage vows
	    I fear that my heart may falter,
	it is because I fear to lose
	    the freedom I hold dear.
	And then a barrier rises up
	as love battles with duty,
	as love battles with duty;
	but I cannot wed another man
	    when he I love is near,
	    when he I love is near.

Our singable translation is fairly literal, partly because our mandate from Ricordi required us to be so, and does not shift the implication of these lyrics. In contrast, Amanda Holden's translation brings them closer to historical reality and the British view of Elizabeth. Holden subtly separates the idea of freedom/liberty from Elizabeth's love for Leicester. In the Italian and in our translation, Elizabeth's freedom has been stolen by her love for Leicester. In Amanda

Holden's translation, Elizabeth fears that her liberty will be stolen by the act of marriage itself. And indeed, married queens did not rule in Elizabeth's time; their husbands did. In Holden's translation, after expressing this fear, Elizabeth states her love for Leicester as *another* reason not to marry the King of France.

Despite the requirement to be fairly literal, elsewhere we too occasionally domesticate by changing the slant of the Italian lyrics to one more familiar to our audience. As mentioned above, we (and also Holden) put a clearer statement of the political problem in the mouth of the character Cecil, the only one of Bardari's characters utterly without mercy for Mary. He is also the one character who never discusses the fictional love triangle that occupies so much of the rest of the opera. Instead, he speaks of the real reason for Mary's execution: her very existence as a rallying point for those Catholics plotting to depose Elizabeth. At the beginning of Act II, he exhorts Elizabeth (No. 7, mm. 20–26):

> E pensi? e tardi? e vive chi ti sprezzò?
> chi contro te raduna Europa tutta,
> e la tua sacra vita minacciò tante volte?
>
> (Still considering? still delaying? and she who scorned you is still alive?
> she who musters all of Europe against you?
> and who threatened your sacred life so many times?)

To point these lines, instead of "scorned," we write "defamed," which has political rather than personal overtones. Instead of "musters all of Europe against you," we write "goads all Europe." "Musters" is clear, but "goads" is more forceful and derogatory. Instead of "threatened your sacred life," we write "whose assassins have stalked you." This is historically correct and more vivid. Our translation of these lines reads:

> You ponder. You waver. And Mary remains alive:
> she who has so defamed you, who goads all Europe,
> turning its kings against you, whose assassins have stalked you . . .
>
> (Herman and Apter, 1997)

We made similar shifts in Cecil's wording throughout our translation. Amanda Holden's translation is:

> Still pensive and doubting . . . while Mary laughs you to scorn?
> She'd have the whole of Europe rise up against you,
> and while she is yet living she'll continue to threaten you!
>
> (Holden, 1998)

"Rise up" is a clearer reference to the Papal Bull than exists in the Italian, and Holden's final line moves into the future tense, more strongly implying what is less clear in the Italian: that Cecil views Mary as an ongoing threat, which must be ended by her execution.

Even after some domestication, in both translations the view of history and of the protagonists' characters remains largely that of the Italian libretto. The idea that Elizabeth, being a woman, would have mainly personal motives for her decision to execute Mary is allowed to stand, as are the motives: jealousy over a love triangle that never existed and rage at being vilified by Mary during a meeting that never took place. Neither English version slides past translation into adaptation.

5.4 Sensibility

Views of love, humor, and morality are often culture-specific. Today's translators of nineteenth-century operas and art songs confront a tremendous change in sensibility. Comprising the overlapping Romantic and Victorian eras, the nineteenth century valued deeply felt emotions, especially the emotion of romantic love. Audiences had little or no problem with fictional characters singing about their feelings without a trace of irony or self-awareness. Today, romantic love is still an ideal, but unexamined emotionality is not. Nineteenth-century emotions can easily seem overly sentimental, and the emoters narcissistic or childish.

The shift to the current point of view was anticipated in a remark attributed to Oscar Wilde (1854–1900) about the death of the heroine Little Nell in the novel *The Old Curiosity Shop* (1841) by Charles Dickens (1812–70): "One would have to have a heart of stone to read the death of Little Nell without dissolving into tears . . . of laughter."

Since Wilde's death, two world wars, rapid scientific and technological change, and the environmental havoc wrought by such change have transformed the generally held worldview to one more ironical and cynical. Translators encountering the gap between twenty-first- and nineteenth-century sensibilities must either bridge it or let it stand.

5.4.1 Love

In the opening number of Act II of *West Side Story* (1957) with music by Leonard Bernstein (1918–90) and lyrics by Stephen Sondheim (1930-), Maria's friends sing that she is not "in love" but "merely insane" (Bernstein and Sondheim, 1957: 141–42). But Maria *is* in love and the audience's sympathy is expected to reside with her.

Maria's friends echo a notion widely held in Western society prior to the nineteenth century, the notion that young love is a deranged state of mind and therefore an unsuitable basis for marriage. The prevailing social compact deemed a suitable basis to be compatibility of social status, finances, beliefs, and manners; from this compatibility, it was thought, would come a settled affection. Sexual infatuation was to be feared and outgrown, for it was likely to undermine the social compact upon which "good" marriages were built.

A change in attitude swept in at the beginning of the nineteenth century. The thrill of young love with its strong emphasis on sexuality became idealized and valued as a basis for marriage. That attitude still prevails. People in the twenty-first century not only respect young love but hope to move from being "in love" to a love that lasts a lifetime. They still marry for money or other practical reasons, but romantic love is the ideal. Middle-aged couples go to therapy sessions to put the "spark" back into their marriages, or divorce if they cannot. This would have seemed insane in the seventeenth and eighteenth centuries.

Although the ideal of romantic love took hold in the nineteenth century, such love did not become the actual basis of marriage, especially among the upper socio-economic classes, until after World War I. That left the sufferers of romantic love to continue looking to literature and the stage for a vicarious experience of what they were denied in real life. Thus the many novels and stage works of the seventeenth through early twentieth centuries about romantic love, and the many operas about little else. The seventeenth- and eighteenth-century works, written before the change in sensibility wrought by the Romantic era, view young love affectionately but mockingly—our dear children will outgrow this phase. After the Romantic revolution, strong emotions are taken dead seriously—literally in tragedies—both by their fictional sufferers and by their contemporary audiences.

Mozart's late eighteenth-century operas fall in with the view that young love is amusingly insane. Mozart himself, after being rejected by one daughter of the Weber family, did not despair but married her sister Constanze. While his tender treatment of the characters Belmonte and Konstanze (a variant spelling of his wife's name) in *Die Entführung aus dem Serail (The Abduction from the Seraglio)* (1782) shows his romantic sympathies, on the whole, his librettos and music take the Enlightenment point of view. For example, there is a distance between the emotions of the characters in *Così fan tutte (The Way They're Made)* (1790) and the emotions expected of the audience. The lovers' feelings are mocked to some extent. And, while audiences are expected to sympathize with Tamino as he falls in love with a portrait in *Die Zauberflöte (The Magic Flute)* (1791), they are also invited to laugh at him. As shown in Figure 5.2, in the middle of the portrait aria, his words are halting and are followed by a complete measure of silence. The literal translation is "I would—would—warmly and purely—what would I [do]?"

FIGURE 5.2 Die Zauberflöte, *No. 3, mm. 40–44.*

When translators eliminate Tamino's confusion, they eliminate the eighteenth-century attitude toward love. Translators Natalia Macfarren (Victorian era), Ruth and Thomas Martin (1941/51), and Andrew Porter (1980) maintain it. The translation of Jeremy Sams (1987) and the English subtitles of Ingmar Bergman's film adaptation (1975) mute it. As would be expected in a version set during World War I, Kenneth Branagh's film adaptation of 2006 abandons the eighteenth-century sensibility. Instead of expressing confusion, Tamino says that, until Pamina is beside him, his love "will never, never find release, will never cease." W. H. Auden and Chester Kallman (1955) also eliminate the confusion: "Oh tell me,—image,—grant a sign—Am I her choice?" J. D. McClatchy's abridged singable version (2004) eliminates the entire section of the aria, both words and music.

In *L'occasione fa il ladro* (*A Thief By Chance*) (1812), composer Rossini and librettist Prividali explicitly state that love is irrational. Parmenione answers his servant Martino's objections to a scheme to steal another man's fiancée with the rapid-fire patter shown in Table 5.3. Since Prividali is mocking something considered laughable today, nothing beyond translation is necessary to make the lyrics comprehensible to a modern audience. However, the nuptials planned at the finale concur with a dead father's wishes and are approved of by a live uncle and live older brother. These family acceptances, so carefully worked out by Prividali, seem unnecessary to us. However, this gap in what is considered appropriate need not be bridged for modern productions to be successful.

Stage works with arranged marriages sometimes include a wooing scene occurring after the marriage has been arranged. In such scenes, the husband-to-be woos the bride-to-be, the subtext being "We're stuck with each other, but I'm willing to be a good husband if you're willing to be a good wife, and we might even begin to like, or perhaps even love, each other." Probably the most famous scene of this type occurs in Shakespeare's *Henry V*, when Henry woos the French princess Catherine of Valois, neither being able to speak or understand each other's language very well.

TABLE 5.3 *L'occasione fa il ladro*, No. 2, mm. 143–56.

Italian lyrics	Literal English translation
Eh! finiscila;	Ah! Stop it;
non odo più consigli,	I listen no more to counsels,
non curo più perigli;	I do not care any more about danger:
Amore bricconcello	Love, the little rogue,
mi ha colto nel cervello;	has taken over my judgment;
e questa cara immagine	and this dear image
mi pizzica, mi stuzzica,	pricks me and prods me,
in petto mi fa crescere	in my breast my heart
dall' allegrezza il cor.	grows from happiness.

	Singable English translation
	Stop! Make no mistake:
	however wise your counsel,
	my logic will refute it,
	for love, the little scoundrel,
	has managed to pollute it.
	This image agitates me,
	animates me, stimulates me
	till my heart is palpitating
	at a devastating rate.
	(Herman and Apter, 2007)

Such a scene also occurs in *L'occasione fa il ladro*, the twist being that Parmenione really has, totally irrationally, fallen in love with Ernestina, and the arranged marriage is not between Parmenione, who is impersonating Alberto, and Ernestina, who is impersonating Berenice, but between Alberto and Berenice. At first, Ernestina's reaction to Parmenione's protestations of love made no sense to us. She says (No. 4, mm. 12–18):

Io m'inchino con rispetto alla vostra gran bontà,
con rispetto alla vostra civiltà.

(I bow my head with respect at your great goodness,
with respect at your civility.)

and (No. 4, mm. 20–22):

È bizzarro, ma grazioso.
(He is eccentric, but gracious.)

Only after we realized that she is assuming that Parmenione is offering courtship to a powerless fiancée were we able to understand her response.

She takes Parmenione's behavior as a great courtesy and kindness, and responds with growing attraction.

Since motivations are not especially important in a farce of any period, we put no extra effort into our English translation to explain the cultural causes of Ernestina's state of mind. However, knowledge of the causes helped us to proceed.

5.4.2 Humor

Humor is very much culture-specific. What is considered hysterically funny in one culture bores or even outrages another. Translators can choose to let the target audience laugh at moments regarded as deeply serious by the source audience, or yawn at moments formerly regarded as hilarious. More often, they strive to elicit the responses originally intended.

A joke guaranteed to fall flat occurs in Scarlatti's *Eraclea* (1700). Because the Baroque audience believed that adults should be past feeling lust, they could find funny the situation of a pompous elderly tutor in love with a young servant girl who is really a boy in disguise. And they could find it funny over and over and over again. *Eraclea* includes five full scenes devoted to this situation. The lyrics are new each time but the situation remains the same, and there is no rising arc of tension. Perhaps two fine comic actors could create such an arc, but they will find no help in the script.

Part of the fifth scene is shown in Table 5.4. It would be funny were it the first such exchange, but it is the fifth.

Perhaps worse for translators than failed jokes is laughter elicited by scenes meant to be serious. This problem sometimes arises for Romantic works. In Weber's *Der Freischütz* (1821), the protagonist Max is a hunter, usually an expert marksman, who has lately been missing all his shots. This is of crucial importance because Max will have to make a test shot successfully in order to win the hand of his beloved Agathe. In an aria, Max sings of the happier past (No. 3, mm. 84–96):

> Durch die Wälder, durch die Auen
>   zog ich leichten Sinn's dahin!
> Alles, was ich konnt' erschauen,
>   war des sichern Rohr's Gewinn.

> (Through the forests, through the meadows,
> I went with an easy state of mind!
> All that I could behold
> was to be won by my sure gun.)

The German lyrics bear an unfortunate resemblance to words in Tom Lehrer's "Hunting Song": "You just stand there looking cute, / And when something

TABLE 5.4 *Eraclea*, No. 53, mm. 1–21.

Original Italian lyrics	Literal English translation
LIVIO: Decrepito Adone, t'ho pur compassione, son tutta pietà.	**LIVIO:** Decrepit Adonis, I do have compassion for you, I am all pity.
ALFEO: Lilletta, Lilletta, che sii benedetta, sei tutta pietà.	**ALFEO:** Lilletta, Lilletta, may you be blessed, you are all pity.
LIVIO: Ti prendo la mano e stretta la tengo. Sta lieto, sta lieto, Alfeo se ne va.	**LIVIO:** I take your hand and hold it close. Be happy, be happy, Alfeo is going off.
ALFEO: Pian, piano, pian piano, già sento che svengo. Deh piglia l'aceto, che Alfeo se ne va.	**ALFEO:** Soft, softly, soft, softly, I already feel I am swooning. Pray, fetch the smelling salts, for Alfeo is going off.

Singable English translation
LIVIO: Decrepit Adonis, I'm brimming with pity, with pity for you.
ALFEO: Lilletta, Lilletta, compassionate and pretty, with pity through and through.
LIVIO: Our hands intertwine and our souls are communing. My pride is swelling. The man is swooning, but he will come to/too.
ALFEO: *(stuttering)* Ge-gently, ge-gently, I'm fainting, I'm swooning. Administer the smelling salts and help me come to/too. (Herman and Apter, 1992b)

moves, you shoot!" (Lehrer, 1953/4: 32). Weber worsens the effect by setting the second line on a lighthearted skipping melody that, for many twenty-first-century English speakers, totally undermines Max's seriousness (see Figure 5.3).

FIGURE 5.3 Der Freischütz, *No. 3, mm. 86–88.*

We translated the German into a neutral contemporary English:

> I was carefree as I hunted
>   through the forest in search of game.
> Not a creature I sighted
>   could escape my rifle's aim.
>   (Herman and Apter, 1986)

This diction, with lyrics such as these, could sometimes be convincingly handled by the performers and sometimes not. Reviews reflected this. *The New York Times* reviewer Will Crutchfield, after watching a performance during the first production of our translation, said simply, "the audience got an enjoyable show" (January 19, 1986). However, after seeing a subsequent production, Anne Midgette, another reviewer at *The New York Times*, said:

> "Freischütz's" only hope of gaining a foothold outside Germany lies in its score. Taken out of its cultural and linguistic context, the drama remained a distant museum exhibit rather than a vivid theatrical experience. (Midgette, January 16, 2001)

Midgette perceived the problem. Perhaps our translation might have played better if it were in a language closer in sensibility to the source text, or otherwise more foreignizing so as to let the audience know that the words are the non-risible expression of the attitude of a different culture. Here is a Victorian translation, that of Natalia Macfarren and Theodore Baker, published in 1904:

> Thro' the forests, thro' the meadows,
> Joy was wont with me to stray:
> Ev'ry bird that roam'd in azure
> Was my rifle's easy prey.
>   (Macfarren and Baker, 1904)

Among the many lyrics in *Der Freischütz* that may provoke unwanted laughter are those sung in Act II as Max prepares to brave the horrors of the Wolf's Glen. He tells Agathe that he has no fear, despite the fact that *"der Häher krächzt, die Eule schwebt"* ("the jay croaks, the owl hovers"). Macfarren and Baker remove the possibility of unwanted laughter by changing the meaning. After having Max say that a hunter faces danger, in place of the jay and owl they write, "The earth his bed, the wood his home." We stayed closer to the original and the sound of *"krächzt"* with "a raven shrieks, a fieldmouse squeaks." Our alternative to "a fieldmouse squeaks," for tenors who cannot sing it with a straight face, is "a thornbush creaks."

There is at least one laugh provoker in *Der Freischütz* about which translators can do nothing other than give advice to the stage director. In Act I, when Max shoots an eagle with a magic bullet, the stage direction says it *"stürzt dann tot zu Maxens Füßen"* ("then falls dead at Max's feet"). NO!! In the first performance of one of our productions, the plopping eagle evoked a burst of uncomfortable laughter. In subsequent performances, the rubber-chicken effect was avoided by having the eagle fall offstage.

5.4.3 Morality

Moral standards change over time. It is almost impossible to reproduce for a modern audience, in either a translation or a production, the shock value that an opera such as Verdi's *La traviata* (1853) had for its contemporary Victorian audience. Certainly Verdi, and Alexandre Dumas *fils*, who wrote the novel and play on which *La traviata* is based, were interested not only in writing a touching love story but in exposing hypocrisy and sexual double standards. Verdi himself was in a relationship with and later secretly married Giuseppina Strepponi (1815–97), a woman with two illegitimate children. At the time, marriage to such a woman was thought scandalous by many. Of course, by the double standards of the time, a man with illegitimate children could marry a "pure" woman without scandal.

La traviata literally means "the fallen woman" and Violetta, the title character, is a courtesan, a salaried mistress to upper-class men, in other words, a high-priced prostitute. Nevertheless, as depicted in the opera and its sources, she has estimable moral worth. By the end of the opera (and conveniently just as she is about to die) Giorgio Germont, a respectable member of the middle class, states he will embrace her *"qual figlia"* ("like a daughter"). Shocking? Critics and censors certainly thought so in both Europe and the United States until the beginning of the twentieth century. That was then. In 1982, Franco Zeffirelli (1923–) directed a film version that made the necessary changes for the transition from stage to screen but was not otherwise altered or censored. It was rated G, meaning even unaccompanied children are welcome to see it.

So deeply ingrained in nineteenth-century culture were double standards that the libretto of *La traviata* rarely refers to them, taking them as a given. Therefore, there is little for translators to work with if they wish to make clear the hypocrisy. The one clear statement comes in Act II, Scene 1, No. 5, mm. 220–25, Violetta sings "*Se pur benefico le indulga Iddio, l'uomo implacabil per lei sarà*" ("Even if charitable God is lenient to her, man will be implacable to her"). We tried to emphasize this line in our singable version by means of parallel structure and off-rhyme: "Merciful God will accept her repentance; merciless man will not relent." Here are some other performable translations:

> Heav'n seem'd to smile on my fond aspiration, but man forgives not, and I am lost.
>
> > (Natalia Macfarren, 1898)

> Though heaven smiled on my love in compassion, man is relentless and I must yield.
>
> > (Ruth and Thomas, Martin, 1946/61: 93)

> Even if God will accept her repentance, men are relentless and she is doomed.
>
> > (Joseph Machlis, 1962: 152–53)

Consider especially the foreignizing diction of Natalia Macfarren. For the foreign sensibility of *Der Freischütz*, Macfarren's diction seemed to be a good possible choice. In *La traviata*, it serves to distance the very statement to which we could and should directly respond.

To get past censorship, even those operas opposed to double standards had to kill off sexually active women. Violetta dies at the end of *La traviata*, as does Mimì, another demimonde heroine, at the end of Puccini's *La bohème* (1896). As Catherine Clément has pointed out, female operatic characters are punished with

> death for transgression—for transgressions of familial rules, political rules, the things at stake in sexual and authoritarian power . . . What is played out for us is a killing . . . there is no liberation. Quite the contrary: [women] suffer, they cry, they die.
>
> > (Clément, 1979; English Translation by Betsy Wing, 1988:10–11)

And with their deaths, nineteenth-century audiences came away with a sense that society's values had been endorsed.

As Clément points out, some transgressions may be against authoritarian power. In *Le médecin malgré lui* (*The Doctor in Spite of Himself*) (1858), in both Gounod's Victorian musical adaptation and Moliere's original play, a woodcutter has gotten himself accepted as a physician. In the seventeenth century, a period when medical theory had little grounding in what we would recognize as science, resentment of doctors was understandably great. The promotion of the woodcutter gave satisfaction to these resentments, which were so strong that Molière could keep his ending no matter how much physicians objected to its "immorality." Not so in the Victorian era. Unlike Molière, librettists Barbier and Carré righteously strip the protagonist Sganarelle of his "doctorhood" at the end. Both the greater security of doctors of our era and the greater cynicism of our audience allowed us to restore Molière's ending. (Our edition does include a performable translation of Gounod's original ending.) We rewrote Barbier and Carré's final dialogue and chose a different chorus to reprise. Barbier and Carré reprised the chorus sung by happy woodcutters and their wives. In our restoration of Molière's ending, the reprised chorus is one from Act III, sung after Sganarelle has given the peasants cheese from his lunch to cure their old sick relative (see Table 5.5). Alert readers will notice some pretty strange words in both the original French and in our singable translation. That is because, in our attempt to convey the sensibility of Molière's farce, we did not translate into contemporary English but into English of the seventeenth century. This temporal foreignization is discussed more fully in Chapter 7.

TABLE 5.5 *Le médecin malgré lui*, No. 11a, mm. 114–45

Original French lyrics	Literal English translation
Morgué, morgué!	'Zdeath, 'zdeath!
vous nous rendez sarvice;	you render us service,
c'est un vrai fromage de roi,	it is truly a royal cheese,
c'est un vrai fromage de roi!	it is truly a royal cheese,
faut que la malade en guarisse,	the illness must be cured,
faut que la malade en guarisse,	the illness must be cured,
ou ben qu'alle dise pourquoi!	or she'd better say why not!
faut qu'alle en guarisse,	must be cured,
morgué! c'est un vrai fromage de roi!	'zdeath! it is truly a royal cheese!
faut que la malade en guarisse,	the illness must be cured,
ou ben qu'alle dise pourquoi!	or she'd better say why not!

Singable English translation
Bidod, bidod!
We all be in your debt, sir.
'Tis a cheddar money can't buy,
'tis a cheddar money cannot buy.
So if she not be any better,
if she kick the bucket and die,
she'd best give a good reason why!
She'd better be better!
Bidod! 'Tis a cheddar money can't buy,
so if she not be any better,
she'd best give a good reason why!
(Herman and Apter, 1979b)

For our reprise, the old lady reappears miraculously cured, and the peasants sing:

> Bidod, bidod!
> We all be in your debt, sir.
>   'Twas a cure no money could buy,
>   'twas a cure that money could not buy.
> Though a sore distemper beset her,
>   when the great physician came by
>   she rose up from where she did lie.
> She could not be better!
>   Bidod! 'Twas a cure no money could buy.
> She be cured of all that beset her
>   and you be the true reason why!
>   (Herman and Apter, 1979b)

And so, licensed by a change in morality, we undid the Victorian Bowdlerization.

In this chapter we have illustrated the principle that each work for the musical stage requires careful consideration overall and at each point within it: whether to let stand, eliminate, replace, explain, minimize, or exaggerate culturally foreign ideas and details.

6

Censorship and taboos

Francesca Billiani opens her article on "Censorship" with this definition:

> Censorship is a coercive and forceful act that blocks, manipulates, and controls cross-cultural interaction in various ways. It must be understood as one of the discourses, and often the dominant one, articulated by a given society at a given time and expressed through repressive cultural, aesthetic, linguistic, and economic practices. Censorship operates largely according to a set of specific values and criteria established by a dominant body and exercised over a dominated one; the former can often be identified with either the state or the Church, or with those social conventions which regulate one's freedom of choice at both public and personal levels. (Billiani, 2011: 28)

More general information on translation and censorship can be found by consulting Billiani's article and her appended bibliography. A discussion of the rewriting, rather than translating, that censorship can cause is given by Lefevere (1992).

In this book, a distinction is made when necessary between a "taboo," a prohibition, explicit or implicit, generally agreed to by large numbers of people within a given culture; and "censorship," a prohibition enforced by some authority, sometimes motivated by a taboo, sometimes motivated by desires specific to the authority. An example of the latter: a publisher's ban on any mention of cookies in a children's book emphasizing good nutrition. Speaking of children's books, one that we translated illustrates just how vast cultural differences can be: written in France, it includes smoking and drinking, two activities unlikely to be allowed an American children's author.

On the musical stage, action, music, words, and ideas can all be subject to taboos and censorship, both those in force at the time and place of a work's creation and those in force at the time and place of its translation. Taboos regarding the first, action, are not usually within the purview of translators. For example, whether or not there should be nudity on stage, either in a work that logically calls for it, such as Richard Strauss's *Salome*, or in works that do not logically call for it, such as several operas directed by Calixto Bieito (1963–), is a decision for the stage director, not the translators.

Even when taboos *are* the province of translators, decisions regarding censorship are often made by others: the commissioners of the translation, an organ of the state, a publisher, an editor, a theatrical organization, performers, or a recording company.

It is usually considered acceptable for translators to undo the censorship of a different culture. For example, few object to productions of Giuseppe Verdi's *Un ballo in maschera* (*A Masked Ball*) (1859) being set in Sweden as Verdi originally intended, rather than in Boston as mid-nineteenth-century Italian censorship nonsensically demanded. Similarly, few object to the restoration of Sganarelle's "doctorhood" in our English translation of the ending of Gounod's *Le médecin malgré lui* (*The Doctor in Spite of Himself*) (1858), as discussed in Chapter 5.

It is often not acceptable for translators to ignore the taboos of their own time and place. Such taboos sometimes required translators to radically change or even destroy an original work. Our own culture, while generally less strict, usually allows more leeway for "offensive" material in texts for reading than in texts for performance. Contemporary translators for singing, therefore, do face censorship, and must negotiate among their own standards and those of others who may have an influence on their work.

6.1 Forbidden music

On August 9–10, 2014, at the Colburn School in Los Angeles, the Ziering-Conlon Initiative for Recovered Voices presented a symposium on "Music, Censorship and Meaning in Nazi Germany and the Soviet Union: Echoes and Consequences." Among other things, the Initiative seeks the recovery and performance of music suppressed by totalitarian regimes. The Nazis banned "*entartete Musik*" ("degenerate music"), by which they meant any piece of music by, about, or otherwise associated with Jews, Negroes, Communists, or anyone else opposed to the Nazi regime, or anyone sympathizing with them; or modernist, especially atonal, music. The Soviet government banned all composers and performers who were not officially sanctioned.

All too humanly, the reaction to suppression and persecution can also result in censorship. For example, many Jews, even seven decades after the Nazi Holocaust, will still not listen to or perform music by Richard Wagner (1813–83), a composer prized by the Nazis and the author of an infamous anti-Semitic tract (1850, revised 1869).

Music can also be banned for religious reasons: all music or certain types of music may be forbidden, either at religious services or at all times. For example, most Jewish synagogues will allow no music other than the *a capella* chanting of prayers during Sabbath services. Thus, the *Avodath Hakodesh* (*Sacred Service*) (1933) of composer Ernest Bloch (1880–1959) can rarely be performed as the composer presumably intended.

Whatever the cause, censorship of music per se rarely affects translation. But it does happen. Evidently convinced of the power of music to move hearts and minds, Soviet censors from the 1950s through the 1970s permitted the publication of the *lyrics* of the Russian singer-songwriter Булат Шалвович Окуджава (Bulát Shálvovich Okudzháva) (1924–97), but forbade publication of the lyrics together with his music or performance of them to his music. Other settings by "official" Soviet composers were allowed! By the 1970s, when state censorship of the songs was rescinded, underground and foreign recordings of his songs had already made Okudzhava famous and beloved. During the period of censorship, translators working outside the Soviet Union were able to translate the songs, but the possibility of repercussions for the composer raised serious moral questions. In such a situation, both the desires and safety of the composer must be considered.

6.2 Forbidden words

6.2.1 Obscenity and euphemisms

Until the late twentieth century, four-letter words were rarely heard on the English-speaking stage. One of the reasons for the multiple re-translations of the Weill/Brecht *Die Dreigroschenoper* (*The Threepenny Opera*) (1928) is that Marc Blitzstein's 1954 translation was accused of "softening the text" and not maintaining "fidelity to Brecht's original German" (*Threepenny Opera*, website). What this verbiage really means is that Blitzstein eliminated four-letter words considered taboo in the United States in the 1950s. Productions in less strait-laced times wished to include Brecht's obscenity and scatology, but found that copyright laws prevented their re-insertion into Blitzstein's translation. In consequence, new translations were commissioned.

Actually, Blitzstein may have been less guilty of censorship than the accusations suggest. Consider "*Das Eifersuchtsduett*" ("The Jealousy Duet") in *Die Dreigroschenoper*. In the critical edition published in 2000 (Weill/ Brecht: 73), Lucy and Polly hurl spoken epithets at each other in the second verse: *"Du Dreckhaufen!"* ("You dungheap!") and *"Selber Dreckhaufen!"* ("Dungheap yourself!"), respectively. The English words in parentheses are both the literal translation and the Michael Feingold translation (1989) included in the critical edition (Feingold: 73). On the original cast recording of Blitzstein's translation, the interchange is reduced to Lucy alone, in the person of performer Beatrice Arthur (1922–2009), saying, "Go peddle your wares somewhere else!" This may or may not have been what was said on stage, since the recording's producers censored the stage script (*Threepenny Opera*, website). Eric Bentley, in an earlier translation, had rendered the exchange as: "Shitpot!" "Shit-pot yourself!" (Bentley, 1949: 60). Ralph Manheim and John Willett, whose 1976 translation was supposedly written to undo Blitzstein's censorship, rendered the exchange as "Little whippersnapper!" "Who's a little whippersnapper?" (1976, published 1994: 50), or at least they did so in the published Arcade Edition. However, in the "Jealousy Duet" posted on YouTube in 2011, which claims to be from the 1976 New York production of that same Manheim/Willett translation, Lucy says "Piss on you!," Polly says nothing, and two "shitpot"s are added elsewhere, one at the end of each verse. As these variants indicate, editing often affects a performable translation as it passes through the hands of the translators, stage directors, performers, publishers, and recording companies.

But is "shitpot" an accurate translation? According to the *Encyclopaedic Muret-Sanders German-English Dictionary* (henceforth *Muret-Sanders*) published by Langenscheidt in 1992, the word *"Dreck"* and all compounds including it are colloquial, not vulgar, in contrast to *"Scheiße"* ("shit"), which is definitely vulgar. If omitting the word, or rendering it as something totally nonvulgar, softens the text, "shitpot" hardens it. There is really no exact equivalent in English. Indeed, at least one critic has called the Manheim/ Willett translation "more shocking than faithful" (Mordden, 2012: 307).

Translators' choices are further complicated by the fact that a word considered obscene or vulgar in one dialect of a language will not be considered so in another. For example, *Muret-Sanders* gives "bloody hell" as a *British* English equivalent for *"verfluchte Scheiße"* (literally, "damned shit"), an incorrect translation into *American* English, which does not consider "bloody" to be obscene (though "hell" alone might suffice for some Americans to consider the phrase too blasphemous for the stage).

The necessity of choosing the proper degree of vulgarity arises for translators of *Das Rheingold* (*The Rhinegold*) (1869), the first part of Richard Wagner's *Der Ring des Nibelungen* (*The Ring of the Nibelung*) (1876). In *Das Rheingold*, Alberich uses the verb *"buhlen"* twice, the first time when he scolds Wellgunde, one of the Rhine daughters, for rejecting him: *"hei! so buhle mit Aalen, / ist dir eklig mein Balg!"* (p. 32); the second time as he is about to plunder the gold and leave the Rhine daughters in the dark: *"So buhlt nun im Finstern, / feuchtes Gezücht!"* (p. 74).

According to *Muret-Sanders*, *"buhlen"* means "to court or woo" and also has an archaic contemptuous meaning: "to have illicit [sexual] relations." The dictionary does not call this verb vulgar, but there are several reasons for "hardening" it in translation. First is the fact that the Rhine daughters call Alberich *"der Garstige,"* whose range of meaning is "the nasty, loathsome, foul, vile, disgusting, filthy, obscene, indecent one" (p. 21). Second is that contempt is a fundamental component of Alberich's character. Third is that Wagner loved archaic words and meanings. And fourth is that there is no forceful way to say "have illicit sexual relations" in English without being vulgar. William Mann's literal translations of the two phrases are

> well then, flirt with eels, / if my skin revolts you (p. 21)
> Then woo in the dark, / damp creatures! (p. 28)
> (Mann, 1964)

We chose to be more forceful:

> Ha! You find me repulsive! / You can go screw an eel! (p. 19)
> You'll fuck in the dark now, / damp little sluts! (p. 50)
> (Herman and Apter, 1983b)

Five other translations of these two lines are shown below. Instead of "screw" and "fuck," the translators chose "wanton," "love" or "lovers," and "mate." Surprisingly, only the two most recent translations eliminate the reference to sex in the second line:

> hei! go wanton with eels then, / if so loathsome am I! (p. 19)
> Then wanton in darkness, / watery brood! (p. 50)
> (Frederick Jameson, 1896)

> Hei! if I am so loathsome/ Give thy love to the eels! (p. 8)
> Go, wanton in darkness, / Water-born brood! (p. 16)
> (Margaret Armour, 1911)

> Get eels for your lovers, / if you find my skin foul! (p. 8)
> Make love in the darkness, / fishified race! (p. 15)
> (Stewart Robb, 1960)

> Eh! Make love with an eel, then, / if he's more to your taste! (p. 9)

Then laugh in the darkness, / nymphs of the waves! (p. 16)

(Andrew Porter, 1976)

Well! If you need a sweetheart, / you should mate with an eel! (p. 6)
Then dance in the darkness! / Out with the light! (p. 9)

(Jeremy Sams, 2002)

As indicated by the above examples, when translators do not censor the thought altogether they often use the word "love" to refer to lust and sex. Cole Porter (1891–1964) satirized this practice in his 1928 song "Let's Do It." Porter's song mentions that various humans and other creatures "do it." The "it" specified is "falling in love." However, Porter is really talking about sex, as made clear, for example, by the results of electric eels doing it (shocks) and of the Siamese doing it (twins).

Using "love" euphemistically is especially problematic for translators of *Das Rheingold* because the distinction between love and lust is one of Wagner's plot points: Alberich recognizes the distinction while the Rhine daughters do not. Therefore, the Rhine daughters mistakenly believe that Alberich will never renounce love (in their minds synonymous with "lust"), and therefore never have the power to forge the gold into a ring:

Wohl sicher sind wir und sorgenfrei,
denn was nur lebt will lieben,
meiden will keiner die Minne.
Am wenigsten er, der lüsterne Alp;
vor Liebesgier möcht er vergeh'n.

(*Das Rheingold*, Scene 1, p. 64.)

(Then we are safe and free of worry,
because whatever lives desires to love,
no one wants to shun love.
And least of all he, the lustful elf;
he is like to die in his greed for love.)

Alberich does renounce love but does not renounce lust, as demonstrated by the appearance of his son Hagen toward the end of the *Ring* in *Götterdämmerung*. He himself makes the distinction in a speech to the gods Wotan and Loge. Note that "*Lust*", in addition to its other meanings, *does* mean "lust":

Habt Acht! Habt Acht!
Denn dient ihr Männer erst meiner Macht,
eure schmucken Frau'n, die mein Frei'n verschmäht,

sie zwingt zur Lust sich der Zwerg,
lacht Liebe ihm nicht!

(*Das Rheingold*, Scene 3, pp. 194–95)

(Beware! Beware!
because your men will be serving my power,
your pretty women, who despise my protestations of love,
will be forced by the lust of the dwarf,
though love doesn't smile on him!)

English is not the only language in which "love" is used euphemistically. In Act III, No. 11 of Giuseppe Verdi's *Il trovatore*, Manrico and Leonora sing of *"gioie di casto amor"* ("joys of chaste love"), a euphemism for marital, as opposed to extramarital, sex. Wishing to stay true to the characters' language register, we translated it with equal euphemism as "the joy of our love" and thought the audience would understand since the "joys of chaste love" are explicitly stated to be what follows the wedding ceremony.

For Natalia Macfarren (1827–1916), a prominent Victorian translator, even the euphemism was evidently too much. The entire thought is censored from her translation (1898): instead of "the joys of chaste love" she says, "forever be mine."

Sometimes translators have to explain a euphemism. Charles Gounod's *Le médecin malgré lui* (*The Doctor in Spite of Himself*) (1858) uses the imagery of Molière's seventeenth-century comedy on which it is based. Consequently, adultery is referred to in many colorful ways, including as a woman's means to be revenged. Similarly, a cuckolded husband is signified by oblique references, including his having a wounded forehead, that is, one bearing a cuckold's horns. No modern audience is likely to understand such references without further explanation. The difficulty can be illustrated with some of the lyrics of Martine's aria, sung after her husband Sganarelle has beaten her. Shown in Table 6.1 are the lyrics, a literal translation, and singable translations by us and the Victorian journalist, dramatist, and translator Charles Kenney (1821–81).

The obvious solution, the word "cuckold," does not fit into Gounod's music. So we translated the thought as "common treatment," another euphemism of the period. In the seventeenth-century parlance we were using, the common treatment of erring husbands was understood to be adultery. Furthermore, the word "common" suggested more than one lover! We added an explanatory footnote so that the soprano could communicate the meaning visually by holding up two fingers to her forehead (the sign for the horns of a cuckold).

TABLE 6.1 *Le médecin malgré lui*, Act I, No. 2, mm. 7–22

Original French text	Literal English translation
Toute femme tient sous sa patte de quoi se venger d'un mari; mais l'atteinte est trop délicate, son front serait trop tôt guéri!	Every woman has in her clutches means to be revenged on a husband; but the attack is too gentle, his forehead would too soon be healed!
Performable English translation (Herman and Apter, 1979b)	**Performable English translation (Charles Kenney, no date)**
Battered women, thrashed by their husbands have means to come by their revenge! Common treatment will not assuage me, 'tis not enough to make amends!	Women's vengeance lacked yet never a good old plan her lord to spite; but all vain were my endeavor: of jealous pangs he'd make too light!

6.2.2 *Other taboo words*

Among current taboo words are those considered insulting to a group of people. Censors howl even if the work as a whole subverts the disparaging meaning. That is why there are repeated attempts to censor the word "nigger" from Mark Twain's *Huckleberry Finn* (1884, United Kingdom; 1885, United States), one of the most anti-racist books ever written.

"Nigger" has not yet arisen in the course of our translations into English. But it most definitely arises in translations from English of Gilbert and Sullivan's popular operetta *The Mikado* (1885), in which the word "nigger" is used twice (Green, 1961: 416, 435). Translations from English are beyond the scope of this book, but we will briefly consider how the word is handled in English-language productions and scores.

The word is first used in No. 5a, mm. 30–32 when, among the people who "never would be missed" is "the nigger serenader, and the others of his race." This is routinely changed to "the banjo serenader, and the others of his race" (Green, 1961: 416), a ridiculous change because the altered phrase is still a racial slur.

The word is used a second time in No. 17, mm. 60–65 when, among the criminals cited by the Mikado is the lady who

> stains her grey hair puce,
>> Or pinches her figger,
>> Is blacked like a nigger
> With permanent walnut juice.

This is routinely changed to the not very funny

> stains her grey hair puce,
>> Or pinches her figure,
>> Is painted with vigour
> With permanent walnut juice.
>> (Green, 1961: 435)

However, there is another alternative, a rewrite of the stanza by Alan P. Herbert:

> stains her grey hair green,
>> Is taken to Dover
>> And painted all over
> A horrible ultramarine.
>> (Quoted by Green, 1961: 435)

Sometimes a word that is not a slur is too close to one that is. In *Le médecin malgré lui*, the protagonist Sganarelle is a *fagotier*. That is, he cuts and binds fagots, bundles of sticks tied together to be used as firewood. The word is etymologically related to "fasces," a bundle of rods bound together around an axe that was used as an emblem of authority in ancient Rome, from whence is derived the word "fascism." Unfortunately, "fagot" is a homonym for "faggot," a disparaging slang term for a male homosexual. Therefore, although the Victorian translation of Charles Kenney uses the word "fagots" freely, Sganarelle usually cannot "bind fagots" in productions of our translation; rather, he must "cut wood."

Speaking of homosexuals, the word "gay" now means "homosexual" almost exclusively in both American and British English, nearly obliterating the earlier meaning of "having or showing a joyous mood." Nonetheless, in our translation of Weber's *Abu Hassan* (1811), when Abu sings a solo to guitar accompaniment, we have him use the phrase "gay guitars," hoping that, in context, the audience will not infer any homosexual connotation.

Even names can take on unwanted resonances. In Mozart's *Die Entführung aus dem Serail* (*The Abduction from the Seraglio*) (1782), the maid Blonde is frequently referred to by the diminutive "*Blondchen*." The corresponding English diminutive is "Blondie," but stage directors almost never allow her to be called that in productions of our translation because the name is so strongly identified with the title character of a long-running American comic strip. Instead, most simply eliminate the diminutive and always call her "Blonde" (or "Blonda" if the name is Anglicized). J. D. McClatchy, in his nonsingable verse translation (2011), calls her "Blanche." This gives her an English name but also loses the diminutive. It also loses the second syllable, an important point when translating for singing to music that expects the name to have two syllables. A one-syllable name cannot be set on the same musical notes as the two-syllable "*Blonde*" or "*Blondchen*."

Just as "fagot" cannot be used at all and "gay" only very carefully, the word "naked" has been subject to censorship even when used in an asexual (or mostly asexual) context. In Puccini's *La bohème* (1896), Rodolfo's response to Mimì's statement that Musetta is well dressed is "*Gli angeli vanno nudi*" ("The angels go naked") (Act II, mm. 416–17). Our translation (to be published) is "Angels, they say, go naked." The anonymous translation published by the English National Opera in 1982 is similar: "Angels are always naked." Others felt the need to tread more carefully: Ruth and Thomas Martin (1954: 128) ("Angels must do without them [dresses]") and Joseph Machlis (1956: 49) ("Someone has paid most dearly!"). David Spencer (1984, revised 2002) and Amanda Holden (2009) avoid the word "naked," but make far more sexually provocative statements: "Yes, but look how she earned it [her dress]" and "How do you think she earns them [her dresses]?," respectively.

6.3 Forbidden ideas

Ideas as well as individual words have been and are subject to taboos and censorship. It is highly unlikely that Stephen Sondheim's *Sweeney Todd* (1979), whose title character is a serial killer, would have been allowed on the Broadway stage in the 1950s. Indeed, Frank Loesser's musical *Guys and Dolls* (1950) softened the stories of Damon Runyon (1880–1946) on which it is based by reducing Runyon's large population of murderous characters to one minor role: Big Jule.

6.3.1 Political censorship

Some political censorship, such as that which changed the setting of Giuseppe Verdi's *Un ballo in maschera* (*A Masked Ball*) (1859), is relatively easy to spot and undo. Other changes motivated by censorship may be harder to spot. Translators must be cognizant of the rules of censorship in force at the time of a work's creation and try to determine whether censorship caused changes. Only then can they decide whether or not to undo them. Also, many works written under censorship include coded messages designed to circumvent it, messages that may have been obvious to the original audience but can require extra emphasis in order to be understood by others.

Mozart's *Singspiel, Die Entführung aus dem Serail* (*The Abduction from the Seraglio*) (1782) was created "just as the news of the American victory over the British at Yorktown was reaching European ears" (Apter, 1982: 16). In *Die Entführung*, the cry for liberty is not directly made, but is encoded, among other places, in a comic duet between Osmin and Blonde about the then outlandish notion of freedom for women. Osmin compares the attitudes of Englishmen and Turks (No. 9, mm. 56–60):

O Engländer, seid ihr nicht Toren,
ihr laßt euren Weibern den Willen.

(O Englishmen, are you not fools,
you allow your women their will.)

Blonde does not answer with a plea just for women, but with a plea for everyone:

Ein Herz, so in Freiheit geboren,
läßt niemals sich sklavisch behandeln,
bleibt, wenn schon die Freiheit verloren,
noch stolz auf sie, lachet der Welt.

(A heart born in freedom
never allows itself to be treated as a slave,
it remains, even when freedom is lost,
still proud of its freedom, laughing at the world.)

Mozart did desire freedom for all. However revolutionary the idea may have been in 1782, it poses no censorship problems for translators today. There is, however, the possibility that modern audiences will miss the revolutionary nature of the work. To help avoid this, we emphasized it by adding words to Blonde's subsequent aria, calling for the bells of freedom to ring. Mozart's music, setting repeats of the final line of the lyrics, rings out the tonic note *G* over and over in apparent agreement with our added meaning (see Table 6.2 and Figure 6.1).

TABLE 6.2 *Die Entführung aus dem Serail*, No. 12, mm. 8–33

Original German lyrics	Literal English translation

Welche Wonne, welche Lust
herrscht nunmehr in meiner Brust!
  Ohne Aufschug will ich springen,
  und ihr gleich die Nachricht bringen,
und mit Lachen und mit Scherzen
ihrem schwachen, feigen Herzen
  Freud' und Jubel prophezeihn.
	What rapture, what pleasure
	governs now in my breast!
	Without delay I want to jump
	and to her at once the news bring,
	and with laughing and with joking
	to her poor, timid heart
	joy and jubilation prophesy.

Singable English translation

I could shout and jump for joy;
I could dance and I could sing!
  Quickly I will run and tell her,
  and the news will soon dispel her
constant crying. No more sighing,
ever after only laughter.
  Let the bells of freedom ring!
(Herman and Apter, 1979a)

Blonde

Allegro

Freud'   und   Ju - bel   pro - phe - zeihn.
Let   the bells of   free - dom ring!

FIGURE 6.1 Die Entführung aus dem Serail, *No. 12, mm. 135–38 and 153–56.*
Source: Herman and Apter (1979a).

6.3.2 Gender roles and sexual stereotypes

Not long ago, the posited ideal family was a nuclear family (almost always Caucasian) with a working father, a stay-at-home mother, and, as satirized in Norton Juster's *The Phantom Tollbooth* (1961), 2.58 children. On stage and screen, those venturing beyond their assigned gender restrictions were ultimately converted to the approved role model or punished with disappointment or even death. The institution of the Hollywood Production Code in the 1930s required onscreen homosexual characters, if they appeared at all, to be indicated by veiled allusions and/or depicted negatively (see <http://en.wikipedia.org/wiki/History_of_homosexuality_in_American_film> and Noriega [1990]). Any homosexuality on the part of performers, producers, directors, composers, and lyricists was a well-kept secret.

The taboo against homosexuality caused unsophisticated audiences to look with suspicion upon adult male alto and soprano voices, sometimes even high tenors. Teenagers on school trips to Mozart's *Le nozze di Figaro* (*The Marriage of Figaro*) (1786) giggled uncomfortably when Cherubino, a boy portrayed by a woman, came onstage.

Some dismiss the effects of onstage or on-screen violations of taboos if conventions or plotlines give "legitimate" reasons for the violations. According to this view, the cross-dressing men in the film *Some Like It Hot* (1959) directed by Billy Wilder (1906–2002) are not really transvestites; they simply have to disguise themselves to escape being murdered by organized crime. Boys dressed up as girls and girls dressed up as boys on the Shakespearean stage were merely a matter of convention, stemming from the prohibition of public performances by women. Castrati were just the result of the audience's desire for high notes projected with masculine force. As for Cherubino, he too is just the result of the operatic convention that women perform as boys in order to mimic unbroken male voices. Nowadays, the frequent performance by women of roles once performed by male castrati is also a mere convention.

But these are all rationalizations. Audience members have always grappled with loaded issues in the "safe" space of the theater, where such issues are frequently presented in disguise. In rendering theater of the past, translators will do well to consider what taboos the original creators may have been addressing, especially if the issues are coded.

Today, homosexual characters appear on television, on film, and on stage, and have been the protagonists of at least two operas: Wallace and Korie's *Harvey Milk* (1995), about the murdered elected openly gay San Francisco City Supervisor (1930–78), and Blanchard and Cristofer's *Champion* (2013), about the gay welterweight prize-fighting champion Emile Griffith (1938–2013). The appeal of opera to homosexual men is openly discussed (see, for instance, Wayne Koestenbaum, *The Queen's Throat: Opera, Homosexuality, and the Mystery of Desire* [1993]). Men are no longer afraid to cultivate alto and soprano voices. In popular culture, the sexually (and racially) ambiguous singer Michael Jackson (1958–2009) remains an icon. On the classical stage, a significant breakthrough occurred with the career of countertenor (male alto) Alfred Deller (1912–79), whose wife and three children put him above homosexual suspicion in most eyes. (Because of his high singing voice, some thought Deller, if not a homosexual, then a castrato. A story attributed to Michael Chance [1955–], like Deller a British countertenor, maintains that a French woman, upon hearing Deller sing, exclaimed, *"Monsieur, vous êtes eunuque,"* to which Deller replied, "I think you mean 'unique', madam").

A few male sopranos can still sing castrato roles, but the roles can also be given to women or to tenors singing an octave down. The very lack of taboos that allows for gender-blind casting can pose both musical and dramatic problems for translators. It can happen that different words are suitable for singing depending on the voice type in question and the position of the musical pitch in the singer's tessitura. It can also happen that a translator may want to vary the words depending on whether it is a woman or a man who is "disguised" as a woman and later undisguised as an ardent male lover, especially if the work is a comedy that pokes fun at the very idea of gender switching. However, it is simply impractical to fine-tune a translation (or an original work) three different ways, for either a single production or for different productions, in order to accommodate a role that might at various times be taken by a male soprano, female soprano, or male tenor. The first production of our English translation of Alessandro Scarlatti's *Eraclea* (1700), with roles for three castrati and a boy soprano, was triple cast, with men and women alternating in several roles. Tenor voices and physiques rendered unbelievable the plot device of men disguised as women. When a woman played a role created for a boy soprano disguised as a girl, the final unmasking of the "boy" made no sense. We are at a loss as to how to revise our translation so as to improve the situation.

However, the gender bending of Baroque operas presents translators with opportunities as well as problems. The boy soprano in *Eraclea* is disguised as a girl wearing a dress with a long train, and that offers an opportunity to create a new musical-verbal joke, quite in keeping with the spirit of the original (see Table 6.3 and Figure 6.2). The contemporary pun on "drag" in the sense of "cross-dressing" is emphasized by the musical setting. First, Scarlatti himself sets the first and third syllables of *"strascinare"* on long notes to indicate the dragging of the train of Livio's skirt, and the English reaps the benefit of this setting. Second, since "dragging" is set upon the same notes as *"strascinare"* and "dragging" has only two syllables while *"strascinare"* has four, we could have two "dragging"s for each *"strascinare."*

TABLE 6.3 *Eraclea*, No. 9, mm. 4–18

Original Italian lyrics	Literal English translation
È pur strano veder con la gonna un ragazzo che faccia da donna strascinare tre palmi, tre palmi di coda; è strano veder con la gonna un ragazzo che faccia da donna strascinare, strascinare tre palmi di coda, strascinare tre palmi di coda.	It is indeed strange to see in a skirt a boy who acts the woman dragging three palm-widths, three palm-widths of train; it is strange to see in a skirt a boy who acts the woman dragging, dragging three palm-widths of train, dragging three palm-widths of train.

Singable English translation
See the petticoats all in a whirl a--round a boy who parades as a girl with long, long laces to bind him, with laces to bind him. With ribbons and laces to bind him, he goes dragging his train behind him, dragging, dragging, dragging, dragging his train behind him, dragging, dragging his train behind him.

(Herman and Apter, 1992b)

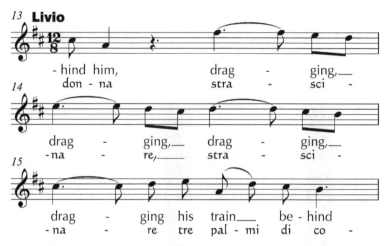

FIGURE 6.2 Eraclea, *No. 9, mm. 13–15*.
Source: Herman and Apter (1992b).

Contemporary mores also allow a freer look at heterosexual lust. For instance, Musetta, in her famous Waltz in Puccini's *La bohème*, describes the lust of men looking at her, desiring her, and undressing her with their eyes. Her wealthy escort-of-the-moment Alcindoro complains that she is singing a *"canto scurrile"* ("indecent song"). Translators should make sure that the audience knows he has grounds for complaint. Consider the second stanza, shown in Table 6.4.

TABLE 6.4 *La bohème*, Act II, mm. 507–22

Original Italian lyrics	Literal English translation

Ed assaporo allor la bramosia sottil che da gl'occhi traspira
  e dai palesi vezzi intender sa
  alle occulte beltà.
Così l'effluvio del desio
  tutta m'aggira, felice mi fa!
	And I then savor the subtle longing that oozes from his eyes
	and from the obvious charms
	he divines the hidden beauty.
	In this way the scent of desire
	all around me makes me happy!

Singable English translation

I feel the air grow heavy with their longing sighs
as their eyes contemplate me,
for they know how to guess from surface graces
    every beauty below.
Desire swirling all around me
    exhilarates me wherever I go.
                    (Herman and Apter, to be published)

Operating in the Puritanical atmosphere of the 1950s, American translators Ruth and Thomas Martin (1954) and Joseph Machlis (1956) indicate lust by the word "desire" but censor the mental undressing. As late as 1982, in an anonymous translation published under the auspices of the English National Opera and the Royal Opera, lust was euphemistically replaced by "love" and there was no mental undressing (English National Opera, *La bohème*, 1982: 79). These translations verbally undercut Alcindoro's reaction.

In the United States, the censorship was lifted in the 1984 version by David Spencer (revised 2002) for the Public Theater in New York. The undressing was shifted to the first stanza:

> What good is fame?
> I'm waited on attentively
> and while each whim is met inventively,
> strip me of my . . . acclaim . . .
> and as I stroll the avenue
> I'd smile if only you knew my name!
> (Spencer, 1984/2002)

The United Kingdom finally had an uncensored translation in 2009, when the English National Opera presented Amanda Holden's version:

> And as I savour all the looks of sly desire
> that appear upon their faces,
> I know that they are lusting for the charms
> I conceal from their sight.
> They can't deny their rampant passion,
> it whirls around me, they want me, I know . . .
> (Holden, 2009)

Contemporary theater may allow frank discussions of sex and permit the entire spectrum of gender identities to appear onstage, but new taboos have arisen: no gender identity may be disparaged and, above all, there is to be no sexism. This creates problems for translators if a work includes sexist characters and ideas, even if the work as a whole is anti-sexist.

One such popular work is Mozart's *Die Zauberflöte* (*The Magic Flute*) (1791) which, critics such as Kristi Brown-Montesano (2007) notwithstanding, is anti-sexist. The opera accepts the gender stereotypes of intellectual male and emotional female, but, using marriage as a symbol of the mystical union of opposites, teaches that both the head (man) and the heart (woman) need to acquire characteristics of the other in order to be complete. The opera begins with the rescue of the male hero Tamino by three women. Two of the principal characters, the male Papageno and the female Pamina, conspicuously exhibit traits deemed uncharacteristic of their sex: cowardice (Papageno) and leadership (Pamina). Both are rewarded, he despite, she because of the gender-role transgression. However, the Queen of the Night, whose desire for power is a typically male attribute, is treated ambiguously. Her quest for power is thwarted, but whether she is otherwise punished is left in doubt at the work's end.

The opera's anti-sexism is conveyed mainly by visual means or by action: Tamino is rescued by women; Pamina leads Tamino through the trials of fire and water; later, she is crowned co-leader of the temple. The explicit sexism of various characters is conveyed verbally, as in a misogynist duet sung by two priests:

> Bewahret euch vor Weibertücken,
>   dies ist des Bundes erste Pflicht;
> manch weiser Mann ließ sich berücken,
>   er fehlte, er fehlte, und versah sich's nicht.
> Verlassen sah er sich am Ende,
>   vergolten seine Treu mit Hohn!
> Vergebens rang er seine Hände,
>   Tod und Verzweiflung war sein Lohn.
>   (*Die Zauberflöte*, No. 11, The Misogynist Duet)

> (Guard yourself against woman's tricks,
> this is the first duty of our covenant;
> many a wise man let himself be inveigled,
> he erred, he erred, and did not realize it.
> He saw himself abandoned in the end,
> his trust rewarded with scorn!
> Vainly he wrung his hands;
> death and despair were his reward.)

The problematic nature of this duet is reflected in the wide range of treatments given to it. It is completely omitted in both Ingmar Bergman's film version (1975), and J. D. McClatchy's singable translation (2004). The villain is changed from "woman" to "lust" in the translation by W. H. Auden and Chester Kallman (1955). Stephen Fry's version made for the film adaptation by Kenneth Branagh (2006) targets women's words rather than women per se. Of course, many translations, from Natalia Macfarren's Victorian version to J .D. McClatchy's non-singable version of 2011, do largely preserve the original meaning.

Oddly enough, translators or directors who intend to reduce the sexism of *Die Zauberflöte* may inadvertently re-introduce it in their zeal to follow the contemporary dictum that spoken dialogue is bad. The Queen of the Night is motivated by more than inherent villainy; her motives are revealed in a speech to Pamina, spoken just before the Queen's famous Act II aria. If this speech is severely cut or eliminated, the Queen exhibits motiveless evil not present in the original. Her complaint is that she was not allowed to inherit an orb of power on her husband's death:

> Übergab freiwillig den siebenfachen Sonnenkreis den Eingeweihten; diesen mächtigen Sonnenkreis trägt Sarastro auf seiner Brust.—Als ich in darüber beredete, so sprach er mit gefalteter Stirne: „Weib! meine letzte Stunde ist da—alle Schätze, so ich allein besaß, sind dein und deiner Tochter."—„Der alles verzehrende Sonnenkres", fiel ich hastig ihm in die Rede,"—„ist den Geweihten bestimmt", antwortete er:—„Sarastro wird ihn so männlich verwalten wie ich bisher.—Und nun kein Wort weiter; forsche nicht nach Wesen, die dem weiblichen Geiste unbegreiflich sind.—Deine Pflicht ist, dich und deine Tochter der Führung weiser Männer zu überlassen".
>
> (*Die Zauberflöte*, Act II, Scene 8)

([Your father] voluntarily gave up the sevenfold orb of the sun to the initiates; Sarastro bears this mighty orb of the sun on his breast. As I pleaded with him on that point, he then spoke with wrinkled brow:

"Wife! my last hour is here—all wealth of which I am in sole possession are yours and your daughter's".

"The all-encompassing orb of the sun", I interrupted in the conversation,

"is allotted to those consecrated", he answered. "Sarastro will administer it in as manly a manner as I have hitherto. And now no further word; seek not after things which are incomprehensible to the womanly spirit. Your duty is to submit yourself and your daughter to the guidance of wise men".)

The treatment of this speech, like that of the misogynist duet, varies widely. Ruth and Thomas Martin (1941/51) and W. H. Auden and Chester Kallman (1955) eliminate it entirely, thereby greatly increasing the perceived sexism of the opera. Interestingly, Auden and Kallman explicitly reveal that they knew what they were doing. They wrote a postscript to their translation, a poem purportedly *by* the Queen of the Night sent *to* the translators, in which the Queen says, "you saw fit to . . . deprive our rage of its dialogue" (Auden and Kallman, 1955, Postscript: 101).

Among the other translations of *Die Zauberflöte* known to us, excluding the two film adaptations and McClatchy's abridged version, only those by us (1982b), Andrew Porter (1980), and J. D. McClatchy (in his nonsingable 2011 verse translation) give the entire speech. The other translators give the speech greatly abridged, possibly in an attempt to cut the dialogue to a minimum while still conveying essential information. Natalia Macfarren's Victorian version, though the earliest, is typical of all such versions, regardless of when they were translated:

> Alas, child, with thy father's death my power ended: he gave the sevenfold shield of the sun to Sarastro, who wears it on his breast.
>
> (Macfarren, no date)

When our translation of *Die Zauberflöte* was first performed in New York City in 1982, that city was one of the leading centers of feminism in the United States. While we were free to express the Queen's motives, we were ordered to tone down some of the sexist remarks in the original. In No. 8, mm. 436–40, Sarastro tells Pamina:

> Ein Mann muß eure Herzen leiten,
> denn ohne ihn
> pflegt jedes Weib aus ihrem Wirkungskreis zu schreiten.
>
> (A man must govern your heart,
> for without him
> every woman is likely to step outside her [rightful] sphere of activity.)

Originally we had written

> Your heart needs guidance from a husband.
> Without a man,
> a woman will exceed the sphere of woman's work.
>
> (Herman and Apter, 1982b)

The stage director and conductor thought that many women, upon hearing the lines above, would leave the theater. So we tried to write something that kept the sentiments of the source while bowing to late twentieth-century theatrical realities:

> Your heart needs guidance from a husband,
> or, like your mother,
> you will never learn to wed desire and duty.
>
> (Herman and Apter, 1982b)

6.3.3 Excretion

Very few musical stage works actually refer to urination or defecation. When words such as "piss" or "shit" or their equivalents in other languages are used, they are usually epithets rather than descriptions of bodily functions. However, Molière did refer to urination several times in *Le médecin malgré lui* (1666) and such references were carefully censored out of Gounod's 1858 musical adaptation. (Gounod did provide a bassoon solo that can be understood as a fart, but, since that is purely musical, it is not the concern of translators.) We decided to restore the references in our edition, in both French and English. Neither the stage director nor the musical director complained. An example is shown in Table 6.5.

TABLE 6.5 *Le médecin malgré lui*, Act III, dialogue between Nos. 12 and 13

Original French dialogue	Literal English translation
Je m'étais amusé dans votre cour à expulser le superflu de la boisson.	I was amusing myself in your garden expelling the excess fluids from drinking.

Performable English translation
I had stopped in your garden to relieve myself o' the superfluidities contingent on bibulation. (Herman and Apter, 1979b)

6.3.4 Race

Not too long ago, opera was an all-white enterprise. As recently as 1935, George Gershwin refused a contract from the Metropolitan Opera in New York for the premiere of *Porgy and Bess* because, instead of a black cast, the Met wanted a white cast performing in blackface. No African-American was allowed to sing at the Met until Marian Anderson (1897–1993) was hired in 1955.

It is probably correct to say that the racist slurs of Gilbert and Sullivan in *The Mikado* (1885) were not intended as such, but were simply an unthinking expression of the view at the time. But some racist remarks in works for the musical stage, such as those referring to the character Monostatos in Mozart's *Die Zauberflöte* (*The Magic Flute*) (1791), *are* intended as such. Unlike the opera's sexist remarks, the racist remarks are *not* contrary to the attitude of the work as a whole. Monostatos is a "Moor." His name means "all alone." He is black and a villain, and, in *Die Zauberflöte* the two are virtually synonymous. However, the libretto also suggests that his mistreatment by society is a prime cause of his villainy. In his aria, No. 13, mm. 15–21, Monostatos's lyrics are "*und ich soll die Liebe meiden, / weil ein Schwarzer häßlich ist!*" ("and I must avoid love / because a black person is hateful!").

Today, most opera casting is color-blind, and it is likely that other *Zauberflöte* cast members, in addition to or instead of Monostatos, will be black. The lyrics and plot that suggest that dark skin is synonymous with evil thankfully now make no sense. However, some still believe that a black man should not have sexual relations with a white woman.

Disagreeing with the view of the source, we nonetheless translated it, but gave an alternate version to be used if the artistic director did not wish the racist idea expressed, or had cast a non-black as Monostatos:

More literal version:
But affection is unwelcome / from a man whose skin is black.

Alternate version:
Why should I be any different? / Do I have a hateful face?

(Herman and Apter, 1982b)

These versions embody the first two of the three main options available to translators in this situation:

1   Translating literally. Since there will probably be other black characters in the cast, "being black" becomes a self-serving excuse for Monostatos. He is not really hated because he is black, but because he is evil.

2   Changing "black" to another quality on which society frowns.

3   Eliminating any societal reason for the hatred of Monostatos.

Translators have tried all the above approaches. The English subtitles to Ingmar Bergman's film version (1975), Andrew Porter (1980), Stephen Fry's adaptation in the 2006 Branagh film, and J. D. McClatchy's nonsingable version of 2011 all mention skin color. W. H. Auden and Chester Kallman (1955), Jeremy Sams (1987), J. D. McClatchy (2004), and Amanda Holden (2007) call Monostatos "ugly" or "disgusting." Natalia Macfarren just says that Monostatos is a "Moor." Ruth and Thomas Martin, using the third option mentioned above, cut out all references to Monostatos's skin color, ethnicity, and facial characteristics,

Why am I not like the others? / No one ever looks at me!

(Martin and Martin, 1941/51: 97)

leaving it to the director and performer to let the audience know why Monostatos is hated. In the "family friendly" production directed by Julie Taymor at the Metropolitan Opera, which used McClatchy's 2004 translation, Monostatos was not only not black but was a nonhuman batlike creature.

The existence of so many approaches exhibits a deep and welcome uneasiness with racism. Eliminating the racism eliminates one of the motivations for Monostatos's evil deeds, but many translators and their commissioners are willing to accept this infidelity to the original script.

6.3.5 Religion

While the principal topic of opera has always been love, some operas include a religious background or theme. Examples are Donizetti's *Maria Stuarda*

(Mary Stuart) (1835) discussed in Chapter 5, Halévy's *La Juive* (*The Jewess*) (1835), Meyerbeer's *Les Huguenots* (*The Huguenots*) (1836), Verdi's *Nabucco* (*Nabuchadnezzar*) (1842) and *I Lombardi alla prima crociata* (*The Lombards on the First Crusade*) (1847), and, more recently, Poulenc's *Dialogues des carmélites* (*Dialogues of the Carmelites*). Interestingly, the last is a French opera composed in 1953 but first performed in 1957 in an Italian translation.

In addition to works with religious themes, works without them can nonetheless include deeply and reflexively religious characters, for example, the rural Czechs in *Prodaná nevěsta* (*The Bartered Bride*) (1866–70) discussed in Chapter 4.

If a work depicts religious or ethnic strife, many will object that it is insufficiently biased for or against one side or the other. In 2014, the furor over *The Death of Klinghoffer* (1991), composed by John Adams (1947–) to a libretto by Alice Goodman (1958–), resulted in the cancellation of a live cinecast by the Metropolitan Opera. This work tells the true story of the hijacking in 1985 of the passenger liner Achille Lauro by members of the Palestine Liberation Front, during which the hijackers murdered the wheelchair-bound Jewish-American passenger Leon Klinghoffer. The opera stirred controversy from its inception, a controversy that essentially ended Alice Goodman's writing career. Since the work is in English, translators into English do not have to be concerned with it. However, it would be interesting to see if Arabic or Hebrew versions could be created without provoking hysteria.

When characters who are adherents of one religion insult characters who are adherents of another, translators must determine how forceful those insults will be. Such a choice must be made when translating Mozart's *Die Entführung aus dem Serail* (*The Abduction from the Seraglio*) (1782). Two of the principal characters in *Die Entführung* are Muslims, the Pasha (speaking role), definitely admirable, and Osmin (bass), definitely a comic villain. Act III, Scene 6 of *Abduction* includes dialogue in which Osmin calls the four captives *"niederträchtigen Christensklaven"* ("vile Christian slaves"). Here, "slaves" is more a term of insult than a description since, although not free to leave, the captives are not considered to be property. Translators vary in their renditions:

Ruth and Thomas Martin (1944/62: 148): The great architect whom you engaged

Elkhanah Pulitzer (2003: 33): That fine young architect you engaged

John Bloch (1957: 65): wretched Christian slaves

J. D. McClatchy (2011: 253): conniving Christian slaves

Edward J. Dent (published 1952: 30): scoundrelly Christian slaves

We chose to give Osmin's hatred full emphasis. Believing that "slaves" does not carry the weight of insult it once did, we translate the phrase as "Christian dogs," but offer "Christian slaves" as an alternative.

When a religion's own adherents, or former adherents, insult it, the result is often considered sacrilege. Such is the case for some of the lyrics in the medieval *Carmina Burana*.

Among the lyrics set by Carl Orff in 1936 is *"Ave, formosissima,"* the eighth stanza of a 33-stanza lyric (Hilka et al., I.2: 53, No. 77.8, 1930–71), a hymn to a soon-to-be nonvirgin. The stanza in the textual variant set by Orff, including the repeated words and phrases in his musical setting, is shown in Table 6.6. In the next to last line, Blanziflor / Blanchefleur is the name of several women in various medieval romances and Helen is Helen of Troy.

TABLE 6.6 *"Ave, formosissima"*

Original Latin lyrics	Literal translation
Ave, formosissima,	Hail, most beautiful,
gemma pretiosa,	precious jewel,
ave, decus virginum,	hail, glory of virgins,
virgo gloriosa,	glorious virgin,
ave, mundi luminar,	hail, light of the world,
ave, mundi rosa,	hail, rose of the world,
Blanziflor et Helena,	Blanchefleur and Helen,
Blanziflor et Helena,	Blanchefleur and Helen,
Venus, Venus, Venus generosa!	Venus, Venus, Venus generous!
(*Carmina Burana*, Hilka et al., I.2: 53, No. 77.8; Orff, No. 24)	

To medievalists, *"Ave, formosissima"* is an obvious parody of a hymn to the Virgin Mary. The paean is addressed to a virgin, and the repeated *"ave"* recalls the opening of *"Ave Maria."* In medieval religious writing, a set phrase praising Mary is "Rose of the World." And she is the mother of Jesus, the Light of the World. To compound the sacrilege, Orff preceded this lyric with:

Dulcissime, ah totam tibi subdo me!
(Hilka et al., I.2: 37, No. 70.15; Orff, No. 23)

(Sweetest one, ah my whole self I yield to you!)

sung by the soprano soloist to the baritone soloist. Therefore, in Orff's song cycle, the hymn is unambiguously sung to someone about to lose her virginity.

Translators are faced with several choices, the first being whether or not to translate such a lyric at all. Next come decisions about whether the sacrilegious nature of the verse is to be eliminated, muted, or reproduced. If the choice is to reproduce, translators must decide whether extra emphasis is needed to make the sacrilege clear to a present-day audience, some of whose members may be unaware of the Marian epithets.

In our translation, we try to reproduce the tone of the original without emphasizing it or toning it down, though we do add "kneel," a word associated with religious services:

> Hail, thou light of all mankind,
>   hail, thou rose emerging,
> hail, thou gem of maidenhood,
>   hail, thou glorious virgin!
> You are beauty unalloyed
>   and we kneel before you:
> you are Helen come from Troy,
> you the avatar of joy,
>   Venus, Venus, Venus, we adore you!
>   (Herman and Apter, 1977/2013)

Since the name "Blanziflor / Blanchefleur" is known to very few today, we domesticated our translation by eliminating it.

Many translators chose not to translate this lyric. It is omitted from most anthologies of medieval poetry, and the translations that accompany printed texts or performances of Orff's cantata are almost all contortedly literal or pseudo-literal versions in which the sacrilege is often indecipherable. Exceptions to censorship-by-omission are George F. Whicher's translation of 1949 (of the entire 33-stanza lyric) and James J. Wilhelm's of 1971, neither of which appear to have been translated with Orff's music in mind. Whicher appears to have understood the sacrilege but his words obscure it:

> Hail, most beautiful of girls,
>   Gem of worth unmeasured,
> Quintessence of maidenhood
>   In one vessel treasured,
> Hail, O dayspring of the world,
>   Hail, rose of creation:
> Blanchefleur, Helen of Troy,
> Blanchefleur, Helen of Troy,
>   Venus' Venus' Venus' emanation.
>   (Whicher, 1949: 53)

The sacrilege is more obvious in James J. Wilhelm's version, where the word "virgin" makes clearer what is going on.

> Hail, most beautiful and good,
>> Jewel, held most dear by us;
> Hail, honor of maidenhood,
>> Virgin, ever glorious—
> Hail, thou light above all lights,
>> Hail, rose of the world—
> Blancheflor and Helen,
> Blancheflor and Helen,
>> Venus, Venus, Venus noble-souled!
>>>> (Wilhelm, 1971: 86)

6.3.6 Disabilities

A recent taboo rejects unsympathetic or mocking portraits of people with disabilities, although the hunchbacked protagonists of Verdi's *Rigoletto* (1851) and Shakespeare's *Richard III* appear to have escaped censorship, as has the evil handicapped Dick Deadeye in Gilbert and Sullivan's *H.M.S. Pinafore* (1878).

However, the taboo does exist, and so when we were commissioned in 2003 to translate Smetana's *Prodaná nevěsta* (*The Bartered Bride*) (1866–70), we were concerned about the inclusion of the stutterer Vašek among the supporting characters. His stutters cannot be easily eliminated in translation because Smetana wrote them right into the music. Removing the stutters would involve replacing them with meaningful syllables and so would significantly change the composer's musical ideas. However, close examination of the libretto and score revealed that nothing in them mocks the stuttering. It is simply there. The other characters laugh, not at Vašek's stuttering, but at his immaturity.

The plot does suggest a reason for Vašek's stuttering: his extremely bossy mother. Indeed, according to the Stuttering Foundation (<http://www.stutteringhelp.org/faq>, accessed September 5, 2014), family dynamics are among the four most common causes of stuttering. All in all, we felt safe in retaining the stuttering in our translation.

Translators for the musical stage must wrestle with self-censorship, censorship by others, and audience reception. They must be especially wary of their own taboos, which may cause them to be unfaithful to the source or to unnecessarily alter the degree of domestication or foreignization of the translation. They must question their own motives carefully whenever changes are made so that a work will become "acceptable" to an audience who would not otherwise be able to experience it, or so that a work will deliver the same "degree of shock" (or lack of it) that it delivered to its original audience.

7

Once upon which time?

In addition to having denotations and connotations, words and phrases have historical resonances and exhibit intertextuality, a term introduced in 1966 by Julia Kristeva (see Alfaro, 1996) to focus on words as dynamic sites rather than as static objects, as intersections of other words and concepts, referring to and even having embedded within them those other words and concepts. In literary works, intertextuality is often consciously manipulated by authors. Every person also exhibits, usually unconsciously, both a sociolect, a variety of language marking him or her as a member of a social group defined by economics, ethnicity, age, or some other criterion, and an idiolect, a variety of language specific to him or her.

All translations exhibit explicit intertextuality in that they are overtly based on other texts. However, the intertextuality of the original text with respect to the source language is unlikely to be the same as the intertextuality of a translated text with respect to the target language. This, according to Lawrence Venuti, is the cause of a major translation difficulty:

Intertextuality is central to the production and reception of translations. Yet the possibility of translating most foreign intertexts with any completeness or precision is so limited as to be virtually nonexistent. As a result, they are usually replaced by analogous but ultimately different intertextual relations in the receiving language. The creation of a receiving intertext permits a translation to be read with comprehension by translating-language readers. It also results in a disjunction between the foreign and translated texts, a proliferation of linguistic and cultural differences that are at once interpretive and interrogative. Intertextuality enables and complicates translation, preventing it from being an untroubled communication and opening the translated text to interpretive possibilities that vary with cultural constituencies in the receiving situation.

(Venuti, 2009: 157)

While reproducing all the intertextuality of the original may be impossible, translators can utilize the possibilities provided by the intertextual references available to them, thereby bringing the linguistic history of the target language, if not of the source language, to bear on their work. Such references can serve as implicit footnotes explaining alien manners and mores, a great help for writers for the stage for whom explicit footnotes are most often not an option.

The employment of words or phrases not in contemporary use, or from a context different from that of the surrounding text, foreignizes a translation. It is no longer "transparent," that is, it draws attention to itself and directs the audience to question the usually unconscious assumptions of more ordinary linguistic formulations. However, many contemporary translators resist such foreignization; they domesticate, rather than foreignize, by utilizing a contemporary standard diction that does not draw on earlier or unusual vocabulary.

Contemporary diction works well when the diction of the source does not differ too much from contemporary diction, or when the subject matter somehow seems contemporary. Translations into contemporary diction may also help smooth disjunctions between the period and culture of the music and the period and culture of the lyrics. Such disjunctions can arise when composers of art songs set lyrics written prior to their own eras, and when opera composers set stories about other times and places to music characteristic of their own eras: for example, Donizetti's *Maria Stuarda*, an opera set in England in 1587 with Italian music composed in 1835.

However, contemporary language is not the only choice. The *King James Bible* of 1611, for example, was written in the language of a century earlier, laying stress on the antiquity of the document and imparting a sense of reverence, weight, and wisdom to the words. It will probably never be known how much of the archaicism was truly intentional and how much was due to the writers' basing their own text on earlier translations (another example of explicit intertextuality).

7.1 Once upon a time

If a work is set in a nebulous mythical past, "long ago and far away," a "never-never" language such as Wardour Street can convey that. Marco Ravasini hit upon another method for his libretto for *La figlia del mago* (*The Sorcerer's Daughter*) (1981, revised 1991), with music by Lorenzo Ferrero.

La figlia del mago was created to introduce children to the conventions of nineteenth-century Italian opera. The simple story tells how the love of a boy and girl prevails by means of magic over the opposition of their two fathers. Much of Ferrero's music sounds as though it was written by Verdi after that composer had first been subjected to torture by twentieth-century atonalism, and then given relief in the form of music reminiscent of that used for Bugs Bunny cartoons. The two-dimensional operatic characters include four singing roles: Princess Soprano, Prince Tenor, Old King Baritone, and Bass the Sorcerer (also a king). There is a silent chorus of soldiers, sailors, several animals, and a sea monster.

In addition to newly invented words, Marco Ravasini's libretto includes words from all eras, especially some of the favorite words of nineteenth-century librettists and modern slang. The result is mythic, heroic, and humorous. For want of a better term, we call such a language "invented." (Wikipedia calls the language "imaginary" [<http://en.wikipedia.org/wiki/La_figlia_del_mago>, accessed October 2014]). It brings to mind not only nineteenth-century operas, but also heroic verse such as the sixteenth-century *Orlando furioso* by Ludovico Ariosto (1474–1533) and contemporary television commercials. While most native Italian speakers find the new words incomprehensible, they do respond with pleasure to the historical and comical resonances. Audiences in other countries should be allowed to share in the fun.

Ravasini's new words vary from possible Italian constructs such as "*doloransia*," in which vowels are dropped from "*dolore e ansia*" ("sadness and anxiety"), to the totally un-Italian "*mareserpa*" ("sea serpent") (feminine) replacing the standard Italian phrase "*il serpe marino*" (masculine). There are also odd forms of real words, such as "*aborrenda*" for both "*aborrente*" ("abhorrent") and "*orrendo*" ("horrendous").

What can translators do with such language? Compound words such as "*mareserpa*" are strange in Italian, but English compounds, whether written as two words ("sea serpent"), a hyphenated word ("warrior-king"), or a single word ("mothballs"), are ordinary words. Also, "sea serpent," combining Germanic "sea" with Latinate "serpent," is not only acceptable but actually more common than the totally Germanic "sea snake." Therefore, creating compound English words that feel strange is not a straightforward task, though mere newness can sometimes be strange enough: "calligamy" ("happy marriage"), composed of two Greek roots. Usually, however, strange (and funny) English compounds require the two parts to clash in some obvious way, such as when the colloquial is joined to the formal, or the archaic to slang: "popcide" ("father murder") and "xenofloozy" ("foreign female of low repute"). Strange compound words in English can also be formed using the portmanteau method of Lewis Carroll's "Jabberwocky," in which two meanings are run together into a single word: in "Jabberwocky," "slimy" and "lithe" are packed into "slithy." For "sea serpent," we pack together "aqua" (Latin root for "water") and "anaconda" (a type of snake, the word perhaps derived from Ceylonese "anacandaia" [*OED*]) and create "aquaconda."

Strange locutions can also be created by taking advantage of the fact that English nouns can be "verbed." Thus in our line "lest by con he loophole loose" ("lest by trickery he find some way to escape"), "loophole," usually a noun, functions as a verb. Abbreviated forms of words can be used: "tuit" for "intuition," "mystere" for "mysterious," and "pelled" for both "compelled" and "impelled"; as can old-sounding, archaic, and esoteric words such as "thou," "hath"; "delice" ("delight"), and "lapideous" ("made of stone"). Brand-new old-sounding words can be invented: "hurst" (past tense of "hoist"), "throught" (past tense of "threatened"), "sprintled" ("shattered"), and "dalliant" ("procrastinating"). The childish temperaments of the two fathers can be underlined by having them declaim infantile expressions:

> Prepare to cry!
> Mud in your eye!
> You took my tyke!
> You take a hike!
> (Herman and Apter, 1993)

Figure 7.1 shows the refrain from Bass the Sorcerer's aria, in which he tells how Old King Baritone will be punished for imprisoning his (Bass's) daughter. Table 7.1 gives translations of the words in Figure 7.1: from invented Italian into standard Italian, from standard Italian into English, and from invented English into standard English.

Bass the Sorcerer

FIGURE 7.1 La figlia del mago, *No. 14, Refrain.*
Source: Herman and Apter (1993).

TABLE 7.1 *La figlia del mago*, No. 14, Refrain

Translation of invented Italian into Standard Italian	Literal English translation of the Standard Italian
Uno spaventoso incantesimo tremendo si abbatterà! Sì, la presunzione del re della terra sarà alfine vittima della magia!	A terrifying tremendous incantation will be cast! Yes, the arrogance of the land king will finally be the victim of enchantment!
Translation of the invented English into Standard English	
Regarding the evil tyrannical land king, let a blast smash him into microscopic pieces. I shall cast a huge tremendous super stupefying spell!	

7.2 Once upon a specific time

Some works may benefit from translation into a language, not of "once upon a time," but of the era in which the works were written or set. Such is the case for *Ma tante Aurore, ou le roman impromptu* (*My Aunt Aurore, or the Impromptu Novel*), a French comic operetta first performed at the Opéra-Comique in 1803. With music by François Boieldieu (1775–1834) and a libretto by Charles de Longchamps (1768–1832), the operetta satirizes the European-wide craze for Gothic novels prevalent at the time, singling out for ridicule *The Mysteries of Udolpho* (1794) by Ann Radcliffe (1764–1823). Radcliffe's novel, the cornerstone of the craze, features a benighted but virtuous heroine living in the Castle of Udolpho, whose north tower is apparently haunted. *Northanger Abbey* (written 1798, revised 1803, first published 1818) by Jane Austen (1775–1817) also satirized gothic novels and also singled out *The Mysteries of Udolpho*.

Familiarity with *Northanger Abbey* suggested the use of period language for our translation of *Ma tante Aurore*, to help our contemporary audience recognize that manners and mores quite different from theirs motivate the characters. One alien idea is that marriage should be a matter of suitability and family alliance, not romantic love; another, that, to protect her reputation, a young woman should never make her preference for a man obvious until his courtship has been sanctioned by her parents or guardians. The comic twist is that an elderly spinster, Aunt Aurore, far from championing the orthodox view of marriage, believes just the opposite.

Bemused by her reading of gothic novels, Aurore will not bestow her blessing (or her money) on the marriage of her niece Julie unless the groom is a romantic hero who has literally swept Julie off her feet and preferably has also saved her from a "fate worse than death." Julie, on the other hand, has taken the conventional path. She is in love with a man totally suitable for an arranged marriage, someone with "name, fame, face, and fortune," who begins his suit by consulting his family and has them write to hers.

Table 7.2 gives a dialogue excerpt translated into period English. Note Julie's worry, in the last line, that she may have prematurely revealed to a man her preference for him.

TABLE 7.2 *Ma tante Aurore*, Act I, Scene 2.

Original French text	Literal English translation	Performable English translation
JULIE: Ah! je serais bien folle de m'occuper d'un homme qui m'oublie, dont je n'ai seulement pas entendu parler depuis deux mois.	JULIE: Oh! I would be very foolish to occupy myself with a man who forgets me, of whom I have heard no one speak for two months.	JULIE: I should be vastly foolish to concern myself with a man of whom I've heard nothing for two mortal months.
MARTON: Excepté par vous et moi, qui en parlons régulièrement tous les jours.	MARTON: Except by you and me, who regularly speak of him every day.	MARTON (ironically): Ah yes, we have not spoken of him daily.
JULIE: Ah! il était de toutes nos parties; son souvenir se mêle à celui de tous mes plaisirs.	JULIE: Oh, he was at all our parties. His memory is mingled with that of all my pleasures.	JULIE: Oh, he was of all our parties. His recollection must necessarily be mingled with that of my pleasures.
MARTON: Sans doute.	MARTON: Without doubt.	MARTON: Necessarily.
JULIE: Tu crois que je l'aime, Marton.	JULIE: You think that I love him, Marton.	JULIE: Marton, you believe I love him.
MARTON: Oh! mon Dieu oui, et vous?	MARTON: Oh, my God, yes, and you?	MARTON: Lord, yes! Do not you?
JULIE: Eh bien, moi aussi; et ce qui m'inquiète, c'est quil ne le croie lui-même.	JULIE: Oh well, me too, and what troubles me is that he may think it himself.	JULIE: Oh well, I do, and what disquiets me is that he may think it himself! (Herman and Apter, 1982a)

We used the same language for lyrics. The first stanza of Valsain's "Romance" from Act I employs the same late eighteenth-century language of "attachment" rather than "love," and an "offer" of marriage:

> Though from the first I looked upon you
>> with something less than perfect detachment,
> only when you had departed I knew
>> how great was my attachment.
> I did not think it vain to believe
>> that you had hinted, circumspectly,
> an offer from me would be well received,
>> and I vowed to propose directly.
>> (Herman and Apter, 1982a)

This is the language of love during an era when society believed "enthusiasm" to be dangerous. The use of that language can help convey the attitudes to an audience without recourse to footnotes.

Another work suitable for translation into period English is the French comic operetta *Le médecin malgré lui* (*The Doctor in Spite of Himself*). Although this is a Victorian work composed by Charles Gounod and first performed in 1858, it is based on Molière's prose farce of the same name first performed in 1666.

Gounod, together with his librettists Paul Barbier and Michel Carré, received the commission for the operetta when the première of *Faust* was postponed, and so, in 1857, they interrupted six years of work on *Faust* to write *Le médecin*. The text includes about two-thirds of Molière's dialogue verbatim. The remainder, slightly trimmed, was transformed into sung lyrics. The librettists then added two love songs and two choral finales.

Gounod's adaptation and our translation are only two of many transformations that Molière's play has undergone over the course of more than three centuries. Most famous among English translations is Henry Fielding's adaptation of 1732, *The Mock Doctor; or, the Dumb Lady Cur'd*, which played at the Theatre Royal in Drury Lane, London.

We needed a language that would translate not only Molière's words but also the cultural assumptions underlying them. Barbier and Carré left Molière's dialogue in seventeenth-century French, but wrote new lyrics in nineteenth-century French. We briefly considered translating into two different periods of English but rejected the idea because, between 1650 and 1850, English had drifted much further than had French. We toyed with translating into a fairly formal modern English with phrases such as "*monsieur*," "*ma foi!*," "*ciel!*," and "*s'il vous plaît*" left in French for a Gallic flavor. This too we found unsatisfactory because a formal modern English, avoiding colloquialisms, would have lost part of protagonist Sganarelle's wide range of diction. Furthermore, modern English, in any register, does not invoke many of the cultural assumptions underlying seventeenth-century French phrases.

Our inspiration came from the euphemisms called "minced oaths," blasphemous interjections made suitable for the stage and elsewhere by leaving out or changing sounds (cf. contemporary "gosh!" for "God!," "gee!" for "Jesus!," and the somewhat obsolete "heck!" for "hell!"). Seventeenth-century French and English minced oaths were quite similar in method of creation and meaning: "*parguienne*" equals "egad," "*diantre*" "deuce," and "*palsanguenne*" "swounds." And so we decided to write our translation in seventeenth-century English.

One example of seventeenth-century manners not well expressed by twentieth-century English is an elaborate ritual regarding hats. If we had translated the work into modern English, the servants Valère and Lucas, on meeting Sganarelle, would have said something such as, "Mister Sganarelle, please put on your hat. The sun might be bothering you." Audiences, though not knowing why, would sense something wrong with that translation. The wrongness inheres in the cultural context. The twentieth-century vocabulary suggests twentieth-century manners, but Valère and Lucas are urging Sganarelle to be the first to put on his hat because they falsely believe him to be their social superior. Sganarelle cannot understand their excessive courtesy. None of these assumptions about hats resonate in modern English, but they are implicit in seventeenth-century English. The lyrics for this incident are shown in Table 7.3, together with our performable translation.

Seventeenth-century English and French culture and customs did not overlap completely; differences did find their way into the fabric of the two languages. For example, English spouses during the Restoration, contrary to their French counterparts, normally used the polite forms of second-person pronouns ("you," "you," and "your"), saving the familiar forms ("thou," "thee," and "thy") for moments of unusual tenderness or anger. Thus, to stay true to seventeenth-century English practice for spouses, we had to reverse Molière's *tutoîment*. In Table 7.4 (p. 138), second-person pronouns are double-underlined in the literal and performable English translations, showing the reversal from familiar to polite and polite to familiar.

An additional problem is posed by the phrase length of the two choruses and love songs written in nineteenth-century French. These were added by the librettists and are not present in the original play by Molière. Both seventeenth-century French and seventeenth-century English differ from nineteenth-century (and present-day) language by employing longer sentences composed of shorter phrases. Gounod's music follows the longer nineteenth-century phrase length, forcing the translated English lyrics to do

TABLE 7.3 *Le médecin malgré lui*, Act I, No. 4, mm. 37–47.

Original French text	Literal English translation
LUCAS: *(à Sganarelle)*	**LUCAS:** *(to Sganarelle)*
Nous venons tout droit de la ville,	We come straight from the village, sir, to
Monsieu, pour avoir votre avis!	obtain your advice!
SGANARELLE:	**SGANARELLE:**
En quoi puis-je vous être utile?	In what way can I be of service to you?
VALÈRE: Monsieur, couvrez-vous,	**VALÈRE:** Sir, cover yourself,
couvrez-vous s'il vous plaît!	cover yourself, please!
LUCAS: Si le soleil vous incommode,	**LUCAS:**
boutez dessus, Monsieu!	If the sun bothers you, put it on, sir!
SGANARELLE: *(Il se couvre.)* C'est	**SGANARELLE:** *(He puts on his hat.)* That's
fait! Peste des saluts à la mode!	done! A pox on fashionable greetings!

Performable English translation
LUCAS: *(to Sganarelle)*
Straightway ha' we come from the village,
sir, for to summon your skill.
SGANARELLE:
I am your very humble servant.
VALÈRE:
But, sir, shade your head from the sun's febrile ray.
LUCAS: I' truth the sun be fiercely beating—
on with your bonnet, pray.
SGANARELLE: *(He puts on his hat)*
Hi-hey! Pox, pester this pother of greeting!
(Herman and Apter, 1979b)

the same. Nonetheless, we tried to suggest seventeenth-century poetry by using favored nature-describing words such as "sylvan" and "silver." When a chorus of *fagotiers* (woodcutters) and *fagotières* (their wives) troops on and sings of rustic pleasures, we translated:

> Sit we where the elm bestows
>   his shady green on the meadow
> and the sylvan streamlet slows,
>   banks of flowers row on row
>   reflected in the silver flow.
>
> (Herman and Apter, 1979b, *Le médecin malgré lui*,
> No. 5, mm. 60–76)

And so we made our language old.

TABLE 7.4 *Le médecin malgré lui*, Act I, No. 1, mm. 132–58.

Original French text	Literal English translation
MARTINE: Je me moque de ta menace!	**MARTINE**: I laugh at thy threats!
SGANARELLE: Ma chère âme, gare au bâton!	**SGANARELLE**: My dear soul, beware of the stick!
MARTINE: Crois-tu me forcer à me taire?	**MARTINE**: Dost thou believe thou canst force me to be quiet?
SGANARELLE: Votre peau, ma douce moitié, vous démange, à votre ordinaire; je vais vous frotter sans pitié!	**SGANARELLE**: Your skin, my better half, Is making you itch, as is usual for you; I will rub you without pity!
MARTINE: Ivrogne,	**MARTINE**: Sot,
SGANARELLE: Ma petite femme,	**SGANARELLE**: My little woman,
MARTINE: sac à vin	**MARTINE**: wine bag
SGANARELLE: je vous rosserai,	**SGANARELLE**: I will beat you,
MARTINE: voleur!	**MARTINE**: thief!
SGANARELLE: je vous étrillerai!	**SGANARELLE**: I will thrash you!
MARTINE: traître! insolent! pendard! infâme! gueux!	**MARTINE**: traitor! insolent one! rogue! infamous one! tramp!
SGANARELLE: Vous en voulez donc, cher trésor de mon âme? eh bien! en voilà! *(Il prend un bâton e la bat.)*	**SGANARELLE**: You want it therefore, dear treasure of my soul? very well! here you are! *(He takes a stick and beats her.)*

Performable English translation
MARTINE: Do you think that I can be frighted?
SGANARELLE: Light o' love, th'art like to be harmed!
MARTINE: What force can force me to be quiet?
SGANARELLE: Is thy skin now plagued with an itch? Then thy loving husband will cure it by scratching it out with a switch!
MARTINE: Thou tosspot!
SGANARELLE: Sweet wife o' my bosom,
MARTINE: Sack o' wine!
SGANARELLE: one wave of my wand
MARTINE: Thou sot!
SGANARELLE: and thy hide will be tanned!
MARTINE: Jackass! Grinning ape! Peacock! Hyena! Swine!
SGANARELLE: Have it as thou wilt, I shall physick thy sickness. And now for the cure. *(He takes a stick and beats her.)*
(Herman and Apter, 1979b)

7.3 Right now

Some translators "make it new." The phrase is most often attributed to Ezra Pound. It is the title of a book of his essays published in 1935, and is included in his Canto 53 first published in 1940, though his use of it almost certainly pre-dates both. In fact, the phrase probably dates back to twelfth-century China (Michael North, *Guernica*, August 15, 2013).

One translator who "made it new" was David Spencer (1954–), who "decided to treat *La Bohème* as if it were a new musical" (1990: 22). Table 7.5 shows an interchange between Marcello and Rodolfo at the beginning of Act I. Note that in Spenser's version, "Marcello" is renamed "Marcel," the character's name in the French novel and play on which *La bohème* is based. By happenstance, in these lines Puccini does a one-time setting of the name as "Marcel," though singers performing in the original Italian would probably pronounce it as in Italian ("mar-CHEL") rather than as in French ("mar-SEL").

TABLE 7.5 *La boheme*, Act I, mm. 111–29

Original Italian text	Literal English translation
MARCELLO: Rodolfo, io voglio dirti un mio pensier profondo: ho un freddo cane. **RODOLFO:** Ed io, Marcel, non ti nascondo Che non credo al sudor della fronte!	**MARCELLO:** Rodolfo, I want to tell you a profound thought: I am terribly cold. **RODOLFO:** And I, Marcel, I do not hide from you that I do not believe in the sweat of one's brow!
Performable translation by David Spencer (1984, rev. 2002)	
MARCEL: This draft is godless torture and worst of all, Rodolfo— My nuts are freezing. **RODOLFO:** Marcel, be grateful you still have them. Mine fell off; I'm just too numb to feel it.	

Thus are the nineteenth-century Bohemians brought into the present.

A nonneutral contemporary diction can also be used to reveal meanings in a source that might otherwise be lost. Such is the case for twelfth-century troubadour lyrics, the direct forerunner of modern popular love songs. Times have changed enough so that the ancestry may not be apparent in literal or "transparent" translations.

Consider the lyric *"Estat ai com om esperdutz"* by Bernart de Ventadorn (fl. late twelfth century). To make the connection between then and now, a radical transformation is required. Table 7.6 shows the first stanza. The surviving music is shown in Figure 7.2. A love song can be made of these lyrics and this music, but the result will not reveal that Bernart's songs are the ancestors of the Blues. What will reveal it is shown in Figure 7.3.

TABLE 7.6 *"Estat ai com om esperdutz"* from Apter (1999: 130–31).

Original Occitan text	Literal English translation
Estat ai com om esperdutz	I have been like a distracted man
per amor un lonc estage,	for a long time because of love,
mas era·m sui reconogutz	but now I have repented
qu'eu avia faih folatge;	that I have been doing folly;
c'a totz era de salvatge,	for I was disagreeable
car m'era de chan recrezutz;	because I had abandoned any singing
et on eu plus estera mutz,	and the more I remained mute,
mais feira de mon damnatge.	the more I acted to my own harm.

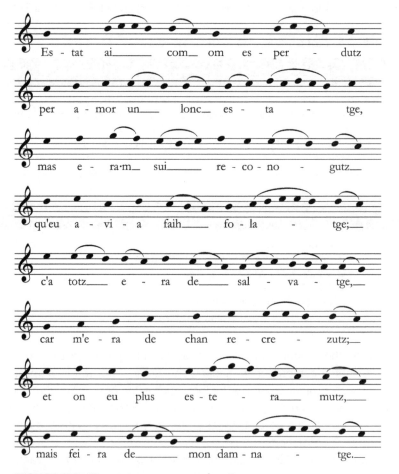

FIGURE 7.2 *"Estat ai com om esperdutz,"*
transcribed by Hendrik van der Werf (1984) from Apter (1999: 134).

FIGURE 7.3 *"Goodbye Blues,"*
An English version of "Estat ai com om esperdutz"
by Bernart de Ventadorn
Words and Music by Ronnie Apter
Arranged by Mark Herman and Jeffry Herman
from Apter, 1999: 1345.

There are other good ways to translate the lyrics of *"Estat ai com om esperdutz."* This translation and musical setting highlights the contemporary resonances; other dictions and musical settings could highlight the differences between our own era and the twelfth century.

Period language can intuitively convey cultural assumptions. For translators of sung lyrics, who are extremely limited in their ability to incorporate footnotes, such language provides a powerful way of conveying necessary information to an audience.

8

Verbal delineation
of character

According to Joseph Kerman (1988: 21), "The composer is the dramatist." Kerman was referring specifically to Claudio Monteverdi (1567–1643), the first great opera composer, but his statement is generally true. However, extended to all composers and compositions for the musical stage, this notion has led to the misconception that sung words, original or translated, do not have to be dramatic and do not have to delineate character. The complex interaction of words and music is discussed in Chapter 12. Here, it will be sufficient to remark that words, while leaving room for the music to do its work, must still carry some of the dramatic burden. Most scripts for the musical stage *are* dramatic and *do* delineate character. Good translations should do the same.

Of course, there have been lyrics written in a mildly poetic, neutral diction intended to not "distract" from the music. Critical theory in the eighteenth and early nineteenth centuries held that simple, nonindividuating language was closer to a postulated Platonic ideal language. In addition, composers were expected to write "portmanteau" arias, portable pieces so non-individuating that they could be inserted into any opera at the whim of a star performer. An example is Edoardo's aria at the beginning of Act II in Felice Romani's libretto *Il finto Stanislao* (*The False Stanislaus*), originally set by Adalbert Gyrowetz in 1818 and later re-used by Giuseppe Verdi for *Un giorno di regno* (*A Day in the Reign*) in 1840:

> Pietoso al lungo pianto
> alfin m'arride amore;
> quella che m'arde il core

mia sposa alfin sarà.
Avrò per sempre accanto
il ben ch'io già perdea!
ah! questa amorosa idea
scordare il duol mi fa!
(*Il finto Stanislao*, Act II, Scene 1)

(Taking pity on my long weeping,
at last love smiles on me;
she for whom my heart burns
will at last be my wife.
I shall have always beside [me]
the treasure that I nearly had lost!
ah! this loving idea
makes me forget my grief!)

By the end of the nineteenth century, such clichéd writing was passé. By then, ideal librettos employed clichés only to indicate the way a particular character spoke, not the way a good librettist wrote. Just about the most clichéd remark in Puccini's *La bohème* (1896) is Mimì's statement in Act II: "*Amare è dolce ancora più del miele!*" ("Love is even sweeter than honey!") (mm. 369–74), written on purpose by librettists Giacosa and Illica to indicate that Mimì is less educated than the Bohemians to whom she is speaking. Verbally individuated characters had become the order of the day.

Presumably, therefore, translators look for verbal character individuations in the source texts and make analogous individuations. However, many do not, perhaps because they believe that music alone should individuate character, or because they fail to note the verbal individuation, or because they are unable to re-create it. Musical constraints sometimes make it difficult to imitate a verbal trait at a specific spot, although it is often possible to compensate by re-creating the trait elsewhere in the translation.

Losing one or another instance of a characteristic speech pattern will not destroy its overall re-creation. Consistent failure will. Overall success or failure can only be judged by considering the entire translation. Nonetheless, examination of specific instances can show what translators can hope to achieve.

8.1 Seventeenth-century French rustics

Charles Gounod's French comic operetta *Le médecin malgré lui* (*The Doctor in Spite of Himself*) (1858) adopts much of the language of the seventeenth-century Molière play on which it is based. In both play and operetta, the character Valère, though a house servant, speaks a French slightly purer than his master's; that is, Valère's speech is more standard and less dialectal. What this would imply in seventeenth-century English—into which we translated *Le médecin*—is debatable, although in John Dryden's *Sir Martin Mar-all* (1667), a servant who speaks upper-class English is revealed to be a gentleman after all. Valère, however, is *not* a gentleman in disguise; he is merely pretentious. Therefore, had we tried to follow Molière's subtle gradations of diction, we might well have falsified his intentions. Further, the effect would probably have been lost on a modern audience. So we conveyed Valère's pretentiousness by exaggerating it:

> **VALÈRE:** Come, come, good sir, leave off this humor,
>   this cicatrix of mind, this tumor,
>   that yet cannot hide your learnèd eloquence.
> > (Herman and Apter, 1979b, *Le médecin
> > malgré lui*, Act I, No. 4, mm. 119–25)

In contrast to Valère, his fellow servants speak a patois. The seventeenth-century English equivalent would be some sort of country dialect. But again, even if we had succeeded in translating into such a dialect, the effect would probably have been lost on a modern audience. An American audience, in particular, might not have understood it. Therefore, for servants other than Valère, we suggested the rural diction by inventing a new, comprehensible dialect based on nonstandard use of the verbs "to be" and "to do." Here is the servant Jacqueline, flirting with Sganarelle:

> **JACQUELINE:** It be true, as the proverbs tell us,
>   when the cat's away, mice will play,
> and do a billy dilly-dally with a willing nanny,
>   then let come what may;
> on a summer day will a summer madness
>   lead a wife astray.
> > (Herman and Apter, 1979b, *Le médecin
> > malgré lui*, Act III, No. 12, mm. 22–37)

Similarly, for a chorus of country people addressing the protagonist Sganarelle as a doctor, we invented a dialectal form of "doctor" to parallel the nonstandard French of "*sarviteur*" (for "*serviteur*") and "*monsieu*" (for "*monsieur*") (see Figure 8.1). The form we invented, "doctorer," also has the advantage of sitting properly on the musical notes. If the stage director wishes, the chorus can carry the dialectal pronunciation all the way to "Sarvent, sar, mister doctorer!"

Ser - vant,   sir,   mi - ster doc- tor - er!
Sar - vi - teur,   Mon-sieu le Doc -teur!

FIGURE 8.1 Le médecin malgré lui, *Act III, No. 11a, mm. 21–23.*

Source: Herman and Apter (1979b).

8.2 Ad libbing in dialect

In the libretto by Franz Carl Hiemer (1768–1822) for Carl Maria von Weber's *Abu Hassan* (1811), four characters have small speaking roles. For two of these roles, the actors are expected to follow the German *Singspiel* tradition of embroidering the written text with comic ad libs. In order to show actors the different directions these ad libs might take, we translated some of the speeches three ways: into dictions recondite, British, and Yiddish. In one such speech between numbers 7 and 8, the servant Mesrur responds to Abu Hassan's claim that he (Abu) will soon follow his supposedly departed wife into the grave:

Original German:
Nicht mutlos, Abu Hassan! Nur ein feiges Gemüt läßt sich vom Mißgeschick überwältigen! Es gibt ja noch so viele schöne Frauen auf der Welt!

Literal Translation:
Not to be discouraged, Abu Hassan! Only a cowardly heart can be overwhelmed by misfortune! There are indeed still so many beautiful women in the world!

Recondite Performable Translation:
Come, Hassan. There is no need for this excessive lugubricity. There are any number of passable women left.

British Performable Translation:
Come, come, Hassan! Don't mope about. Bad for the system. Chin up, chest out, eyes front. Lots of beautiful women left, you know.

Yiddish Performable Translation:
A young, strong man like you? Ridiculous! Listen, there's a girl in the harem, a little pudgy but a real bargain, and if you—

(Herman and Apter, 1980)

8.3 Wagner's *Das Rheingold*

The verbal differentiation of character in Richard Wagner's *Der Ring des Nibelungen* (*The Ring of the Nibelung*) (1876) is Wagner's own. While the music and stage action also differentiate the characters, the libretto carefully gives the different characters different speech patterns. These differences are especially obvious in *Das Rheingold* (*The Rhinegold*) (1869), the first part of the four-part *Ring*, because three characters, Fafner (a bass), Alberich (a baritone), and Loge (a tenor), repeatedly express their resentment toward other characters. Since their emotion is the same, differences in speech *content*, though they do exist, are minimized, more clearly revealing differences in speech *patterns*.

In what follows, several translations are cited to illustrate successes and failures in differentiating speech patterns.

8.3.1 *Fafner*

Fafner is one of the two giant brothers who build Valhalla, Wotan's castle and fortress, also known as the Hall of the Slain. In the aftermath of the construction, Fafner murders his brother Fasolt and then, transformed into a dragon, sleepily guards the ring and the rest of the Nibelung hoard until he is killed by Siegfried.

Of the three characters being considered, Fafner's diction is closest to neutral. For instance, in a speech to his brother in Scene 2 (p. 107), given right in front of the gods, he simply states that he wants them dead, and that he will achieve that result by taking away the goddess Freia, the only one who can grow the golden apples responsible for the gods' eternal youth. Fafner gloatingly depicts what the gods will look like as they age. Here are a few lines of this speech, together with a literal translation:

> . . . siech und bleich doch sinkt ihre Blüte,
> alt und schwach schwinden sie hin,
> müssen Freia sie missen.
> Ihrer Mitte drum sei sie entführt!

> (. . . however, their bloom will decline, [turn] sickly and pale,
> old and weak, they will fade away
> if they must do without Freia.
> So she must be carried off from among them.)

A good translation of these lines should incorporate Fafner's comparatively simple and direct diction.

Frederick Jameson, who used a mythologizing Wardour-Street, did not do well in rendering Fafner's directness:

> . . . pale and blighted passeth their beauty,
> old and weak waste they away,
> if e'er Freia should fail them.
> From their midst let us bear her away!
> (Jameson, 1896: 74)

Jameson's inversions make it hard to understand what Fafner is saying. Furthermore, it is unclear what a failure on Freia's part entails: Freia's failing the gods is very different from their having to do without her. While it might seem to be beating a dead horse to complain about a translation from 1896, Jameson's translation remains important because it is still widely available. In fact, a comic novel of 2012 sends its main character to the library to read the libretto of Wagner's *Ring*. He encounters Wardour Street, which he calls "some obscure dialect of Middle English" and refuses to "wade through [it]" (Holt, 1987: e-book location 396).

Because Fafner is direct, translations that eschew Wardour Street do fairly well at characterizing him:

> Sick and pale, their beauty will vanish,
> Soon they'll pass [,] old and worn out
> if their Freia is taken.
> So I say we should carry her off!
> (Stewart Robb, 1960: 24)

> Think of them grown ailing and ugly,
> old and weak, wasting away:
> lacking fruit, lacking Freia.
> Let us take her and be on our way!
> (Herman and Apter, 1983: 74)

> All the gods would sicken and die,
> Old and weak, they would perish
> if they lived without Freia!
> And that's why we will take her away!
> (Jeremy Sams, 2002: 12)

All three convey Fafner's directness. We concentrate somewhat more on Fafner's gloating than do the others.

8.3.2 Angry Alberich

Alberich is a Nibelung dwarf, the title character, the Nibelung of *The Ring of the Nibelung*. Like Fafner, he says what he means, but with some differences. In Scene 1 (pp. 38–39), he excoriates the Rhine daughters:

> Ihr schmählich schlaues,
> lüderlich schlechtes Gelichter!
> Nährt ihr nur Trug,
> ihr treuloses Nickergezücht?

> (You shameful, deceitful,
> loose, evil riff-raff!
> Do you feed only on deceit,
> you treacherous nixie brood?)

Alberich is as direct as Fafner but, unlike Fafner, Alberich is characterized by a piling on of pejorative words, by a tendency to vulgarity (see Chapter 6), and, when angry, by alliteration on *sch*, a sound he can spit out. Although "*Nickergezücht*" is not vulgar, its pronunciation causes a disgusted pursing of the lips. These are traits for which translators should find analogues.

Stewart Robb does not fully capture Alberich's sound for these lines:

> You shocking, wily,
> wicked, disorderly riff-raff!
> Brood of the nixies,
> treacherous breeders of lies!
> (Robb, 1960: 10)

While there is the *sh* of "shocking" and the harsh *ch* of "treacherous," the spitting anger is softened by alliteration of the soft sound of *w* and by the *u*-sound of "brood," done with lips much more loosely held than German *ü*. "Riff-raff" is a good choice for the pejorative "*Gelichter.*"

Jeremy Sams uses *ch* and *t* wherever he can, as analogies to repeated *sch:*

> You evil breed of
> treacherous, lecherous bitches.
> Teasing and cheating,
> lying. That's all you know!
> (Sams, 2002: 7)

Andrew Porter uses *sh* and *s*, as do we:

You shameless, slippery
underhand, infamous wenches!
Shifty and sly,
you treacherous watery tribe!
                    (Andrew Porter, 1976: 11)

You shifty, shameless,
sickening, simpering bitches!
Spawn of the Rhine,
you're raised from the cradle on lies!
                    (Herman and Apter, 1983: 11)

Both Porter and we do well at capturing Alberich's relentless piling on of straightforward pejoratives. Neither Porter nor we manage to capture the sonic bite of "*ihr treuloses Nickergezücht.*"

8.3.3 Poetic Alberich

Alberich has a second speech pattern, different from, yet somehow compatible with the first. When in despair, his speech can take poetic flights, as when he warns Wotan not to steal the ring (Scene 4: 233–34):

Hüte dich, herrischer Gott!
Frevelte ich, so frevelt' ich frei an mir:
doch an Allem was war, ist und wird,
frevelst, Ewiger, du—
entreißest du frech mir den Ring!

 (Watch yourself, imperious god!
If I sinned, then I sinned only against myself:
but against all that was, is, and shall be,
you will sin, immortal one,
if you rashly tear away my ring!)

Alberich is still direct and pejorative—"*herrischer*" means "imperious, overbearing, peremptory," but he also uses the religious terms "*Gott*" (God) and "*Ewiger*" (immortal being). These in turn push "*freveln,*" the principal meaning of which is "to commit a crime," over to its religious meaning of "to commit sacrilege or blasphemy," "to sin." Alberich is claiming that Wotan's theft would be of Biblical proportions, against all that ever has existed or will exist. Of all the other characters in *The Ring*, only Erde speaks in such sweeping terms.

Any translation approaching literal should be able to capture the serious nature of Alberich's warning. The words "god," "sin," and "all that was, is, and shall be" assure the presence of mythic qualities. The poetic quality, however, is more difficult to attain, requiring careful attention not only to words but also to musical setting (see Figure 8.2).

FIGURE 8.2 *Das Rheingold, Alberich, Scene 4: 233–34.*
J = Frederick Jameson (1896: 172–73)
P = Andrew Porter (1976: 57)
H&A = Herman and Apter (1983: 172–73)
S = Jeremy Sams (2002: 24)

Jameson and Porter change the music in an acceptable way by splitting an eighth note into two sixteenth notes to accommodate "and shall" underlying German "*und*." In the next to last measure, Sams's "dare" is shown underlying German "*-sest*." This poor setting, placing "dare," a word with a relatively heavy burden, on a relatively short sixteenth note, is not necessarily Sams's, since the available libretto does not show how Sams might have changed Wagner's rhythm to accommodate "dare."

As for the words, Jameson's phrase "sinn'st, eternal one, thou" is an awkward wrenching of order-bound English syntax, apparently in an attempt to follow Wagner's word placement. We too have an inversion, "Sinner am I," but it is still easy to understand, and avoids setting the relatively weak word "if" on "Fre-."

Sams's opening, "You beware, tyrannous god," has "You" on a downbeat, with the result that Alberich could sound childish if performed by an unskilled actor: "You beware"—"No, *you* beware." He (like us) tries to tie the mythic quality of "*war, ist und wird*" to a longer span of notes with "all things that were, that have been, and will be," but his lack of parallel structure harms the poetry.

Porter's two adjectives, "proud, cruel," in the second measure have a weaker effect than the single adjectives "o'erweening," "almighty," and "tyrannous." His phrase "you are planning a crime" is too weak to end on a high F. Although "*freveln*" can mean "to commit a crime," the mythic "sin" seems required on so poignant a musical note.

We lose the meaning of "seizing" or "stealing" in the next to last measure by saying "beware of the ring" instead of "if you steal the ring," but thereby achieve a more menacing tone.

Everyone wisely ends on "ring!"

As mentioned before, translation is a process of gain and loss. These excerpts from translations of Alberich's poetic flight illustrate that there is no perfect and no best translation.

8.3.4 Loge

Loge is the god of fire. He is not one of the Æsir-Vanir, the more powerful gods with whom he has formed an uneasy alliance. His protector is Wotan, chief of the Æsir-Vanir, who finds Loge's tricks and cunning useful. Loge's speech, unlike that of Alberich, is never vulgar or pejorative; unlike that of both Alberich and Fafner, it is also almost never direct. Instead, Loge is sly, clever, and evasive, characteristics evident in Table 8.1. He is the most difficult of *The Ring's* characters to individuate verbally.

TABLE 8.1 *Das Rheingold*, Scene 4, pp. 307–9

Original German text	Literal English translation
Ihrem Ende eilen sie zu,	They rush to their end,
die so stark im Bestehen sich wähnen.	those [gods] who imagine themselves to be so strong.
Fast schäm' ich mich, mit ihnen zu schaffen,	I'm almost ashamed to deal with them,
zur leckenden Lohe mich wieder zu wandeln,	to change myself again into tongues of flame,
spür' ich lockende Lust:	I feel a tempting lust
sie aufzuzehren, die einst mich gezähmt,	to consume those who once tamed me,
statt mit den Blinden blöd zu vergeh'n,	instead of idiotically expiring with those blind ones,
und wären es göttlichste Götter!	even if they may be the godliest gods!
nicht dumm dünkte mich das!	that wouldn't seem stupid to me!
Bedenken will ich's: wer weiß was ich tu'?	I'll think it over: who knows what I'll do?

The speech in Table 8.1 is an aside, but, even though the other gods are not listening, Loge says nothing vulgar. The most pejorative word he uses is *"Blinden"* ("blind ones"). He does not directly say that the gods are idiotic; instead, he implies it by declining to "idiotically expire" with them. By saying "even if they may be the godliest gods," he suggests that they are not. When speaking of his own future actions, he is indirect and undecided. Rather than say, "That would seem intelligent to me," he uses litotes: "That wouldn't seem stupid to me." Rather than say, "I'm not ashamed to deal with them [the gods]," he says, "I'm almost ashamed to deal with them." These are the verbal indications of Loge's character, which translators should strive for.

The same four singable translations considered for Alberich, plus a fifth by Stewart Robb (1960), provide useful examples of successes and failures.

All except Jeremy Sams say something close to "rather than blindly sink with the blind," a reasonable approximation. Sams says, "rather than follow them like a fool" (2002: 30), which does keep away from vulgarity and name calling, but does not indirectly suggest that the gods are fools.

Three of the translations keep the suggestion that the gods may not be the godliest, two by Wagner's means, Andrew Porter by sarcasm:

> e'en were they of gods the most godlike (Jameson, 1896: 215)
> although they're so gracious and god-like! (Porter, 1976: 71)
> If they were of gods the most godly (Herman and Apter, 1983: 215)

Two do not:

> although they are gods the most godlike (Robb, 1960: 70)
> magnificent gods though they may be (Sams, 2002: 30)

The litotes of "that wouldn't seem stupid to me" fares poorly with everyone:

> not ill were it, meseems! (Jameson, 1896: 215)
> I think that is the thing! (Robb, 1960: 70)
> I think that might be best! (Porter, 1976: 71)
> I'd still serve them the same. (Herman and Apter, 1983: 215)
> In fact, that's an idea! (Sams, 2002: 30)

Only Jameson reproduces it, and his involution makes the meaning hard to decipher in the heat of performance. In the others' attempts, including ours, Loge sounds as direct as Fafner.

The most difficult to reproduce of Loge's indirections is *"Fast schäm' ich mich, mit ihnen zu schaffen"* ("I'm almost ashamed to deal with them,") because the musical setting does not have quite enough notes for an English equivalent (see Figure 8.3).

Loge

Mässig bewegt [Moderately animated]

J:	A-shamed am I	to share in their deal-ings
R:	I feel a shamed	to share in their ac-tions
P:	A-shamed I'd be	to share in their deal-ings
H&A:	I'm al-most a-shamed	to share in their deal-ings
S:	I'm quite a shamed	to be their ac-com-plice

FIGURE 8.3 Das Rheingold, *Loge, Scene 4: 307.*
J = Frederick Jameson (1896: 214)
R = Stewart Robb (1960: 69–70)
P = Andrew Porter (1976: 71)
H&A = Herman and Apter (1983: 214)
S = Jeremy Sams (2002: 30)

When Loge's words are mis-translated as "I'm ashamed," the translators not only lose Loge's speech pattern, but also falsify his meaning and his character. He is *not* ashamed of his shady dealings. It is unclear why Robb, Porter, and Sams rendered the line as they did, since "I'm not ashamed," closer to Loge's actual meaning, fits the musical notes. (Jameson would not have used a contraction.) However, even "I'm not ashamed" is not the exact equivalent of "I'm almost ashamed," which claims that Loge approaches shame, but does not reach it, a subtle and important distinction. Including "almost" does entail a musical cost: as shown in Figure 8.3, we had to add an extra eighth-note G-natural.

8.4 Changing a speech pattern

Richard Wagner, when creating the character of Alberich, used different speech patterns depending on whether Alberich is enraged or despairing. Occasionally, translators can similarly change a character's speech pattern when the character's state of mind changes, whether such pattern changes exist in the original or not.

In Mozart's *Die Zauberflöte* (*The Magic Flute*) (1791), Pamina has a spell of madness as a cumulative result of her mother's commanding her to kill Sarastro, an attempted rape by Monostatos, and her belief that Tamino has deserted her. She contemplates suicide, and speaks to a dagger as if it were her betrothed:

> Du also bist mein Bräutigam—
> durch dich vollend' ich meinen Gram!—
> (No. 21, mm. 45–49)

(You are my bridegroom—
through you I end/complete my misery!—)

To indicate Pamina's deranged state of mind, we altered the contemporary English diction we usually assigned her and had her sing such archaic words as "thine," "thy," "whate'er," and "betide," and pronounce "beloved" as "be-LUH-ved":

I shall be thine whate'er betide:
belovèd bridegroom, behold thy bride!
                    (Herman and Apter, 1982b)

For an added insider-joke, there is the suggestion that characters veer toward Wardour Street only when they are insane.

As Richard Rodgers and Oscar Hammerstein said in 1960, referring to the two lead characters in *Oklahoma!* (1943): "we had to write in their words, not ours" (quoted online at <http://www.npr.org/2000/04/29/1073526/npr-100-oklahoma>, accessed on November 30, 2014). Translators should do no less.

9

Multiple translations

U nlike re-translations, discussed in Chapter 4, multiple translations are
purposefully designed to elucidate one or more specific aspects of the
original. A re-translation is the one version of choice for a specific occasion,
while multiple translations are frequently all collected in one place, and may
even all be by the same translator.

Multiple translations are needed because, as Ezra Pound (1885–1972)
maintained, "a translation can always and only be *one view* of the original"
(Pound, paraphrased by Apter, 1984/87: 7). Where one translation might attempt
to render literal meaning, another might strive to mimic poetic form, another
to elucidate hidden meanings, another the cultural ambience. Where one
translation might emphasize the cultural differences between the source and
target cultures, another might emphasize similarities. In pursuit of his own idea,
Pound sometimes made several differing translations of the same poem.

Because singable translations are almost always written to pre-existing
music, and that music tends to follow the form of the original words, singable
translations usually must do likewise. Multiple singable translations, unlike
those of spoken poetry, say, will therefore generally differ in characteristics
other than form. However, as discussed below for translations of the songs of
the troubadour Bernart de Ventadorn, if a set of multiple translations includes
both singable and nonsingable versions, these may differ markedly in form.

Douglas R. Hofstadter (1945–) famously devotes an entire book, *Le Ton
beau de Marot* (1997), to multiple translations of a single poem written in
a particularly tight form. But even before considering the form, Hofstadter
provides not one but two different literal translations. One is in readable
English; the other sacrifices readability to express multiple meanings of
individual words. The poem by the French poet Clément Marot (1496–1544),
is shown together with Hofstadter's two literal translations in Table 9.1.

TABLE 9.1 Clément Marot's "Ma mignonne"

Clément Marot A une Damoyselle malade	Literal translation 1 To a Sick Damsel	Literal translation 2 My sweet/cute [one] (feminine)
Ma mignonne,	My sweet,	My sweet/cute [one] (feminine),
Je vous donne	I bid you	I [to] you (respectful) give/bid/convey
Le bon jour;	A good day;	The good day (i.e., a hello, i.e., greetings).
Le séjour	The stay	The stay/sojourn/visit (i.e., quarantine)
C'est prison.	Is prison.	[It] is prison.
Guérison	Health	Cure/recovery/healing (i.e., [good] health)
Recouvrez,	Recover,	Recover (respectful imperative),
Puis ouvrez	Then open	[And] then open (respectful imperative)
Votre porte	Your door,	Your (respectful) door,
Et qu'on sorte	And go out	And [that one (i.e., you (respectful) should] go out
Vitement,	Quickly,	Fast/quickly/rapidly,
Car Clément	For Clément	For/because Clément
Le vous mande.	Tells you to.	It (i.e., thusly) [to] you (respectful) commands/orders.
Va, friande	Go, indulger	Go (familiar imperative), fond-one/enjoyer/partaker
De ta bouche,	Of thy mouth,	Of your (familiar) mouth,
Qui se couche	Lying abed	Who/which herself/himself/itself beds (i.e., lies down)
En danger	In danger,	In danger;
Pour manger	Off to eat	For/in-order-to eat
Confitures;	Fruit preserves;	Jams/jellies/confectionery.
Si tu dures	If thou stay'st	If you (familiar) last (i.e., stay/remain)
Trop malade,	Too sick	Too sick/ill,
Couleur fade	Pale shade	[A] color pale/faded/dull
Tu prendras,	Thou wilt acquire,	You (familiar) will take [on],
Et perdras	And wilt lose	And [you (familiar)] will waste/lose
L'embonpoint.	Thy plump form.	The plumpness/stoutness/portliness (i.e., well-fed look).
Dieu te doint	God grant thee	[May] God [to] you (familiar) give/grant
Santé bonne,	Good health,	Health good,
Ma mignonne.	My sweet.	My sweet/cute [one] (feminine).
(Hofstadter, 1997: 1b)	(Hofstadter, 1997: 2b)	(Hofstadter, 1997: 4b)

The form of Marot's poem is bound by many rules. Here is Hofstadter's "original list" as printed in his book (Hofstadter, 1997: 1a):

1   *The poem is 28 lines long.*
2   *Each line consists of three syllables.*
3   *Each line's main stress falls on its final syllable.*
4   *The poem is a string of rhyming couplets: AA, BB, CC, . . .*
5   *Midway, the tone changes from formal ("vous") to informal ("tu")*
6   *The poem's opening line is echoed precisely at the very bottom.*
7   *The poet puts his own name directly into his poem.*

Poetic versions of "*Ma mignonne*" can conform to or diverge from any or all of the rules, and be more or less literal. Hofstadter's book includes versions by many people, exhibiting many degrees of conformity and diversion. The first two, by Hofstadter himself, are shown in Table 9.2.

TABLE 9.2 Poetic versions of Clément Marot's "*Ma mignonne*"

Version 1	Version 2
My sweet dear,	Cutie pie,
I send cheer—	Herewith I
All the best!	Wish you well,
Your forced rest	In your cell.
Is like jail.	It's like jail
So don't ail	When you ail.
Very long.	Hope you make
Just get strong—	Jailbreak
Go outside,	Straightaway.
Take a ride!	'Twill be gay,
Do it quick,	Without doubt,
Stay not sick—	Once you're out.
Ban your ache,	"Quick!" says Clem,
For my sake!	"Flush your phlegm!"
Buttered bread	Think of ham,
While in bed	Eggs and jam—
Makes a mess,	Pretty posh
So unless	Stuff to nosh;
You would choose	But no way,
That bad news,	If you stay
I suggest	Stuck abed,
That you'd best	With those med-
Soon arise,	ical folks
So your eyes	Making pokes.
Will not glaze.	"One needs sun-
Douglas prays	light and fun!"
Health be near,	So say I,
My sweet dear.	Cutie pie!
(Hofstadter, 1997: 6b)	(Hofstadter, 1997: 7b)

The four translations in Tables 9.1 and 9.2 each give different insights into the original poem. The first literal translation in Table 9.1 does not attempt any formal equivalence but does clearly show that the poem is a kindly get-well note. The second literal translation in Table 9.1 elucidates all sorts of denotations and connotations but loses any sense of the poem as a poem and stifles any emotional response. The first rhymed version in Table 9.2 reproduces form as exactly as possible, matching the three syllables per line and the couplet rhyme scheme. To achieve greater naturalness, it does not try to imitate the switch from you-formal ("*vous*") to you-familiar ("*tu*"), and is not strictly literal: "jam" has become "buttered bread" and "Clément" has become "Douglas." Also, the position of the name has been shifted from the midpoint of the poem to near the end. The second rhymed version is even less literal and less consistent in diction. (Marot's diction is consistent.) It lightheartedly begins "cutie pie," and flippantly (Hofstadter's characterization) spreads both "med-ical" and "sun-light" across two lines. Further, Hofstadter considers the "jail-" in "jailbreak" to have two syllables. This version does attempt an analogue of the switch from formal to familiar via diction levels: formal, old-fashioned "herewith" and 'twill in the first half, the more casual "posh," "nosh," and "no way" in the second half. The idea of praying for the child's good health has been dropped. Other insights into meaning, form, and tone abound in the many other translations of "*Ma mignonne*" to be found throughout Hofstadter's book.

A set of rules can be developed to describe the forms of any poem or set of poems operating under related conventions. For instance, such a set can be created to describe the customary form of the love songs of the medieval troubadour Bernart de Ventadorn (fl. ca. 1150 to 1180 AD), who lived in Southern France and wrote in the composite of southern French dialects known as Old Occitan.

Here are five rules regarding Bernart's customary form that we have determined from a study of his lyrics:

1 The lyrics are divided into stanzas, eight being the most common number of them.

2 Each stanza of a particular lyric includes the same number of lines, except for one or two shorter stanzas, called *tornadas*, at the end. Not all of the lyrics have *tornadas*.

3 The corresponding lines of each stanza have the same number of syllables. The *tornadas* usually mimic the final lines of a stanza as to number of syllables.

4 Every stanza has the exact same, usually complex, end-rhyme scheme. In many lyrics, every stanza also has the exact same rhyme syllables. The end-rhymes of the *tornadas* are usually the same as those of the last two lines of a regular stanza. Many stanzas also have irregularly placed internal rhymes.

5 Particular lyrics sometimes have nonce rules, such as that the sixth line of every stanza ends with the same word, or that specified pairs of lines end in words sharing an etymological root.

There are also conventions unrelated to form. It was understood that love songs were addressed to a noble lady who was not the wife of the troubadour. Because of this, her identity was to be kept secret. Consequently, the lyrics are rife with multiple meanings and *double entendre*, made possible because so many words in Old Occitan have multiple meanings. Further, the multiple meanings and *double entendre* are conveyed as wittily as possible.

Finally, it should be remembered that the lyrics are not poems to be recited but songs to be sung, with appropriate word-music interactions.

It is obviously impossible to reproduce all the aspects of a love song by Bernart, plus the basic literal meaning, within a single English translation. A rhyme scheme by Bernart may have one or more end-rhyme sounds requiring sixteen words each, difficult or impossible for rhyme-poor English.

Music, consisting only of musical pitches, has survived for some of Bernart's songs. Based upon little evidence, scholars argue about the rhythmic scheme: two popular theories are (1) that one or more of the rhythmic schemes called "musical modes" were applied by the singer, and (2) that the music was sung in a close approximation of speech rhythm. In order to write a translation intended to be sung to extant music, a decision must first be made about rhythm, whether to follow one or another of the current theories or to ignore them. For those lyrics for which no music is extant, translators can either choose an extant troubadour melody compatible with the lyrics in question or supply new music.

In *Sugar and Salt* (1999), Ronnie Apter offers multiple translations of each of Bernart's forty-three extant lyrics. For most of the lyrics, there are two translations: one highly literal, the other free-verse. For five of the lyrics, there are singable translations rather than free-verse translations. For one lyric, there are literal, free-verse, and singable translations. One of the singable translations, discussed in Chapter 7, transforms Bernart's lyric into a modern blues song with suitable new music. The other five singable translations are set to reconstructions of the lyrics' own extant music. Apter's book is accompanied by a CD on which are performed the singable English translations, together with sung examples that demonstrate the effects of conflicting theories about medieval performance practices.

The literal translations list multiple meanings of words and phrases in an effort to show the double and triple meanings characteristic of troubadour song, and make no effort to copy the form or portray the beauty of the originals. The free-verse translations do attempt to portray the beauty (and wit) of the originals but make little effort to copy form. The singable translations of necessity copy the form at least partially, and also attempt to demonstrate the interaction of words and music.

Unfortunately, we could not find sufficiently differing translations of any one lyric by Bernart to enable a useful analysis of the critical possibilities offered by multiple translations. Therefore, the analysis below considers translations of stanzas from three different lyrics.

Multiple meanings are especially prevalent in *"Anc no gardei sazo ni mes."* Table 9.3 shows the first two stanzas in Old Occitan, together with Apter's extremely literal English translation. The symbols < > enclose a set of multiple meanings and the symbol | separates the meanings in the set. The symbol / separates a multiple meaning within another one. [ ] enclose an English word added to aid comprehension.

In the lyric, *"esplei"*, the last word of the second stanza, means "tool, utensil" before it means "revenue, profit" or "service, practice, exercise." According to Louis de Landes's *Glossaire erotique de la langue français, "outil"* ("tool") was used for "penis" in the Middle Ages. Old Occitan *"esplei"* was very likely to have been used similarly (Apter, 1999: 64–65).

The "one view" offered by Apter's literal translation is of the multiple and sometimes contradictory meanings that Old Occitan makes possible. *"lo dezir ab pauc d'esplei"* says simultaneously that the speaker's desire is not fulfilled and that it comes from his sexual organ. *"c'aquel tems senhorei"* says simultaneously that he rules the season and that, no, the season is in charge.

To explain wit is not to be witty. For Apter, to reproduce even some of the wit required a free-verse translation:

> I never saw a season
> (flower up or under
> or shoot poking out by the spring)
> but that when love came
> in spouting joy
> thought I that season ruled
> before
>> I'd have called him a fool
>> who told me I would be love's pawn
>> till I could die
> but now
>> I feel, I know
>> all other ills are nothing
>> to a tool's desire
>>> (Apter, 1999: 62)

TABLE 9.3 "*Anc no gardei sazo ni mes*," first two stanzas

Original Old Occitan text	Literal English translation
Anc no gardei sazo ni mes ni can flors par ni can s'escon ni l'erba nais delonc la fon, mas en cal c'oras m'avengues d'amor us rics esjauzimens, tan me fo bels comensamens qu'eu cre c'aquel tems senhorei.	I never \<considered|observed\> a \<period|season\> or \<month|crop|dish\>, either when [the] \<flower|menstrual period\> appears or when it hides or the grass is born beside the fountain, but [that] at whatever moment a rich joy came to me from love, it was so beautiful a beginning to me that I believe that \<I rule/ruled that time|that season prevails\>.
Be l'agra per fol qui·m disses tro aras, qu'en sui tan prion, que ja·m tengues tan deziron amors qu'eu morir en pogues; mas aras sen e sui sabens que totz autres mals es niens vas lo dezir ab pauc d'esplei.	Indeed, I would have held him for a \<fool|chess bishop\> who would have told me, until now, that I am in it so \<deep|far advanced\> that love would always keep me so greatly desirous that I could die of it; but now I am \<knowledgeable|wise\> and I feel that all other ill is nothing compared to the desire \<with so little exercise/advantage|from so small a tool\>. (Apter, 1999: 63)

The free-verse translation compensates for the ugliness of the literal translation. The literal translation allows readers to understand that certain choices in the free-verse translation do not deviate from the literal meaning, but instead emphasize one or another of the multiple meanings. Also, when the free verse does deviate from the original meaning, even readers who do not know Old Occitan can see what has been added and left out, and can speculate on the reasons why.

Neither version, together or apart, conveys Bernart's skills in rhyme and meter. Every line of this five-stanza lyric is octosyllabic. Each seven-line stanza rhymes *abbaccd* on the same rhyme sounds. That calls for ten rhymes each on *a*, *b*, and *c*, and five each on *d*. Rhyme-poor English cannot reproduce this.

One translator who did attempt to imitate most if not all of the form was Barbara Smythe (1882–?). Her translation of stanzas 4, 5, and 6 of *"Ara no vei luzier solelh"* is given in Table 9.4, together with the original Old Occitan and Apter's literal translation.

From the literal translation, it is obvious that there are fewer multiple meanings in this lyric than in the one given in Table 9.3. However, the form is even more intricate. Again there are eight syllables per line, this time rhyming *abbcddef*, with the same rhyme syllables repeated from stanza to stanza. However, in each stanza the *a* rhyme word is etymologically related to *c*, the first *b* rhyme to the first *d*, the second *b* to the second *d*, and *e* to *f*.

Smythe maintains the eight syllables throughout, using iambic tetrameter. She also maintains the *abbcddef* rhyme scheme, though she maintains the same rhymes only for two stanzas, then switches to a different set of rhymes for the next two stanzas, and so on (see Table 9.4: same rhymes in stanzas 5 and 6, different rhymes in stanza 4). She also maintains the etymological relationships between the rhyme words for each stanza, mostly through the use of "-ing" words, perhaps the only way to do so in English and still rhyme. However, she thereby is forced into some nonstandard uses of the progressive tense. She gets the main meaning of the Old Occitan words but loses some nuances. Apter's poetic translation of stanzas 4, 5, and 6 does get the nuances, but can only suggest, rather than reproduce, the original form:

> Hear these
> the lamentations of a lover
> wracked in the fearful wrath
> they've roused
> My pleasures their alarm
> Another's joy their disgust
> May I gain no better justice
> than roundely
> to rout my attackers
>
> Day and night, restless, uneasy
> I note notes

TABLE 9.4 "Ara no vei luzier solelh," stanzas 4, 5, and 6

Original Old Occitan text	Literal English translation	Poetic translation by Barbara Smythe
D'aquestz mi rancur e·m corelh qu'ira·m fan, dol et esglai e pesa lor del joi qu'eu ai. e pois chascus s'en corelha del l'autrui joi ni s'esglaya, ja eu melhor dreih no·n aya, c'ab sol deport venz' e guerrei cel qui plus fort me guerreya. (Apter, 1999: 74, 76)	I recriminate and complain about these people that they cause me chagrin, grief, and horror, and any joy which I have pains them, and then each of them complains about or takes fright at the joy of anyone else. May I never have better justice than through <pleasure|amusement|sport|[or possibly a type of song]> alone I conquer and combat those who attack me most strongly.	And of such people I complain Who make me sorrowful and sad, For they are grieved when I am glad, And whene'er they are complaining And on others' joy look sadly, I behold their grief right gladly Since my delight can thus annoy Those who oft are me annoying.
Noih e jorn pes, cossir e velh, planh e sospir; e pois m'apai. on melhs m'estai, et eu peihz trai. mas us bos respeihz m'esvelha, don mos cossirers s'apaya. fols! per que dic que mal traya? car aitan rich' amor envei, pro n'ai de sola l'enveya!	Night and day I think, worry, and wake, I lament and sigh, and then am appeased. The more I am better off, the worse I suffer. However, one good <respite|hope> <animates|wakes> me, by which my pre-occupied mind is appeased. Fool! why <do|did> I say that I suffer ill? for I wish so rich a love I have benefit from only the desire of it!	By night and day I weep and wake And sigh, but soon I cease to grieve, And count it joy ills to receive, For good hope doth gently wake me And it swiftly cures my grieving; Sure, 'tis joy I am receiving, 'Tis happiness e'en to desire Such a love as I'm desiring.
Ja ma domna no·s meravelh si·lh quer que·m do s'amor ni·m bai. contra la foudat qu'eu retrai, fara i genta meravelha s'ilh ja m'acola ni·m baya. Deus! s'er ja c'om me retraya ("a! cal vos vi e cal vos vei!") per benanansa que·m veya? (Apter, 1999: 74, 76)	My lady should never be surprised if I ask her that she give me her love and kiss me. Against the folly that I <recount|reproach> she would do a gracious miracle if she ever embraced or kissed me. God! if only it will ever be that someone should <say of me|reproach me [with]> "Ah, how I saw you and how I see you!" for the good fortune that <I would evidence|he would see in me)! (Apter, 1999: 75, 77)	Marvel not, lady, if I take Such joy in you, but give me leave To love you; if you do, believe, Happiness will overtake me, Grief henceforth I shall be leaving And all men will be believing That to a high love I aspire Since to yours I am aspiring. (Smythe, 1911: 53)

strain strains
burden burdens
and then am appeased
(but suffer worst where I am best)
Madman! Why do I say I suffer ill
when I desire so rich a love
desire itself is requital?

Indeed
my lady shouldn't marvel
if I ask a kiss to work
miracles against my madness
Kissed, clasped, glad
would I recount my blissfulness?
Would any say, "How changed you are!"
when I appear?

(Apter, 1999: 74, 76)

Apter lightly suggests the etymological root pairings with "note notes," "strain strains," "burden burdens," and "kiss kissed." The rhyme is even more lightly suggested with "disgust justice," "uneasy appeased," "madness glad," and "kiss blissfulness," plus some alliteration and assonance. "Roundely" is an attempt to suggest both "roundly" and "roundel," in an analogy to the meaning spread of Old Occitan "*deport*" ("pleasure|amusement|sport|[or possibly a type of song]").

The discussion so far of Bernart's lyrics do not indicate that they were songs to be sung rather than poems to be recited. However, all of Bernart's lyrics were meant to be sung, and tradition holds that he composed the music himself, except perhaps for the debate lyrics. Melodic pitches for eighteen of his lyrics have survived; the music must be re-constructed by supplying time values for the musical notes. Since Smythe's translation has the same number of syllables and rhyme scheme as the original Old Occitan, the music for "*Ara no vei luzier solelh*" (see Apter, 1999: 78) could in theory be re-constructed so that Smythe's translation would be singable, though it is doubtful that that is what Smythe had in mind when she wrote her translation.

In singable translations, literality, or at least nuance, will usually be sacrificed to a greater extent than in free-verse translations. Some wit is also likely to be sacrificed. Although there must be some formal equivalence if the original music is to be used, even some of the formal complexity, especially that of repeated rhymes, is usually abandoned. Despite the losses, only singable translations can convey to a modern audience that Bernart's songs were indeed songs.

Table 9.5 gives stanzas 1, 3, and 5, together with literal translations, of "*Can par la flors josta·l vert folh*." The rhyme scheme of each 8-line stanza is *ababccdd*. The first six lines of a stanza have eight syllables; lines 7 and 8 each have ten. Not only are the same rhyme sounds carried over from stanza to stanza, but the rhyme word in line 6, "cor," is the same for every stanza.

TABLE 9.5 *"Can par la flors josta·l vert folh,"* Stanzas 1, 3, and 5

Original Old Occitan text	Literal English translation
Can par la flors josta·l vert folh e vei lo tems clar e sere e·l doutz chans dels auzels pel brolh m'adousa lo cor e·m reve, pos l'auzel chanton a lor for, eu, c'ai mais de joi en mo cor, dei be chantar, pois tuih li mei journal son joi e chan, qu'eu no pes de ren al. (Apter, 1999: 246, 248)	When the flower appears close by the green leaf and I see the ⟨bright|clear⟩ and ⟨calm|clear⟩ season, and the sweet song of the birds through the wood ⟨sweetens|softens|tempers⟩ my heart and ⟨re-awakens|revives⟩ me, since the birds sing according to their ⟨custom|law|fashion⟩, I, who have more of joy in my ⟨heart|core|will|courage|desire|spirit|memory⟩, ought indeed to sing since all ⟨my|half⟩ ⟨day|day's work⟩ are joys and songs, for I don't ⟨think|worry⟩ about anything else.
Be sai la noih, can me despolh, el leih qu'eu no dormirai re. lo dormir pert, car eu lo·m tolh per vos, domna, don me sove; que "lai on om a so tezor, vol om ades tener so cor". s'eu no vos vei, domna, don plus me cal, negus vezers mo bel pesar no val.	I know well at night when I undress that I shall not get any sleep in bed. I lose the sleeping because I ⟨am deprived of it|deprive myself of it⟩ for your sake, lady, whom I call to mind; for "there where one has his treasure, one always wishes to keep his ⟨heart|etc.⟩." If I do not see you, lady, about whom I ⟨care|inflame myself⟩ most, no sight ⟨is worth|aids⟩ my fine thought.
Tals n'i a qued an mais d'orgolh, can grans jois ni grans bes lor ve; mas eu sui de melhor escolh e plus francs, can Deus me fai be. c'ora qu'eu fos d'amor a l'or, er sui de l'or vengutz al cor. merce, domna! non ai par ni engal. res no·m sofranh, sol que Deus vos me sal! (Apter, 1999: 246, 248)	Such men there are who have more pride when great joy or great good comes to them, but I am of better ⟨sort|conduct|manners⟩ and more frank when God does me good. For if formerly I may have been at the ⟨brink|outskirts⟩ of love, now I have come from the edge to the ⟨heart|etc.⟩. Thanks, lady! I have no peer nor equal. Nothing is lacking to me if only God ⟨safeguard|reserve⟩ you for me. (Apter, 1999: 247, 249)

For our singable English version, we set the original pitches in a 2/4 rhythm of our own invention. This accords with none of the current theories about the original rhythm, but we chose it because it stimulated our inventive process for the singable translation. We usually followed the original syllable count and kept the original rhyme pattern, but changed the rhyme sounds from stanza to stanza. As in the original Old Occitan, we kept the same end-word for line 6 in every stanza, substituting English "core" for Old Occitan "*cor*." The presence of music helped us reproduce the metrical variety of the Old Occitan, which pits varying positions of stress against strict syllable count. The pattern of accents in our metrical setting for stanza 1, given musical phrase by musical phrase, is:

Sww S Sww S	Line 1
wSww S Sw S	Line 2
Sw Sww Sw S	Line 3
wSww Sww S	Line 4
Sw S Sww SW–	Line 5
SW Sw Sww S	Line 6
Sww SW Swsw S	Line 7
wSw S SwW Sw S	Line 8

where S   a strong (accented) syllable, a downbeat
       w   a weak (unaccented) syllable, a nondownbeat
       s   a downbeat less accented than usual because of its position in the phrase
       W   a nondownbeat more accented than usual because of its position in the phrase
       –   possible enjambment to next line.

The resulting song, with the Old Occitan of the first stanza and the English translation for stanzas 1, 3, and 5, is shown in Figure 9.1.

The predominant foot is a dactyl, Sww, but there are many nondactylic feet to offset them. There are four stresses each (capital and lower-case S in the diagram above) for lines 1–3, 5, and 6. There are only three for line 4 ("my heart is relieved and revived" in stanza 1), but the missing fourth stress is compensated for by a bar of rest. Lines 7 and 8 each have five stresses. Therefore, in homage to Old Occitan, the metrical pattern is much more varied than, say, lines of only iambic tetrameter or pentameter would have produced.

The important word "*cor*" ("heart"), the end-rhyme of the sixth line of every stanza, is repeated as "core" and rhymed in our translation, and given extra musical emphasis by both being held and underlying a musical ornament called a melisma, as shown in Figure 9.2. Also shown in Figure 9.2 are two other examples of melismas used for word painting, both in stanza 1: "pour out" is set on a melisma that "pours out" and "turned" is set on a melisma that "turns."

FIGURE 9.1 *An English version of "Can par la flors josta·l vert folh"*
by Bernart de Ventadorn.
Stanzas 1, 3, and 5.
Original pitches transcribed by
Hendrik van der Werf (1984) from Manuscript G.
Translated and with musical note time values set
by Ronnie Apter and Mark Herman.
Source: Apter (1999: 250–51).

FIGURE 9.2 *Melismas to emphasize and "paint" words.*

Figure 9.3 shows the variance in enjambment between lines five and six. In measures 20–21 of stanza 1, "pour out" involves enjambment between "pour" and "out." In stanza 3, there is no enjambment between "stored" and "I." In stanza 5, there is enjambment between "more" and "on." The varying enjambment adds greater rhythmic variety to the song.

FIGURE 9.3 *Variations in enjambment.*

A subtle example of word-music interaction can be seen from our translations of line 5, different in stanza 5 from our translations in every other stanza. As can be seen in stanzas 1 and 3, mm. 17–19, the first two measures proceed without a break to the third measure (see Figure 9.4). This pattern holds for all the stanzas not shown. Not so for stanza 5. There, the English words are "All is changed. Now I am no more on love's brink." The period after the word "changed" requires the singer to take a break at that point in the music. Therefore, at the word "changed," musically, all is changed.

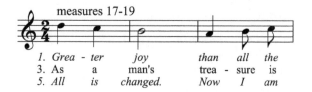

FIGURE 9.4 *All is changed at "changed."*

In these ways and others not discussed here, the translation of *"Can par la flors josta·l vert folh"* attempted to suggest Bernart's intricate mating of words and music.

Via multiple translations, many, if not all, aspects of the original Old Occitan can be carried over into English: the meaning via a literal translation; the emotional feeling, wit, and some of the form via a free-verse translation; and more of the form and the fact that the lyric is a song rather than a poem via a singable translation. However, the full formal complexity remains locked in the original, probably impossible to re-create in English.

10

When the music is missing

Lyrics, whether printed or digital, take up less storage space than music and sometimes survive when their music does not. In some oral traditions, such as that of the Saami discussed below, music is never written down, and can disappear when performers die. Music for operas and musicals may be lost because no one bothered to archive music cut from various revivals, or even the entire score. For example, editors working on critical editions, such as Ricordi's Verdi edition, have discovered much lost music, some of it rightly forgettable, some not.

In consequence, those who make singable translations may encounter lyrics whose music is partially or completely missing. When partially missing, the notation for what survives may not provide sufficient information for performance.

When faced with missing music, translators can employ a number of strategies:

1 Omitting the lyrics.

2 Translating the lyrics into spoken verse or prose.

3 Translating the lyrics into words spoken over music from elsewhere in the score or from another composition by the same composer or from another composer of the same period or with the same style.

4 Finding suitable existing music to which the lyrics may be sung.

5 Reconstructing the music from the clues left by the incomplete notation, sometimes with the help of scholarly theories.

6 Commissioning new music.

Omitting the lyrics is the simplest solution. If they contain nothing important for characterization, plot development, or dramatic construction, it is also the best solution.

Next simplest is translating the lyrics into spoken verse or prose. Myrdene Anderson (2005) has done this for Saami *yoiks*. The Saami of Northern Europe (formerly called Lapps) never write down the music of *yoiks*. No two performances are the same, and performance per se is considered to be an inextricable part of the piece. Further, performances include sounds in addition to or instead of actual words, and words that are incantatory rather than constituting any narrative. Here is a transcription of part of a *yoik* chanted by Mari Boine in 1994, quoted by Anderson together with Anderson's translation:

> Gumpet holvot
>
> Ealán ealán beaivvis beaivát
> ealán ealän beaivvis beaivát
> oainnán oainnán maid dal buktibehtet
> oainnán oainnán maid dal hutkabehet
> ealán ealán beaivvis beaivát
>
> The wolves howl
>
> I live, live from day to day
> I live, live from day to day
> I wait to find out what you bring
> I wait to see what you come up with
> I live, live from day to day
> (Anderson, 2005: 214–15)

We use the same strategy for most of the recitatives in the Baroque opera *Eraclea* (1700), with music by Alessandro Scarlatti (1660–1725) and words by Silvio Stampiglia (1664–1725). Scarlatti's music for one quartet and all the recitatives except the farcical ones has been lost. However, the words of the recitatives cannot be eliminated; they are essential to the drama. And so, we translate the no-longer-accompanied recitatives into loose, unrhymed spoken dramatic verse, centering around a norm of iambic tetrameter. This expedient works fairly well for some passages, particularly for sections of stichomythia, in which single alternating lines or half-lines are given to alternating characters who are having a dispute. In Table 10.1, the speakers are 15-year-old Princess Flavia and her 14-year-old sister Princess Irene. They are rivals in love.

Although the passage in Table 10.1 and many others proved to be successful individually, the strategy of translating into spoken verse was unsuccessful for

TABLE 10.1 *Eraclea*, Act II, Scene 12

Original Italian text	Literal English translation
FLAVIA: Tu di Damiro amante?	**FLAVIA:** You [are] a lover of Damiro?
IRENE: E tu d'Iliso?	**IRENE:** And you of Iliso?
FLAVIA: Bella finezza, Irene,	**FLAVIA:** Beautiful finesse, Irene,
Amare un che mi sprezza.	To love someone I despise.
IRENE: Flavia, bella finezza	**IRENE:** Flavia, beautiful finesse
Un che sià in odio mio, chiamar tuo	To call someone I hate your
bene.	sweetheart.
FLAVIA: Forza è d'amor,	**FLAVIA:** It is the strength of love,
che su quest' alma impera.	which rules my soul.
IRENE: Forza è di genio,	**IRENE:** It is the strength of the spirit,
che al mio cor sovrasta.	which dominates my heart.
FLAVIA: Ah Irene, Irene.	**FLAVIA:** Ah Irene, Irene.
IRENE: Ah Flavia, Flavia.	**IRENE:** Ah Flavia, Flavia.

Recitable English verse
FLAVIA: Aha! Damiro's admirer.
IRENE: Oho! Iliso's worshiper.
FLAVIA: Fine behavior, Irene,
to love my despiser.
IRENE: Fine behavior, Flavia,
to cherish someone who calls me names.
FLAVIA: The power of love rules my spirit.
IRENE: The force of attraction commands my heart.
FLAVIA: *(simultaneously with Irene)* Oh, Irene, Irene!
IRENE: *(simultaneously with Flavia)* Oh, Flavia, Flavia!
(Herman and Apter, 1992b)

the performance as a whole. Scarlatti's treatment of recitative varies flexibly from very speech-like with occasional chords to fully accompanied musically structured vocal lines with complex musical backgrounds. This flexibility allows Scarlatti's arias, almost all of which are in *da capo* form, to follow recitatives composed in a variety of musical structures. The *da capo* form, largely developed by Scarlatti himself, is in the pattern *ABA'*. *A* is a first section of music and words, *B* is a second section with different music and words, and *A'* is a repetition of the first section with variations and ornamentations. The *A* section is usually twice as long as the *B* section, which means the *B* section occupies only one-fifth of the entire aria. When the recitatives are spoken, the remaining sung music is forever in the same *da capo* form: *ABA'*, *ABA'*, *ad nauseam*. The intervening spoken dialogues do not supply enough variation. A strategy other than translating into spoken verse, had one been possible, might have been a better choice.

We employ the third strategy, translating into verse spoken over existing music, for an aria for the character Trénitz in Charles Lecocq's French operetta *La fille de Madame Angot* (*Madame Angot's Daughter*) (1872). An Act II aria for Trénitz had been eliminated in the tinkering the creators did between the opening in Belgium and the first performance in Paris. Available librettos give all the lyrics, but the music has been lost. For the first production of our English translation, producer Ruth Bierhoff and stage director David Ostwald felt that the performer they had cast as Trénitz deserved a bigger part. The four of us decided to give him a verse translation of the aria to be declaimed over music taken from the operetta's *Entr'acte* between Acts II and III. Our translation gives him the "deboned" pronunciation used for his dialogue (see Chapter 3), although the surviving lyrics switched to ordinary French. Table 10.2 shows the original French, a literal translation, and the chantable English lyrics. Figure 10.1 shows the beginning of the aria; the syllables that should fall on downbeats are capitalized.

TABLE 10.2 *La fille de Madame Angot*, Act II, No. 8a, Stanza 1

Original French text	Literal English translation
Gloire au pouvoir exécutif!	Glory to the executive power!
Il est actif, expéditif;	It is active, expeditious;
rien de plus communicatif	nothing communicates more
que mon pouvoir exécutif.	than my executive power.
Des pouvoirs qu'on chante à la ronde	Of powers sung all around,
n'est-ce pas le plus portatif,	it is the most portable,
le plus distributif,	the most distributed,
le plus persuasif,	the most persuasive,
le plus impératif,	the most imperative,
et le plus primitif.	and the most primitive.
Il remonte, c'est positif,	It harks back, positively,
à la création du monde.	to the creation of the world.
Gloire au pouvoir exécutif!	Glory to the executive power!
(Lecocq, 1872: 136)	

Chantable English lyrics
Glowy to the executive powah
that wins the day and rules the houah.
It educates, elucidates,
stimulates, and facilitates.
It innovates and communicates
and legislates and it adjudicates.
Evah since the world was created,
this is the powah to be venerated.
Glowy to the executive powah.
(Herman and Apter, 1989: 136–37)

Allegretto moderato

Trénitz

GLO - wy to the e-XE-cu-tive pow-ah that

WINS the day and RULES the hou-ah. It E-du-cates, e-LU-ci-dates,

FIGURE 10.1 La fille de Madame Angot, *beginning of Trénitz's Aria.*

David Bowles also uses the third strategy. He translates Aztec poetry (Bowles, 2014) and recites it over the music to *Toxcatl*, a ballet composed by Carl Seale (1936–2014) based on an Aztec ceremony and incorporating elements of traditional Meso-American music together with indigenous instruments (Bowles, December 2014, personal communication. For more information on *Toxcatl*, see: <https://apps.lib.utpa.edu/archon/index.php?p= core%2Fsearch&q=Toxcatl&content=1>; for more information on research regarding pre-Columbian Meso-American music, see: <http://mexicolore. co.uk/aztecs/music/>, both accessed December 3, 2014).

The fourth strategy for dealing with missing music is to find suitable alternative existing music to which the lyrics may be sung. In the case of a lyric by a troubadour for which no music exists, it may be possible to find an extant melody with matching syllable counts for a different lyric by the same or a different troubadour.

Consider the lyric *"Pro ai del chan essenhadors"* by Jaufre Rudel (fl. second quarter of the twelfth century) (Wolf and Rosenstein, 1983: 126–29). The lyric contains seven stanzas, each with eight octosyllabic lines. No music is extant for this lyric, nor for a different lyric by Jaufre Rudel with eight-line octosyllabic stanzas. However, the extant musical pitches (van der Werf, 1984: 288*) for "*Pois tals sabers mi sortz e·m creis*" (Pattison, 1952: 195) by Raimbaut d'Aurenga (c. 1147–73) fit an eight-line octosyllabic stanza. It is therefore possible for translators to make a singable translation of Jaufre's song using Raimbaut's extant music. Figure 10.2 shows the musical pitches for the first two lines, underlain with both Raimbaut's and Jaufre's words for the first stanza.

FIGURE 10.2 *Raimbaut d'Aurenga's music and Jaufre Rudel's lyrics*
Original pitches transcribed by Hendrik Van Der Werf (1984: 288).*

As can be seen in Figure 10.2, and as previously mentioned in Chapter 9, the surviving music conveys musical pitches and some ornaments for the melody line, but does not indicate rhythm, instrumental accompaniment, or vocal timbre. Rhythm can be supplied by a musicologist, by the translators (see below), or can be left up to the performers. Instrumental accompaniment and vocal timbre are definitely for performers rather than translators to choose. Theories (Apter, 1999: 32–35) regarding vocal timbre postulate everything from a pure, white sound to an ululating, microtonal Arabic sound. The pure, white timbre is favored by countertenor Russell Oberlin, who can be heard singing "*Chanson Do·ill Mot Son Plan E Prim*" by Arnaut Daniel (fl. fourth quarter of the twelfth century), accompanied by a viola da gamba, at <http://www.pandora.com/russell-oberlin/courts-kings-troubadours-medieval-renaissance-music>. The Arabic timbre is favored by the Clemencic Consort, who can be heard singing the songs of several troubadours at <http://www.allmusic.com/album/troubadours-mw0001821276>. Both websites were accessed December 8, 2014.

As for rhythm, translators may choose to follow one of the three most common theories regarding troubadour songs, that they were sung (1) in a speech-like rhythm, (2) with one syllable per musical beat except that the last syllable in a line could be held longer and be followed by a rest, and (3) in one of the medieval rhythmic modes. There were six such rhythmic modes, not to be confused with melodic modes, all in triple time (Apter, 1999: 285), which medieval performers were expected to know and apply as needed.

Or, considering the sparse evidence for any of the theories, translators may choose to ignore them all, and simply create a rhythm they like, as we did when making singable translations of troubadour lyrics.

Whatever rhythm is chosen will very much influence subsequent word choices in the target language. Consider the first two lines of a lyric by the troubadour Marcabru (c. 1127–48):

> *Pax in nomine Domini!*
> Fetz Marcabrus los motz e·l so
> > (de Jeanne, 1909: 169)

> *(Peace in the name of the Lord!*
> Marcabru created the words and the music)

Figure 10.3 on the next page shows how different the songs can be depending on the rhythms chosen.

The final strategy is to replace missing music with newly composed music. For the recitatives of *Eraclea*, it may be possible for a skillful composer to study the extant recitatives of other Scarlatti operas and compose new music in a matching style, or else in a modern but still blending style. Conversely, completely new music having little or nothing to do with the original medieval music could be composed. Two examples are our blues setting for Bernart de Ventadorn's "*Estat ai com om esperdutz*" (see Chapter 7), and Carl Orff's famous setting for some of the medieval lyrics of *Carmina Burana*.

Various strategies can be used to make singable translations when music is missing in whole or in part. Translators should be guided by sensitivity to the work as a whole, but their choices will often be limited by circumstances and the preferences of those commissioning the translation.

10.3a *One syllable per beat*

10.3b *Rhythmic mode according to Gennrich (1958: 28)*

10.3c *Rhythmic mode according to Davenson (1967: 23)*

10.3d *Rhythmic mode according to Collins et al. (1982: 122)*

FIGURE 10.3 *Four reconstructions of the first two lines of Marcabru's "Pax in nomine Domini."*

11

Verbal and musical form

Two aural systems determine sense and arouse emotion on the musical stage, the verbal and the musical, each with its own formal properties. When words are sung, verbal and musical forms may re-inforce, ignore, or conflict with each another. They re-inforce each other when, for instance, the musical setting pauses at rhymes; they conflict when the musical setting enjambs rhymes, as shown for Puccini's *La bohème* below. Sometimes a composer deliberately alters the verbal form, as shown below for a Rachmaninoff chorus.

Translators too, sometimes alter, indeed, must often alter, the verbal form of the source language to one more congenial to the target language, especially when translating from a largely multisyllabic or relatively rhyme-rich language into largely monosyllabic rhyme-poor English. These alterations, discussed in detail below, typically take the form of spreading a single syllable over notes originally setting multiple syllables, and dropping some rhymes. When altering the verbal form, translators should carefully consider how the source text and music work together, and try to maintain their relationship.

11.1 Rhythm

When composers set text, they are free to add, subtract, repeat, or change the words in order to obtain the rhythmic effects they desire, or even to ask their librettists for verse in a different meter or prose with a different rhythm. Translators customarily must take the musical rhythm as given, and match it syllable for syllable, stress for stress, and burden for burden. Translators of sung lyrics are not allowed to render French alexandrines by iambic pentameters or to switch to prose. In a domesticating translation, they must mimic the foreign rhythms embodied in the music without contorting those of the target language. In a foreignizing translation, they might accept, even emphasize, distortion.

11.1.1 Syllable count

In English, most of the basic word stock has been worn down to monosyllables. Simple concepts and strong emotions, both abundant on the musical stage, usually call for monosyllabic words. "Passion" is usually *not* a substitute for "love," nor is "bipedal appendages" for "legs." Yet many works are written in languages in which simple and emotional words are multisyllabic.

One solution for translators into English is to spread the English monosyllable over two, or even more, notes (see Figure 2.1 in Chapter 2). This change in poetic rhythm is usually masked by the music. Alternatively, in a comic situation, the oddity of multisyllabic words may be acceptable. In the example below, from our translation of Verdi's *Un giorno di regno* (*A Day in the Reign*) (1840), "eyeball," "elbow," and "torso" stand in for Italian *"testa"* ("head"), *"gambe"* ("legs"), and *"braccio"* ("arm"):

> We will fill a wooden barrel
>   full of high explosive powder.
>   Not a Roman could be prouder
> of the resulting Roman candle.
> We will seat ourselves astride it.
>   We will bid ourselves good night.
> Within our hands we hold the fuses,
>   which we then proceed to light.
> Boom! an eyeball! Boom! an elbow!
>   Boom! a torso taking flight!
> This is the weapon that I choose
>   if you insist upon a fight.
>   (Herman and Apter, 1983a, *Un giorno di regno*, No. 19, mm. 115–38)

Sometimes, neither spreading a syllable nor using a polysyllabic diction will work. Such is the case when, in Verdi's *La traviata* (1853), Violetta sings *"Addio del passato."* "Addio" is three syllables in Italian; the English equivalents, "goodbye" and "farewell" and even the informal "so long," boast only two. Ruth and Thomas Martin, beginning their translation with "farewell," padded the line with the word "then" to fill up the third syllable: "Farewell then, to illusions" (Martin and Martin, 1946/61: 197–98). There is another solution, not requiring padding. Verdi's music tends not to depict particular words, or even phrases, but to express the emotion of an entire verbal passage over one or more sections of an aria. Therefore, translators of his operas are usually free to move thoughts around within an aria. By moving the thought of *"Addio del passato"* forward eight measures, the literal English translation, "Farewell to the past," fits the music without any need for padding (see Figure 11.1).

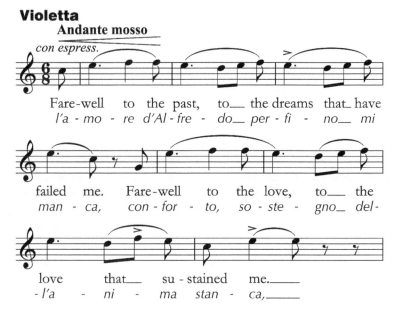

FIGURE 11.1 La traviata: "Addio del passato," *No. 8, mm. 137–45.*
Source: Herman and Apter (1981).

Moving the opening thought eight bars forward does not leave translators with nothing to say at the beginning of the aria. Thoughts from the middle of the stanza are just as easily moved to the beginning (see Figure 11.2).

FIGURE 11.2 La traviata: "Addio del passato," *No. 8, mm. 129–37.*
Source: Herman and Apter (1981).

"*Addio del passato*" is a meditation on an emotion. More of its meaning can be retained by repositioning ideas than by attempting, and failing, to reproduce them *in situ*.

11.1.2 *Stress and burden*

Stress, also called accent, is the relative force with which a syllable is pronounced. The English language possesses both word stress and sentence stress. Multisyllabic words are pronounced with different stresses on different syllables, and different words within a sentence receive different stresses depending on their grammatical function, all according to complex rules. Spoken French, by contrast, is a language with almost no word stress, and fewer points of sentence stress than English; almost all spoken French syllables are pronounced with the same force.

However, music itself is a stressed "language." In the typical four-beat measure, the first beat receives the primary stress, the third beat receives a lighter secondary stress, and beats two and four are unstressed. In fact, in most sequences of four notes of the same duration beginning on a downbeat, the first note will receive the most stress, the third less stress, and the second and fourth the least. (Very fast sequences of four, say sixteenth notes in 4/4 time, will stress only the first note.) Thus, sung French, due to musical stress, is more like spoken English (and sung English) than spoken French.

Despite this lessening of difference, some aspects of spoken prosody are necessarily reproduced when a language is set to music. The most difficult rhythms to mimic in English are those of languages whose prosodies, both spoken and sung, are very different from those of English. For example, all Czech words are stressed on their first syllables, except in prepositional phrases, where the preposition receives the stress. As a result, for both single words and phrases, the stress pattern / × × × (strong weak weak weak) is common in Czech. This pattern is very uncommon in English, which most naturally falls into iambic (× /) or trochaic (/ ×) patterns. Anapests (× × /) and dactyls (/ × ×) are also fairly easy to achieve in English, but a higher proportion of unstressed to stressed syllables is hard to come by.

The solution is to follow the musical stresses and replace the second unstressed Czech syllable—the third note—with an English syllable having a very light burden.

Burden—also called verbal weight—is related to the quantities of Classical Greek metrics, and refers to the length of time and/or physical effort required to say or sing a particular syllable. It is both absolute and relative: absolute in that, for any syllable, there is a minimum time required to say or sing it, and if insufficient time is allotted, a syllable cannot be sung; relative in that a long stressed syllable can sound bad if it is not held long enough relative to the length of an adjacent short unstressed syllable, even if it is possible to sing the long syllable in the time allotted. Taking relative burden into consideration means that, except in very unusual circumstances, it is inadvisable to set the word "strengthen" in a four-beat measure so that "strength-" occupies one beat and "-en" three beats. However, in a very protracted setting over three measures, "strength-" could receive eight beats and "-en" three without anything sounding wrong.

In English, stress and burden usually increase together, making even lightly stressed syllables impossible to sing in the time duration of a sixteenth note. However, there are exceptions, and if a stressed syllable has an unusually short burden, it is singable on the third sixteenth note on which an unstressed (or very lightly stressed) Czech syllable is set.

Figure 11.3 shows an example from Bedřich Smetana's opera *Dvě vdovy* (*Two Widows*) (1874/77). The first notes setting the prepositional phrase beginning with Czech "*po*" are two sets of four sixteenth notes. The short-burdened English words set on the third note of each set are "shot" and "lot." These two words each consist of a short vowel between single consonants ("sh," though consisting of two letters, represents only one consonantal sound), and are surrounded on both sides by vowels and not by other consonants: "a shot and," "a lot of." This allows them to be pronounced much more quickly than a word such as "blast," which is bounded on both sides by double consonants, or "soup," which includes a long vowel.

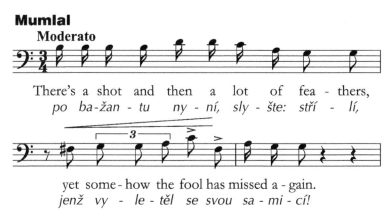

FIGURE 11.3 Dvě vdovy (Two Widows), *I.iii: 54–55*.
Source: Herman and Apter (1984).

Even languages closer to English than Czech, such as German and French, have burden patterns that deviate from those common in English. In particular, compared to those in German and French, the burdens of unstressed final English syllables, such as "-tion" and "-tive," tend to be long. Sung French (unlike spoken French) frequently has a very short unstressed final "-e," and German has short "-e" and "-en." When these occur in the middle of a phrase, translators can replace them with the little words of English: "a," "the," "of," "is," and so on. However, such words cannot replace short-burdened syllables that end phrases.

Some translators try to solve the problem with final "-ing," frequently distorting word order or using an unnatural progressive aspect to do so—and the burden of "-ing" is too long anyway. It is usually better to comb English for its scattered wealth of light final syllables. Using examples from our own translations, these include:

(a) short-voweled personal pronouns in unaccented position:

> What do toil and sweat avail us
> when both flesh and spirit fail us?
> > (Herman and Apter, 1980, *Abu Hassan*, #1, mm. 26–29)

> **OMAR:** Take my heart!
> **FATIMA:** You do me credit.
> **OMAR:** Know my mind!
> **FATIMA:** I haven't read it.
> > (Herman and Apter, 1980, *Abu Hassan*, #6, mm. 30–35)

(b) "-es," the third-person present singular ending for verbs and plural ending for nouns:

> This fact be true the world around;
>   'tis not a man's purse that bewitches.
> What if his purse be empty found,
>   so long as he fill his britches.
> > (Herman and Apter, 1979b, *Le médecin malgré lui*, #7, mm. 88–96)

(c) "-le," the verb, noun, and adjective suffix:

> **FRONTIN:** If you were offered silk and sable,
>   would you cleave to your love for Frontin? . . .
> **MARTON:** Were I to dine at the master's table,
>   who should be my partner if not my Frontin?
> > (Herman and Apter, 1982a, *Ma tante Aurore*, II.iii, #8: 152–53)

(d) "-er," the verb, noun, and adjective suffix:

> What are you hiding?
>   Is there some treachery undercover?
>   If I discover you have a lover,
> I will unleash my ax and hack him limb from limb!
> > (Herman and Apter, 1980, *Abu Hassan*, #7, mm. 51–60)

and a host of multisyllabic English words that just happen to have very short unstressed final syllables: "bosom," "hyena," "sofa," "millennia."

In addition to finding short unstressed syllables, translators into English sometimes have to match long unstressed syllables. Such syllables do not occur naturally in English, but they do in Czech. The ' mark in Czech, which can be positioned over any syllable in a word, means that the syllable should be held twice as long as a Czech short syllable. It does *not* mean that the syllable should be stressed. In fact, as already stated, Czech words are always stressed on the first syllable. This gives some Czech words a very un-English syncopation that is often mis-heard by English speakers. Figure 11.4 shows the pronunciation of the composer Leoš Janáček's last name.

FIGURE 11.4 *Pronunciation of "Janáček."*

There are two ways to handle long unstressed syllables in English. One way is to find a short unstressed syllable that can be syncopated and stretched out, such as the "-ti-" in "Pitiful" in Figure 11.5.

FIGURE 11.5 Dvě vdovy (Two Widows), *I.vi: 121.*
Source: Herman and Apter (1984).

A second way is to find a stressed syllable that sounds natural in the syncopated position. In Figure 11.6, the "emp-" of "plate empty" has both word and position stress, word stress because it is the stressed syllable of "empty," and position stress because, as an adjective following a noun, the less usual position in English, it is given about the same stress as the noun rather than less. It is set on a long half-note. Since, in English, long burden generally goes with stress, "emp-" sounds natural despite the fact that it is in the same position as an unstressed Czech syllable.

FIGURE 11.6 Dvě vdovy (Two Widows), *II.v: 215.*
Source: Herman and Apter (1984).

11.2 Rhyme and closure

Most pre-twentieth-century works for the musical stage pair musical metrics with poetic metrics. Phrase closure for both is usually marked by rhyme. While rhymed originals should generally be translated into rhymed English, the spirit rather than the letter of the relationship between words and music should dictate the stanza form. The whole point of stanza form is to group and separate ideas.

11.2.1 Less rhyme than the original

It is the rhyme scheme demanded (or allowed) by the music, rather than the rhyme scheme of the original verse, that should dictate the rhyme scheme of a translation. The two rhyme schemes could be identical, say an *aabb* pattern, in which case translators should probably stick to couplets.

Another typical rhyme scheme for lyrical verse is *abab*. If the musical setting allows the *a* rhymes to be dropped, yielding a properly closing stanza rhymed *abcb* (also designated more generally *xbxb—x* indicating a non-rhyming line), there is no reason not to change the rhyme scheme in order to avoid a contorted translation.

Verdi's treatment of lyrics first discussed in Chapter 4 (Table 4.2, Verdi's *Il trovatore*, No. 11, mm. 155–76) provides a good illustration of music both echoing and altering the rhyme scheme of the original. The stanza rhymes *abab*, with feminine *a* rhymes stressed on the next-to-last syllable and masculine *b* rhymes stressed on the last syllable. There is also strong assonance: *"amarti"* in the first line and *"frenarmi"* and *"martir"* in the second line:

Era già figlio prima d'amarti;
   non può frenarmi il tuo martir!
Madre infelice, corro a salvarti,
   o teco almeno corro a morir!

Each of the lines has a caesura, or break, in the middle. Verdi's music splits each line at the caesura, sets the rhymes at the ends of musical phrases, and repeats the final line with variations, creating an eleven-line *musical* stanza rhymed *xaxbxaxbBXB*, where the capital letters indicate repeated lines or phrases:

Era già figlio
   prima d'amarti;
non può frenarmi
   il tuo martir!
Madre infelice,
   corro a salvarti,
o teco almeno
   corro a morir,
   o teco almen corro a morir,
o teco almen,
   o teco a morir!

The musical setting, like the original verse, places the rhymes at the ends of lines, but, by separating them, gives them less prominence. The *"amarti-frenarmi-martir"* assonance, due to the proximity of the words, is a sonic component of the verse as strong as the rhymes. The *a* rhymes never regain their prominence. The *b* rhymes do regain their prominence when the final *b* rhyme is repeated twice at the end, effectively increasing the number of *b* rhymes from two to four.

Our singable translation, like the original, includes four instances of the *b* rhyme ("-ide"), but eliminates the less prominent *a* rhyme. Since the musical phrasing adds more possible end-rhyme sites, compensatory sonic connections are provided by weak end-rhyme ("suffer-mother"), end-of-line repetition ("mother-mother," "you-you"), and assonance ("may," "stay" and "save"; "die" and "side"):

Though you may suffer,
I cannot stay here;
she is my mother,
   you are my bride.
Unhappy mother,

I swear to save you
or to die with you
   there at your side,
    to die with you, there at your side,
to die with you,
   to die at your side!
          (Herman and Apter, 2002)

11.2.2 *The same or more rhyme than the original*

Fashion may dictate against converting a rhyme scheme from *abab* to *xbxb* even if logic does not. During the Victorian and Edwardian eras, the unwritten rules for the translation of all poetic forms into English called for an exact imitation of the rhyme scheme (and of the original meter), whether or not required by the music and however convoluted the result (see Apter, 1984: 86–89). Chapter 3 included an example demonstrating how a slavish reproduction of rhyme can harm a translation. Nonetheless, twentieth-century opera translators such as Edward J. Dent (1876–1957) still attempted to reproduce rhyme exactly as in the original.

In a duet in Mozart's *Die Entführung aus dem Serail (The Abduction from the Seraglio)* (1782). The Englishwoman Blonde argues for women's freedom while the Turk Osmin demands that women be totally subservient to men. Here are some lyrics from the middle of the duet (No. 9, mm. 64–68), together with a literal translation:

BLONDE: bleibt, wenn schon die Freiheit verloren,
   noch stolz auf sie, lachet der Welt.
OSMIN: Wie ist man geplagt und geschoren,
   wenn solch eine Zucht man erhält!

(**BLONDE:** she remains, even if freedom is lost,
   still proud of herself, laughing at the world.
OSMIN: How one is plagued and bothered
   when encountering such a race!)

As in the previous example, the rhyme pattern is *abab*, with *a* feminine and *b* masculine. However, in this case, the *a* rhymes cannot be ignored. Mozart has the two characters sing the two *a*-rhyme words, "*verloren*" and "*geschoren*," simultaneously, thereby requiring some sort of sonic connection between them. Dent's translation, published in 1952 but probably written earlier, uses the rhyming words "languish" and "anguish":

BLONDE: Yes, even if captive we languish,
   hold up our heads, laugh at our fate!

OSMIN: They must live in torment and anguish
if marriage is that sort of state.
(Dent, 1952: 13–14)

Unfortunately, having found his rhymes, Dent obviously believed that no further effort was necessary. His inversion of English word order and elimination of a necessary pronoun in Blonde's lines render them virtually incomprehensible.

Our own translation uses assonance/off-rhyme for the *a* rhymes ("prison-treason") and an identity for the *b* rhymes ("slave-slave"):

BLONDE: and even confined by a prison,
her head is high. She is no slave.
OSMIN: To let women rule you is treason:
a man must be master and woman his slave.
(Herman and Apter, 1979a)

Occasionally, even in rhyme-poor English, it is possible to create a translation with the same or even more true rhymes than the original. Table 11.1 gives an example from the medieval lyrics of *Carmina Burana*, some of which, including the lyric shown, were set to music by Carl Orff. The English verse translation is more highly rhymed than the Latin original: *ababcdcd* rather than *ababxdxd*.

TABLE 11.1 *Carmina Burana, "Fortuna rota volvitur."*

Original Latin lyrics	Literal English translation
Fortune rota volvitur: descendo minoratus; alter in altum tollitur; nimis exaltatus rex sedet in vertice— caveat ruinam! nam sub axe legimus Hecubam reginam. (Hilka et al., 1930–71, I.1: 16.3; Orff, 1936, 2.3)	The wheel of Fortune turns: one thrust down, the other borne up high, all too exalted; the king sits at the top— let him beware ruin! for beneath the wheel we read: Queen Hecuba [deposed mythological Queen of Troy].

Verse Translation by Herman and Apter
The wheel of Fortune whirls in space: rank riffraff reach the summit, distinguished leaders fall from grace as their fortunes plummet. King, beware, lest your gold crown tarnish and prove hollow. Fortune's wheel can bring kings down; when it turns, you'll follow. (Herman and Apter, 1977/2013)

11.2.3 Alternatives to true rhyme

Translators into a rhyme-poor language should be adept at using rhyme's cousins to create recognizable stanza forms, that is, to signal the close of a line or stanza. These partial rhymes include off-rhyme ("line-time"), weak rhyme ("major-squalor"), half rhyme ("kitty-pitted"), and consonant rhyme ("slat-slit"), any of which can be used alone or in combination with other devices such as assonance ("get ready") and alliteration ("Peter Piper picked a peck of pickled peppers"). In particular, true feminine rhyme, such as "hidden-bidden" and "litany-Brittany," tends to be not only hard to find in English but also to produce a not-always-welcome comic effect à la Gilbert and Sullivan.

Here is a translation of a selection from Verdi's *Un giorno di regno* (1840) with extensive use of partial rhyme. The original Italian verse rhymes *xaax*, with the *a*-rhymes feminine:

> **CHEVALIER:** Ah, my friends, I am transmuted
> from the man you knew in Paris,
> from the madcap of the barracks,
> from a soldier to a statesman, a philosopher and king.
>   (*Un giorno*, No. 4, mm. 2–10; Herman and Apter, 1983a)

"Paris" and "barracks" are half rhymes, in the positions of the true rhymes of the original. However, the first three lines are also tied together by assonance on "am", "transmuted," "man," "Paris," "madcap," and "barracks." The longer fourth line, devoid of half rhyme or assonance, signals by its difference the close of the stanza and the musical section.

11.2.4 Radically changing the original rhyme scheme

If the music allows it, a rhyme scheme can undergo a change more radical than *abab* to *xbxb*. Consider the Vaudeville Finale of *The Abduction from the Seraglio*, which was discussed from a different viewpoint in Table 2.1 of Chapter 2. Our English version has a rhyme scheme *(a₁a₂bccb)* radically different from that of the German source *(abbacc)*. The subscripts on a_1a_2 indicate a half-rhyme, with a_1 feminine ("praises") and a_2 masculine ("-mazed"). The original German and the English version are reproduced here:

> Nie werd' ich deine Huld verkennen,
> mein Dank bleibt ewig dir geweiht;

an jedem Ort, zu jeder Zeit
werd' ich dich groß und edel nennen.
Wer so viel Huld vergessen kann,
den seh' man mit Verachtung an.

(Mozart/Stephanie, Die Entführung aus
dem Seraglio, No. 21a, mm. 1–14)

I'll pay you tribute with my praises,
and all the world will be amazed
that you have nobly set us free.
Now I will be forever in your debt.
It is ignoble to forget
an act of magnanimity.

(Herman and Apter, 1979a)

Not only has the rhyme scheme been changed, but the above-mentioned masculine–feminine half-rhyme has been created ("praises-amazed"), and a German feminine rhyme word ("nennen") has been changed to an English masculine one ("debt"). An analysis of Mozart's music shows why such changes are allowable (see Figure 11.7 on the next page).

Every line of the German text is end-rhymed and receives its own musical phrase, the end of which is signaled by a rest, a long note, or both. Our English translation follows this scheme, although it changes the rhyme scheme. The first change couples the first two lines together via the a_1a_2 half-rhymes. This is allowed by the music because the first two lines are set off from the rest of the stanza by the relatively long rest after "geweiht" (m. 5). The third and fourth lines (second half of m. 5 through first half of m. 10) are run together musically, the end of the third line being signaled only by the long note on "Zeit" (m. 7). The music, therefore, does not require the lines to end-rhyme to each other. We do provide some sonic matching by rhyming the end of line 3 ("free" in m. 7) to an internal "be" in the fourth line (downbeat of m. 8). The end-rhyme match for "free" is delayed until the end of the final line of the stanza ("magnanimity"). This leaves the fourth and fifth lines to be end-rhymed. However, the German fourth line ends in the two-syllable feminine "nennen," while the fifth line ends in the one-syllable masculine "kann." We could have created another masculine–feminine half-rhyme as we did for the first two lines. Instead, we took advantage of the fact that "nen-," the first syllable of "nennen," is held for four beats, the longest held syllable in the entire stanza. Because of its length and the fact that it is spread over two musical notes (m. 9), it is easily replaced by two English syllables ("in your"), allowing a masculine rhyme at the end

Belmonte

FIGURE 11.7 Die Entführung aus dem Serail, *No. 21a,*
mm. 1–14.

Source: Herman and Apter (1979a).

of the fourth line ("debt" in m. 10) to match the masculine end-rhyme of
the fifth line ("-get" in m. 12) without changing the music.

Although Mozart's music allows the radical change in the rhyme scheme,
English translations adhering to the original rhyme scheme can of course
also be created. As mentioned in Chapter 2, we provide performance
groups with one such translation as an alternative to the translation
discussed here.

11.2.5 Eliminating rhyme

It is possible for a translation to dispense with rhyme altogether if care is taken that the sound patterns interweave closely enough that internal sonic connections override the lack of rhyme at musical phrase endings. Table 11.2 shows a highly rhymed original from Verdi's *La traviata* (1853) *(aabcbc)* together with unrhymed singable translations by Joseph Machlis and us. The difference in syllable-count between the original and the two singable translations is due to differences in the syllabic underlay; the musical notes for all three versions are exactly the same.

TABLE 11.2 *La traviata*, No. 10, mm. 78–101

Original Italian lyrics	Literal English translation

Parigi, o cara, noi lasceremo,
la vita uniti trascorreremo,
  de' corsi affanni compenso avrai,
 	
la tua salute rifiorirà.
  Sospiro e luce tu mi sarai,
tutto il futuro ne arriderà.
	We will leave Paris, oh beloved,
	to spend our life together,
	you will be compensated for your
	  past sufferings,
	your health will again bloom.
	Breath and light you will be to me,
	all the future will smile on us.

Singable translation by Joseph Machlis (1962: 350–51)	**Singable translation by Herman and Apter (1981)**

Far away from Paris, we'll find
  contentment,
always together, ever devoted.
 	
Turmoil and sorrow we'll leave behind
  us.
Safe in my keeping, you'll bloom
  again.
You'll be my treasure, my guardian
  angel.
Golden our future, radiant our life!
	In a cottage, in the country, we will
	  live together,
	caring for each other, misery
	  forgotten.
	We will leave the crowded city for
	  a quiet garden;
	we will be contented in a world of
	  love.
	I shall be your breath and you shall
	  be my sunlight,
	blooming like a flower into health
	  again.

Machlis's version includes weak internal rhymes on "together," "treasure," and "future," and assonance on the short *e*'s of "contentment," "together," "ever," "again," and "treasure." The long *i*'s of "behind" and "life" are probably too far apart for the ear to hear them as assonance.

Our own translation is sonically tied together by the alliterating hard *c*-sounds of "cottage," "country," "caring," "crowded," "quiet," and "contented," the hard *g*-sounds of "together," "forgotten," and "garden," and the irregularly placed rhyme alternatives ("cottage-forgotten," "together-other," "forgotten-garden," "crowded-flower"). The sonic connections are re-inforced because two of the rhyme alternatives function as end-rhymes. The words of one set, "forgotten-garden," actually come at the ends of verbal and musical phrases. The words of another, "together-other," though not at the ends of verbal phrases, are nonetheless at the ends of musical phrases, signaled by Verdi's setting of the penultimate syllables on relatively long quarter notes (see Figure 11.8).

FIGURE 11.8 La traviata, *No. 10, mm. 78–89.*
Source: Herman and Apter (1981).

11.2.6 Alliteration

Alliteration, called *Stabreim* in German and famously used by Richard Wagner throughout his *Ring* cycle (1876), is the repeated use of a particular consonant or consonant cluster, usually as the initial sounds of stressed syllables in close proximity. Also, all initial vowels are considered to alliterate. As mentioned, the preceding example included alliteration on hard *c*'s and hard *g*'s.

When sonic closure is dependent on alliteration rather than rhyme, it is also more dependent on the music. Figure 11.9 shows a passage from *Das Rheingold* (1869), including Wagner's lyrics and our singable translation.

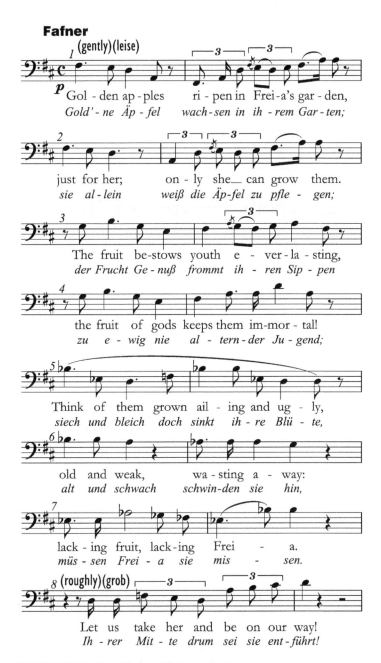

FIGURE 11.9 Das Rheingold, *Scene 2: 74.*
Source: Herman and Apter (1983b).

Each of the eight lines of verse in Figure 11.9 is allotted two bars of music, and each line is separated from the others by musical rests. In both languages, lines are bound by alliteration on *g* and *fr*. English also has *w* and German also has *v* (spelled *w*), *bl*, *z* (spelled *s*), *schw*, and *m*. Both German and English include words with initial vowels. Line 8 closes the stanza for three reasons. First, it and line 6 are alliteratively isolated, lacking the *g*, *fr*, and *bl* sounds of the other lines. Second, lines 8 and 6 are the only two which end on stressed syllables. Third, and most tellingly, only line 8 ends on a downbeat. Both aural systems, the verbal and the musical, combine to achieve sonic closure.

11.2.7 Conflicting verbal and musical closures

When verbal and musical structures conflict, the effect is much stronger than that caused by enjambment in spoken verse. In a rejected draft, we tried to express Alfredo's confusion in a translation of some lines from Verdi's *La traviata* (1853). Librettist Piave's Italian stanza (No. 7, mm. 698–700) consists of three ten-syllable lines plus a nine-syllable line, all four lines broken by a caesura after the fifth syllable (indicated below by the symbol ‖) and rhymed as follows:

```
_____ ‖ _____a
_____ ‖ _____a
_____ ‖ _____b
_____b ‖ _____c
```

Verdi followed this pattern by placing the second *a*-rhyme and the *c*-rhyme on downbeats, thereby dividing the stanza into two units of two lines each. Instead, we divided the stanza into a fifteen-syllable line, a nine-syllable line, and a fourteen-syllable line:

```
_____a ‖ _____a ‖ _____b
_____c ‖ _____c
_____c ‖ _____d ‖ _____e
```

The result is shown in Figure 11.10. Note that our *a*-rhymes *(confusion-passion)* and *c*-rhymes *(vengeance-senses-frenzy)* are *not* true rhymes. The new setting makes Alfredo sound confused because the verbal phrase endings conflict with the musical line; they run past musical breaks and end in the middle of musical phrases. We found the translation interesting, but eventually decided that the setting was too far from Verdi's nineteenth-century style. Therefore, we more closely imitated the match of phrase and rhyme pattern of the original in our final English version.

FIGURE 11.10 La traviata, *No. 7, mm. 698–700.*
Source: Herman and Apter (1981).

11.2.8 Rhyme as a creator of aural shape

Giuseppe Verdi loved to compose ensembles in which several characters sing at the same time. Usually, he creates musical consonances at the ends of phrases, when some or all of the characters sing rhyming sounds simultaneously. Rhyme joins with the music to create an aural shape despite the fact that the simultaneous singing of disparate texts renders most words incomprehensible. Translators, like the composer, must rely on the music, acting, and previous plot developments to communicate what is going on. Translators should also follow the composer in lining up the rhymes and assonances, so that the singers can blend their voices more easily and the audience can discern the aural shape.

In the following example from our translation of a septet in Verdi's *Un giorno di regno* (1840) (No. 24, mm. 1–83), the Chevalier, pretending to be a king, has given orders preventing the marriage of his estranged love, the Marquise, to the Count. The lines below show the lyrics for the various characters. These lyrics are repeated in whole or in part in a series of intricate verbal meshings, with different sets of characters singing simultaneously at various times, and landing on rhyme words simultaneously or not. The permutations take up almost twenty-one pages of the piano-vocal score. Most of the time, the audience hears at least two sets of different words at once. However incomprehensible, the words do help the singers to act and the director to block. For example, Édouard and Juliette may be standing by the Marquise when their lines reflect hers, and cross to talk to the Count when their lines reflect his:

> **CHEVALIER:** I have put her on the defensive.
> She is trembling with consternation.
> But she will thaw.
> Yes, her anger soon will thaw.

> **MARQUISE:** I am trembling, apprehensive.
> Shall I answer his provocation?
> His inventiveness inspires me with awe.
> This is not what I foresaw.

> **JULIETTE and ÉDOUARD:**
> She is trembling, apprehensive,
> and the Count would voice his indignation.
> It is sticking in his craw,
> but a monarch's word is law.

> **COUNT:** My displeasure is quite extensive.
> I would voice my indignation.
> It is sticking in my craw,
> but a monarch's word is law.

> **BARON and TREASURER:**
> She is trembling, apprehensive,
> But a monarch's
> word is law.
> His word is law.

11.3 Repetition

Repetition, both musical and verbal, is an important element of almost all musical genres, serving various functions. Many composers end an aria with repeats of the aria's final part, just as many singers of popular music end a song with repeats of the song's final part. Wagner's repeated leitmotifs are important structural components of his fifteen-and-a-half-hour *Ring* (1876).

Usually, verbal repetition involves phrases, but it can sometimes involve a single word repeated from stanza to stanza. While repetition in the original should usually be indicated in some way in a translation, exactly matching the repetition of the original might either be impossible or preclude re-creating other aspects of the source.

11.3.1 General concepts versus concrete detail

Some languages, such as English, are more comfortable with concrete detail, while others, such as Italian and French, are more receptive to general concepts. Therefore, an Italian or French phrase may be repeated many times in a piece of music and not sound over-used to an Italian or French speaker; matching repetitions in an English translation may bore a native English speaker even if every word fits the music. In such cases, translators into English have two choices: (1) finding another phrase, perhaps one deviating far from literality, which does bear repetition in English; or (2) substituting English specificity for Italian or French generality by replacing the many repeats of a small number of Italian or French words with fewer repeats of a greater number of English words. The latter, in the words of Donald Pippin previously quoted in Chapter 2, gives translators a

> golden opportunity to expand, to probe, to clarify, to bring into focus something that in the original is often vague, generalized, abstract. (Pippin, 1998)

We took advantage of such a "golden opportunity" in our translation of a duet from Verdi's *Un giorno di regno* (1840). In this duet, the beginning of which is shown in Table 11.3 on the next page, Baron de Kelbar is challenging Treasurer Montroc to a duel.

11.3.2 Repeating rather than padding

If it is impossible or undesirable to expand meaning as in Table 11.3, translators can be faced with extra notes on which they have to put words. A little bit of padding, such as with added "then's" and "now's," may be acceptable. However, the extra notes can sometimes be usefully filled with a repetition. Figure 3.3 in Chapter 3 shows Amanda Holden's translation of a line from Donizetti's *Maria Stuarda* (1835), which repeats the first three words when the source does not: "Oh have mercy, oh have mercy! Oh be moved to grant her grace!" (Holden, 1998).

TABLE 11.3 *Un giorno di regno*, No. 19, mm. 1–32

Original Italian lyrics	Literal English translation
Tutte l'armi si può prendere	If he [Montroc] could get hold of all the weapons
de' due mondi e vecchio e nuovo,	of both the old world and the new,
me lo bevo come un ovo,	I would suck him like an egg,
me lo voglio digerir,	I would digest him,
me lo bevo come un ovo,	I would suck him like an egg,
me lo voglio digerir,	I would digest him,
me lo bevo come un ovo,	I would suck him like an egg,
come un ovo, come un ovo,	like an egg, like an egg,
me lo voglio, me lo voglio,	I would, I would
me lo voglio digerir,	I would digest him,
me lo bevo come un ovo,	I would suck him like an egg,
come un ovo, come un ovo,	like an egg, like an egg,
me lo voglio, me lo voglio,	I would, I would,
me lo voglio digerir,	I would digest him,
sì me lo voglio, me lo voglio digerir,	yes, I would, I would digest him,
sì me lo voglio digerir.	yes, I would digest him.

Singable English translation

I will not dispatch you publicly.
An affair of honor should be private.
Therefore, Montroc, I challenge you
  to meet me in a duel
at a peaceful spot where the world will not
  note the passing of a fool.
You will thrust and I will parry;
then your counter will miscarry
and a very ordinary
  cut will knock your blade askew.
You will thrust and I will parry;
then your counter will miscarry
and a very ordinary
  cut will knock your blade askew.
  And in a twinkling it is curtains for you
  as with a flourish I run you through.
(Herman and Apter, 1983a)

11.3.3 Indirect indication of repetition

It is sometimes possible for a translation to indirectly indicate repetition when exact repetition is impossible or undesirable. For example, Alfredo's famous toast (No. 2, mm. 182 et seq.) in Verdi's *La traviata* (1853) begins with the repeated word "*libiamo*" ("let us drink"). The three syllables of "let us drink," with the stress on the third syllable, cannot substitute for the three syllables of "*li-bia-mo*," with the stress on the second syllable. Nor could we find another repeatable three-syllable English word or phrase with the correct meaning, stress, burden, and consonantal liquidity. Therefore, we suggest the repetition indirectly, repeating only the first English word "to" and alliterating on the initial "l" of the second word (see Figure 11.11). Additional repetitions of the word "to" and further alliterations on "l" re-inforce the idea of repetition in the minds of the audience.

FIGURE 11.11 La traviata, *No. 2, mm. 204–14.*
Source: Herman and Apter (1981).

11.3.4 Altering the meaning of a repeated phrase

The meaning of some phrases must be altered before they can be repeated in a translation. In Mozart's *Die Entführung aus dem Serail* (*The Abduction from the Seraglio*) (1782), Osmin gloats over what will happen to the protagonists (No. 19). He repeats the single word "*schnüren*" and the phrase "*schnüren zu*," which means "strangle." But "strangle" and "strangle you" are virtually impossible to sing repeatedly at the speed required. "Hang you" has no hard sounds to match the "ts" sound of the German "z" in "*zu*," and therefore loses much of the ferocity. Other phrases that preserve the literal meaning, such as "by the neck"—"by the, by the, by the neck!"—also do not work. To preserve the genuine (albeit comic) ferocity in English, we changed the method of execution and, not coincidentally, substituted English rhyme for some of the German repetition (see Figure 11.12).

FIGURE 11.12 Die Entführung aus dem Serail, No. 19, mm. 65–88. *Source:* Herman and Apter (1979a).

11.3.5 Repetition as a contributor to meaning

The repetition of a phrase can influence or even change its meaning. In Gounod's *Le médecin malgré lui* (*The Doctor In Spite Of Himself*) (1858), Sganarelle offers to help Jacqueline take vengeance on her husband by cuckolding him. In duet No. 12, both repeatedly sing the words *"pas assez"* ("not enough"). As the phrase is repeated by the two in close harmony, the brisk pace of the music retards and decrescendos, a change strongly suggesting that some kind of love-making is occurring. The implications of the repeated phrase shift from "We can't do enough to get even with my/your husband" to "Not enough caresses, caress me some more." In order to follow Gounod's shift in meaning, translators must find a target phrase that functions like "*pas assez*" when repeated. The literal English translation, "not enough," does not work despite having the correct number of syllables, stress pattern, and burdens, because the final unvoiced "f" sound of "enough" is too abrupt to fade away on a retard and decrescendo. A different phrase, "very well," ends in a liquid consonant that works musically. And, though it seems to have a different meaning, "very well" in fact preserves the meaning of the duet as a whole. In conjunction with the music, repetition shifts the implications from "I know very well how to get even with my/your husband" to "Very well, I'll have an affair with you":

> 'Tis their husbands who be wrong
>> when women long to rebel,
> 'tis their husbands who be wrong
>> when women long to rebel.
> Do they slight us, we must fight 'em:
>> truth will out and time will tell,
>> time will tell, time will tell
> that a woman has her weapons
>> and a woman wields 'em well,
>> very well.
> Very well, very well, very well . . .
>> (Herman and Apter, 1979b: 191–93)

11.3.6 Distorted repeats

One reason for not repeating in a translation exactly as in the original is that the music for the repeated verbal phrases, while fitting the repeated original words, distorts the repeated translated words. However, if the composer distorts the original repeated phrases to achieve some effect, so may the translators.

In the quintet (No. 4) of *L'occasione fa il ladro* (*A Thief by Chance*) (1812), composer Gioacchino Rossini (1792–1868) distorts words and sets the characters' rhythms against each other during the repeats to emphasize the confusion of the situation. The opening measures of the section in question are shown in Figure 11.13. In these measures, all five characters sing the words in the same rhythm shown for Berenice. In the repeat shown in Figure 11.14, the musical rhythm distorts both the original Italian and our English. (The two lowest voices [not shown] sing in the same rhythm as Alberto.)

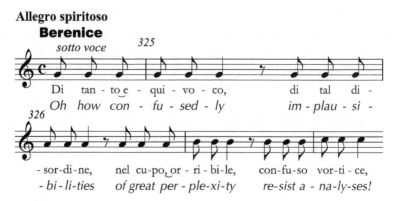

FIGURE 11.13 L'occasione fa il ladro, No. 4, mm. 324–28.
Source: Herman and Apter (2007).

FIGURE 11.14 L'occasione fa il ladro, No. 4, mm. 336–39.
Source: Herman and Apter (2007).

11.4 Dynamics and crests

Musical dynamics or the crest of a phrase will often dictate where certain meanings must fall.

Figure 11.15 gives an example involving musical dynamics, showing translations by Morton Siegel and Waldo Lyman (1956) (a) and us (b) of a line from Mozart's *Die Entführung aus dem Serail* (*The Abduction from the Seraglio*) (1782). In German, the condemnatory *fortes* are motivated by the meaning of *"häßlich"* ("hateful") and *"Rache"* ("revenge"). The dynamics make no sense on "man" and "neighbor," though a musical director could ask the performers to change the dynamics to accommodate Siegel and Lyman's words. Our translation, "Revenge is hideous and hateful," allows Mozart's dynamic markings to maintain their function.

FIGURE 11.15 Die Entführung aus dem Serail, *No. 21, mm. 95–97.*
Source: (a) Siegel and Lyman (1956: 175); (b) Herman and Apter (1979a).

An example involving musical and verbal crests is shown in Figure 11.16, which shows a line from Weber's *Der Freischütz* (1821). The literal meaning of the German is "Reddish gray, scarred branches stretch out to me their giant fist." In this context, the word *"graue"* ("gray") resonates with *"Grauen"* ("horror"). The words follow the music, with a false crest at the *forte* on *"mir."* The true crest arrives at the *double forte* on *"Riesenfaust."* If the translation does not place a word capable of being mistaken for a phrase ending on the *forte*, a subtle musico-verbal formal conjunction is lost. The words of the English phrase apparently end at the *forte* with the word "night," but then continue on to the *double forte* and the word "clutch." In order to achieve the false and true crests, we had to abandon the image of the giant fist.

11.5 When the composer ignores the verbal form

Music is more strongly perceived than words, and musical form is more strongly felt than verbal form. When the two forms are different, translators may find it convenient to follow the musical form. However, if the clash of musical and verbal form is a significant feature of the work, translators should preserve it.

FIGURE 11.16 Der Freischütz, No. 10, mm. 178–82.
Source: Herman and Apter (1986).

In *La bohème* (1896), Puccini often does not place rhymes at the ends of musical phrases, although the effect is not as strong as that of the enjambment in the possible translation of *La traviata* discussed above. Table 11.4 shows some lines from Act I, when the friends are burning one of Rodolfo's plays in a vain attempt to warm themselves. The lines are set up to show the poetic form, which rhymes *abacbddc*, with *a*, *b*, and *d* feminine, and *c* masculine.

TABLE 11.4 *La bohème*, Act I, mm. 300–315.

Original Italian lyrics	Literal English translation
COLLINE:	**COLLINE:**
Scoppieta un foglio.	A page is crackling.
MARCELLO:	**MARCELLO:**
Là c'eran baci!	There are kisses there!
RODOLFO:	**RODOLFO:**
Tre atti or voglio	Now I want three acts
d'un colpo udir.	to hear at one stroke.
COLLINE:	**COLLINE:**
Tal degli audaci	Thus the bold
l'idea s'integra.	ideas are united.
ALL THREE:	**ALL THREE:**
Bello in allegra	Beautifully in happy
vampa svanir.	blaze to vanish.

As depicted in the schematic below, only the masculine *c*-rhyme words ("*udir*" and "*svanir*") both occur at the ends of musical phrases. The second of each of the feminine *a*, *b*, and *d*-rhyme words ("*voglio,*" "*audaci,*" and "*allegra*") occurs in the middle of a musical phrase, therefore with diminished sonic prominence. Further weakening even the prominence of the *c* rhymes are the orchestral interludes (indicated by dashed lines) that interrupt the vocal exchange:

COLLINE:
Scoppieta un foglio.
MARCELLO:
Là c'eran baci!
– – – – – 1-measure interlude
RODOLFO:
Tre atti or voglio d'un colpo udir.
– – – – – 6-measure interlude
COLLINE:
Tal degli audaci l'idea s'integra.
ALL THREE:
Bello in allegra vampa svanir.

Our performable translation retains only the *c* rhymes ("blow-go"):

COLLINE:
The pages crackle.
MARCELLO:
Those were the kisses!
– – – – – 1-measure interlude
RODOLFO:
And now three acts at a single blow.
– – – – – 6-measure interlude
COLLINE:
Bold integration, a new conception.
ALL THREE:
Blazing with glory, that's how to go!
(Herman and Apter, in press)

The rhymes Puccini buries in the middle of lines and interrupts with orchestral interludes are not completely lost. They still provide some sonic glue, however subliminal, which helps hold the passage together. We too provide some glue with "crackle-acts," "integration-conception," and "blow-bold."

Sometimes music completely transforms the original verse. A good example is *"Задремали волны"* (*"Zadryemalyi volnï"*), a poem by K. R., the pen name of Grand Duke Konstantin K. Romanoff (1858–1915). It was set to music by Sergei Rachmaninoff (1873–1943) as the fourth of his *Шесть хоров для женского хора с фортепьяно* (*Six Choral Songs for Treble Voices and Piano*) (1895).

Figure 11.17 shows the poem, together with an approximate English pronunciation. The first four-line stanza describes moonlight on quiet waves; the second four-line stanza expresses a simile in which the sea is flickeringly ablaze just as joy brightly illuminates grief.

	Trochee 1	Trochee 2	Trochee 3 fem. rhyme / masc. rhyme			Trochee 1	Trochee 2	Trochee 3 fem. rhyme / masc. rhyme	
1	За-дре-	-ма-ли	вол-ны,	*a*	1	Zá-drye-	-má-lyi	vól-nï,	*a*
2	я-сен	не-ба	**свод,**	*b*	2	yá-syen	nyé-ba	**svód,**	*b*
3	све-тит	ме-сяц	пол-ный	*a*	3	svyé-tyit	myé-syats	pól-nïi	*a*
4	над ла-	-зурь-ю	**вод.**	*b*	4	nád la-	-zúr'-yu	**vód.**	*b*
5	Се-ре-	-брит-ся	мо-ре,	*c*	5	Syé-rye-	-bryít-sa	mó-rye,	*c*
6	тре-пет-	-но го-	**-рит,**	*d*	6	tryé-pyet-	-nó go-	**-ryít,**	*d*
7	так и	ра-дость	го-ре	*c*	7	ták i	rá-dost'	gó-rye	*c*
8	яр-ко	о-за-	**-рит.**	*d*	8	yár-ko	ó-za-	**-ryít.**	*d*

FIGURE 11.17 *"Задремали волны"* (*"Now the waves are drowsing"*), *the poem.*

In Figure 11.17, the poetic feet are separated and the stresses and rhymes indicated. Each line ends in a rhyme, the scheme being *abab cdcd* with *a* and *c* feminine and *b* and *d* masculine. The *d* rhyme is actually an identity: *"-ryít."* All eight lines are in trochaic trimeter, that is, each line has three poetic feet and each foot is a two-syllable trochee stressed / × (strong weak), with two deviations: four-syllable words, such as the first word of the poem, receive a secondary weaker stress on one of their stressed syllables; and, in order to make rhymes *b* and *d* masculine, the lines ending in the *b* and *d* rhymes drop the final unstressed syllable of the third trochee. There is another point of sonic interest: between lines 6 and 7, there is a similarity in the sounds of the masculine and feminine end-rhyme words *"go-ryít"* and *"gó-rye,"* meaning "afire" and "grief," respectively.

The structure of the poem as set by Rachmaninoff is very different. The composer repeats words, breaks up the lines, and stretches syllables over multiple notes, thereby changing the meter and eliminating one end-rhyme. He also eliminates a word from line 6 in one of the two singing parts (Sop = Soprano and Alt = Alto) and sometimes sets unexpected syllables on downbeats. In our opinion, Rachmaninoff makes the poem far more interesting than it originally was.

Rachmaninoff's setting is shown in Table 11.5. Only the transliterated pronunciation is given to save space. Syllables falling on musical downbeats are capitalized. Syllables spread over more than one note are indicated by repeating the vowel, as in "*-RYI-it*" in line 8b. Italics indicate syllables which, by being spread, cause a masculine rhyme to be *feminized* (lines 6.(Alt) and 8b). An end-rhyme word made into an internal rhyme (line 7b/8a) is underlined.

TABLE 11.5 Rachmaninoff's setting of "*Zadryemalyi volnï*"

	Za-drye-má-lyi vólnï	Rhymes	Spread Syllables
1.	Za-drye- -MA-lyi vol-nï,	*a*, feminine	
2.	ya-syen NYE-ba svod,	*b*, masculine	
3a.	svye-tyit MYE-syats,		
3b.	mye-syats POL-nïi	*a*, feminine	
4.	nad la- -ZUR'-yu vod.	*b*, masculine	
5.	Sye-rye- -BRYIT-sa mo-rye,	*c*, feminine	
6. (Sop)	trye-e-E-pyet-no go-ryit,	*d*, masculine	trye-e-E-
6. (Alt)	go-o- *-RYI-i-it,*	*d*, *feminized*	go-o- *-RYI-i-it*
7a.	tak i RA-dost'		
7b/8a.	<u>go-rye</u> YAR-ko	*c*, feminine (<u>go-rye</u>), made <u>internal</u>	
8b.	o-za- *-RYI-it,*	*d*, *feminized*	*-RYI-it*
8c.	YAR-ko o-za-RYIT.	*d*, masculine	

In the first stanza, Rachmaninoff interrupts what had been trochaic trimeter by changing line 3 to two half-lines of trochaic dimeter (two poetic feet per half-line), 3a and 3b, both with feminine endings. He does this by repeating the word "*myé-syats*" (moon).

In the second stanza, he goes further in interrupting the trochaic trimeter:

(1) His first new line, called 7a in the above diagram, consists of the first two words of the original line 7.

(2) His second new line 7b/8a consists of the last word of the original line 7 and the first word of the original line 8. The last word of the original line 7, *"gó-rye,"* is in fact an end-rhyme word. By moving it, Rachmaninoff loses a *c* end-rhyme and creates an internal rhyme.

(3) His third new line 8b consists of the last word of the original line 8.

(4) The three new lines, 7a, 7b/8a, and 8b, containing four syllables, four syllables, and three syllables, respectively, would naturally become three dimeter lines, with endings that are feminine, feminine, and masculine. But Rachmaninoff wants all three to be feminine, and therefore adds an extra musical "syllable" in order to feminize line 8b. That is, he spreads the single Russian syllable *"-RYIT,"* in line 8b, over two notes, feminizing it to *"-RYI-it."*

(5) For musical closure, Rachmaninoff then repeats the original line 8 (new line 8c), in this case preserving the masculine ending of the final rhyme (actually, as mentioned above, the identity *"-RYIT"*).

The composer also creates a difference between the soprano and alto parts in line 6, eliminating the first word from the alto part. He then changes the meter by spreading the syllables of both the soprano and alto parts over several notes.

Rachmaninoff additionally changes the meter of the original poem by setting unexpected syllables on the downbeats of musical measures. In words set to music, the main stresses fall on syllables that are set on downbeats. Normally, one would expect such syllables to be the stressed syllables of rhyme words, such as the *"vól-"* of *"vól-ni"* in line 1. But it is not *"vól-ni"* that is stressed in line 1. Instead, it is the third syllable, *"-MÁ-"* of the first word, *"za-drye-MÁ-lyi."* The tension between the expected and actual stresses creates an unsettling effect that reinforces the idea of waves rocking erratically.

Rachmaninoff's rhythmic subtlety goes beyond changing the meter of the original poem. The song is written in three-quarter time, and the piano introduction further suggests the quiet rocking of waves by a triplet figure with every third note tied to the first note of the next triplet (see Figure 11.18).

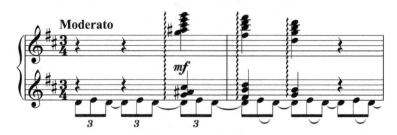

FIGURE 11.18 *Triplets suggest rocking waves.*

However, when the voices first enter at the end of the sixth measure of the song, they are not in triplets, but in duple time, that is, eighth and quarter notes (see Figure 11.19). The tension between the two rhythms intensifies the sense of waves, perhaps slapping the bottom of a boat that moves in a counter-rhythm. The tension between the rhythms of the voices and the piano continues throughout the song.

FIGURE 11.19 *Voices in duple time.*
Source: Herman and Apter (2009).

Where does all this leave translators?

Those who believe in strict verbal lockstep would say that the translation should include an exact matching of the trimeter and end-rhyme scheme of the original poem, yet also work when lines are repeated and the verbal form distorted as required by Rachmaninoff's music. In practice, such a translation is impossible.

Rather, a translation should strive to carefully follow the musical form and be informed by sensitivity to the interaction of the music with the sound and sense of the words. Our performable translation of the song, together with a literal translation of the Russian words, is shown in Table 11.6. In the performable translation, syllables falling on musical downbeats are capitalized. We added extra syllables, marked off by underlines, to fill up the notes on which Rachmaninoff spread syllables; unlike in Rachmaninoff's Russian setting, in our English translation there is always only one syllable per musical note.

TABLE 11.6 "Now the Waves Are Drowsing."

Literal English translation	Singable English translation
1. Have-dozed-off waves,	1. Now the WAVES are drows-ing
2. clear firmament,	2. in the QUI-et night,
3a. shines moon,	3a. a-zure WA-ters
3b. moon full	3b. glim-mer BRIGHT-ly
4. on azure water.	4. in the FULL moon LIGHT.
5. Becomes silvery the sea,	5. Sil-ver MOON-beams fall-ing
6.(Sop) flickeringly afire.	6.(SOP) set the WAVES a-blaze be-neath.
6.(Alt) afire,	6.(ALT) waves a-BLAZE be-neath.
7a. just as gladness	7a. Like a MOON-beam
7b/8a. grief brightly	7b/8a. driv-ing DARK-ness
8b. illuminates,	8b. from the O-cean,
8c. brightly illuminates.	8c. JOY makes light of GRIEF.

(Herman and Apter, 2009)

Another change between the English translation and the original Russian is that the feminine end-rhymes are dropped, which makes the end-rhymes *xaxa xbxb*, where *a* is a true masculine rhyme ("night" and "light" ending lines 2 and 4) and *b* is a masculine assonance ("beneath" and "grief" ending lines 6 and 8c). To these are added additional rhymes, off-rhymes, and assonances, mostly internal: "brightly" in line 3b, "like" in line 7a, "driving" in line 7b/8a, and another "light" in line 8c; also the weak rhymes "azure," "glimmer," and "silver" in lines 3a, 3b, and 5, and the assonance "waves" and "ablaze" in line 6.

The only lost thought is that of the "firmament" in the original poem's second line. "Flickeringly" in line 6 is absent from the translated words, but the rhythm of the music strongly creates that idea without the presence of the actual word (see Figure 11.20).

Also lost is the sound play on *"go-ryít"* ("afire") (original line 6) and *"gó-rye"* ("grief") (original line 7), partially replaced with alliteration in line 7b/8a ("driving darkness").

Finally, instead of repeating the idea of "brightly illuminates" at the end, some suspense is created by keeping the first part of the simile going longer,

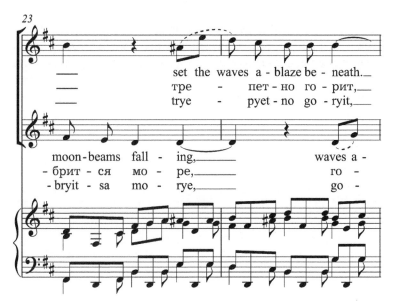

FIGURE 11.20 *Flickering rhythm.*
Source: Herman and Apter (2009).

all the way through the last of Rachmaninoff's newly created line 8b. The conclusion of the simile, "joy makes light of grief" arrives only on the last musical phrase (line 8c). That is, the idea is emphasized by saving it for last, rather than by repeating it as Rachmaninoff did (see Figure 11.21).

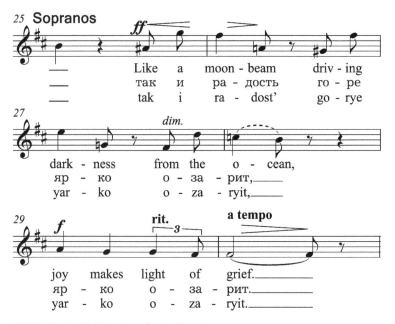

FIGURE 11.21 *Keeping the simile going.*
Source: Herman and Apter (2009).

Given the many constraints imposed on singable translations, translators should be free to alter the form of the source lyrics, both to make the form more congenial to the target language and to follow any formal changes imposed by the music. However, if matches or clashes of musical and verbal form are important to the structure of a work, the translators should re-create them.

12

Music and meaning

Many have been fascinated by the synergistic interplay of words and music. Opera has been considered by Patrick J. Smith (1975), among others. Peter Newmark cites a Bach cantata:

> [T]he "breathtaking beauty" which Richard Stokes highlights in the second aria of J. S. Bach's *Cantata No. 82, Ich habe genug* (1727) *(It is enough for me)* becomes the interpretation, not of the "original" text or music, but of the unparalleled word-music relationship. (Newmark, 2013: 61)

The American musical-comedy team of composer Richard Rodgers (1902–1979) and lyricist Oscar Hammerstein (1895–1960) have commented:

> [T]he choice of the proper words to express an emotion is an extremely delicate one. If the composer were to try to explain the emotion in musical terms independent of words, he would find it difficult enough. Imagine then the problem involved in trying to make the semantic expression and the musical thought meet, each one valid by itself and both satisfactory and complete in combination. The hoped for result is a dramatic musical expression in which one component is ideally enhanced by the other and the total result has far greater meaning in the final communication with the listener and viewer.
>
> (Rodgers and Hammerstein, 1958: 7–8)

As discussed in the previous chapter, music can totally alter the metrics and rhyme scheme of a poem. However, music not only changes words, but is also changed by them. According to lyricist Hammerstein:

My belief about words and music is that when a melody is good to hear, it can take on any color the lyric gives it. My favorite example is a song by Irving Berlin called "Blue Skies". It is a bright, optimistic lyric, as the title suggests. Hum the melody slowly, without the happy words and you will immediately realize that it has the quality of an Oriental lament! (Hammerstein, 1945: xviii)

"Blue Skies," composed in 1926 by Irving Berlin (1888–1989), opens with a minor chord and proceeds unconventionally to a G-major chord (see Figure 12.1). It is surprising that such music is anything *other* than a lament.

Blue Skies

FIGURE 12.1 *"Blue Skies."*
Source: Berlin (1926).

Because music and words interact synergistically, translators for the musical stage must take care that their words maintain the interaction. It is as important as reproducing meaning and adhering to structural form.

12.1 Inherent and acquired meaning in music

Some consider music to be entirely abstract, to have no "meaning" other than that acquired from words or circumstances associated with it, or from other pieces of music of which it is reminiscent. However, even if only acquired, the meaning *does* exist. Unless the words and music conflict on purpose to make a dramatic point, translators should usually work with rather than against that meaning.

There is at least one "meaning" that music can communicate completely independently of words: differing or similar melody lines, harmonies, or rhythms can indicate how close or far apart characters are psychologically. Figure 12.2 shows an excerpt from the Act II finale of *Die Entführung aus dem Serail* (*The Abduction from the Seraglio*) (1782), in which Mozart sets Blonde's rant apart in her own time world of 12/8, while the other three characters sing in 2/2. Far from ranting, Belmonte and Pedrillo are begging forgiveness, while Konstanze is grieving at Belmonte's lack of faith in her (the "it" in Konstanze's line is her heart).

FIGURE 12.2 Die Entführung aus dem Serail, *No. 16, mm. 230–31.*
Source: Herman and Apter (1979a).

Music can acquire meaning by defying convention. Eighteenth-century servants were expected to know their musical as well as their social places. The higher, more difficult music was reserved for singers portraying the nobility. Consequently, in *Die Entführung*, Konstanze's vocal line always lies above that of her servant Blonde whenever the two are singing in ensemble. However, in a solo aria, Mozart sends Blonde up to a high E (No. 8, mm. 90–91), a full tone higher than anything Konstanze ever sings. For the few in Mozart's audience both musically adept and politically conscious, the high E signaled Mozart's egalitarian beliefs.

By defying a conventional definition of "good" music, composers can make fun of their own. In *Die Entführung*, the Pasha is the only nonsinging character. His first entrance in Act I, Scene 6, accompanied by the female protagonist Konstanze, is heralded by the raucous march of the chorus of Janissaries (No. 5). The march, played mostly *forte*, calls for the entire orchestra, including timpani and the eighteenth-century staples of "Turkish" music: a large drum, triangles, and cymbals. During this march, the chorus also sings *forte:*

> Singt dem großen Bassa Lieder,
>   töne, feuriger Gesang;
> und vom Ufer halle wider
>   unsrer Lieder Jubelklang!
>
> (Sing songs to the great Pasha,
> reverberate, spirited singing;
> and from the shores let resound
> our songs' rejoicing ring!)

This is an orchestral-choral racket, but the Pasha calls it "*diese bezaubernde Musik*" ("this enchanting music"), a commentary on the Pasha's bad musical taste. (No wonder he is a non-singing character!)

The most famous example of music acquiring meaning by association is Richard Wagner's use of leitmotifs in *Der Ring des Nibelungen* (*The Ring of the Nibelung*) (1876). Starting with the first low E-flat, the first sound heard in the *Ring* and the beginning of the first leitmotif, every leitmotif is associated with some idea, object, or character that is either onstage or otherwise relevant when the leitmotif is first introduced, or, in a few cases, during a subsequent hearing of the leitmotif. Once he has introduced them, Wagner alters the leitmotifs, and their meaning, by distorting them musically, associating them with new ideas, and combining them.

In *Петя и волк* (*Peter and the Wolf*) (1936) by Sergei Prokofiev (1891–1953), the musical association is straightforward: in a prologue, the orchestra plays, and the narrator explicitly states, the motifs assigned to each character.

Music can acquire meaning from the name of a musical instrument. Horns are usually associated with hunting, but they can also be used literally to signify horns on the head, that is, cuckoldry. Mozart utilizes the horns in this way in *Le nozze di Figaro* (*The Marriage of Figaro*) (1786), during Figaro's Act IV rant against the inconstancy of women: "*Aprite un po quegl' occhi*" ("Open your eyes a little") (Trowell, 1992: II: 1198).

Music can re-inforce the meaning of words as well as acquire meaning from them. For example, music in the form of dotted eighth and sixteenth notes can provide a sense of ease and laziness beyond that expressed by words. The reason for this musical association is perhaps a psychological connection between the reluctance of lazy people to do anything and the apparent reluctance of the eighth note to end, extended as it is by an additional sixteenth note. A good example of this association occurs in the song "Lazy River" (1930) by Sidney Arodin (1901–48) and Hoagy Carmichael (1899–1981) (see Figure 12.3).

FIGURE 12.3 *"Lazy River."*
Source: Arodin and Carmichael (1930).

In Bedřich Smetana's *Prodaná nevěsta* (*The Bartered Bride*) (1866–70), Kecal's unrelenting wheedling is expressed more by music than by words (see Figure 12.4). Note his repetitive and obsessive use of just three notes: the tonic, fifth, and octave of a major chord. The stiff foursquare quarter and half notes display his pomposity as well.

FIGURE 12.4 Prodaná nevěsta (The Bartered Bride), *I.3, mm. 811–19.*
Source: Herman and Apter (2003).

Many such examples exist; they are a staple of sung lyrics.

12.2 The physical act of singing

12.2.1 *High notes and low notes*

Like composers, translators for the musical stage must consider the physical limitations of the human voice. Vowels and consonants are produced by air expelled from the lungs, passing through the vocal cords, and exiting through the oral or nasal cavities, modified along the way by different positions of the lips, tongue, and teeth. When a musical pitch is required outside the central portion of a singer's vocal range, the shape of the oral cavity limits what vowels and consonants the singer can produce. The soft palate (behind the hard palate at the back of the throat, also called the velum) must be raised higher and higher as the pitch goes up; the jaw must usually be dropped as the pitch goes down. Vowels are called "front," "central," and "back" depending on which part of the tongue is raised when they are pronounced; and "high" and "low" depending on how high the relevant part of the tongue is raised (Stageberg, 1965: 10–21).

The most "natural" English vowel, requiring the least modification of the lips, tongue, and teeth, is that of "ah" (Adler, 1965: 8). It is a low central vowel for which the tongue is virtually flat (Stageberg, 1965: 16), and one of the easiest vowels to sing, serviceable for most musical pitches. The schwa, the vowel of "f*u*dge," a slightly higher central vowel than that of "ah" (Stageberg, 1965: 14), is also easy to sing. More information is available in the books by Adler and Stageberg and in several entries in Hoch's dictionary (2014).

In general, the easiest vowels for very high notes are the high-front vowels: the highest front vowel of "f*ee*" and the second highest of "f*i*t." "Ah" and the schwa are also usually serviceable. The best vowel for very low notes is the low back vowel of f*ou*ght, for which the jaw is dropped. However, other variables affect the ease of pronouncing vowels, such as the consonants that surround them, and whether or not those consonants are voiced, that is, pronounced with vibrating vocal cords. Except when whispered, all vowels are voiced. Often, the only way to tell if a consonant-vowel combination is singable on a certain musical pitch is to actually sing it.

Whatever the pitch, whatever the sound, singing takes physical effort. And sometimes that very effort can contribute to meaning. For example, in Mozart and Schikaneder's *Die Zauberflöte* (*The Magic Flute*) (1791), the Queen of the Night sings ferociously difficult high coloratura during her famous Act II aria. On a recording, this may sound as if the Queen were laughing happily. The notes are so high (up to F), the tones so pure, that it is hard to connect them with anger. However, during a live performance, the only kind possible when the opera was created, the audience sees the soprano contorting her face as if in anger to reach the high notes. Also, she must move her diaphragm rapidly up and down to separate the notes, so her upper body seems to be shaking with rage. The translation required is minimal: give the Queen an "ah" as Mozart did and get out of her way (see Figure 12.5):

FIGURE 12.5 Die Zauberflöte, *No. 14, mm. 24–31.*
Source: Herman and Apter (1982b).

What should translators do when composers set hard-to-sing syllables on very high or very low notes? That depends on the sound the composer intended the performer to produce. An instance where we believe that the composer intended the soprano to have a pleasing sound occurs in a passage in Verdi's *La traviata* (1853). Most sopranos make no attempt to pronounce the Italian syllables, those of "f*oo*l" and "f*oa*l," on the high notes, not out of laziness but out of sheer physical inability. To make pronunciation easier, in our translation we set the schwa and "ah" on the high notes (see Figure 12.6).

Violetta

FIGURE 12.6 La traviata, *No. 2, mm. 586–93.*
Source: Herman and Apter (1981).

A similar problem arises in a duet in Bedřich Smetana's *Prodaná nevěsta* (*The Bartered Bride*) (1866–70). Mařenka, enraged at her boyfriend Jeník, sings:

Tak ošemetný muž jsi ty, nechci o tobě vědět!

(So deceitful a man are you, I do not want to know about you!)
(*Prodaná nevěsta*, III.7, mm. 1115–23)

The "*-dět*" (pronounced "*-dyet*") of the last word "*vědět*," though an unaccented syllable, is first set on a high A and then even higher on a high C. The vowel of "*-dět*" is low front, though not the lowest front (Stageberg, 1965: 16). It is probably still possible to raise the soft palate high enough to sing "*-dět*" on the high A, but perhaps not on the high C. In that case, the soprano must modify the vowel to produce the pitch. We set the syllable "*-ful*" and Amanda Holden set the syllable "you" on the high notes (see Figure 12.7). Both incorporate fairly high back vowels requiring rounding of the lips (Stageberg, 1965: 16), which may impede pronunciation on the high C. Even if a soprano finds it possible, singing the syllables on such high pitches is very difficult. Therefore, in Czech and in both English translations, she is likely to modify the vowels and consonants to ones easier to sing.

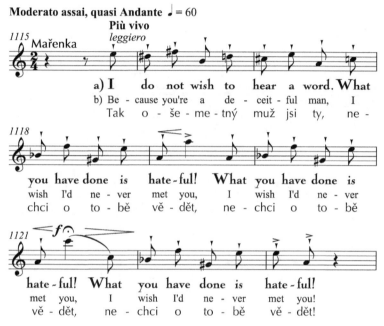

FIGURE 12.7 Prodaná nevěsta, *III.7, mm. 1115–23.*
Source: (a) Herman and Apter (2003) and (b) Holden (2006).

In a coloratura run, the same vowel sound may be set on both very high and very low notes. In this case, translators should choose the vowel that sounds best overall, not the best vowel for the highest or lowest note. For example, while the vowel of f*ee* is easy to sing high, when spread over a long run it resembles a fire siren. Hence, our translation of a melisma sung by the Marquise in Verdi's *Un giorno di regno* (1840), on which we set an "ah" vowel (see Figure 12.8).

FIGURE 12.8 Un giorno di regno, *No. 13, mm. 13–14.*
Source: Herman and Apter (1983a).

Of course, if a composer intentionally sets a melisma on a "poor" vowel, the translators should do likewise. Mozart obviously wanted Osmin to sound like a 500-pound bass canary (see Figure 12.9).

FIGURE 12.9 Die Entführung aus dem Serail, *No. 19, mm. 146–68.*
Source: Herman and Apter (1979a).

Extreme pitches can give translators a chance to add musical-verbal jokes. In a duet in *Die Entführung* (No. 9), the following interchange occurs between Blonde and Osmin:

BLONDE: Fort, laß mich allein!
OSMIN: Wahrhaftig, kein'n Schritt von der Stelle,
    bis du zu gehorchen mir schwörst.

BLONDE: Nicht so viel, nicht so viel, du armer Geselle,
und wenn du der Großmogul wärst.

(**BLONDE:** Go, leave me alone!
OSMIN: Truly, no step from this place [will I take],
till you swear to obey me.
BLONDE: Not very much [will I swear], not very much, you miserable
fellow,
even if you were the Great Mogul.)

The Great Mogul was the ruler of the former Mongol Moslem Empire in what
is now India.

Mozart sets this interchange using both high and low notes, which we took
advantage of in our translation:

BLONDE: Go, leave me alone!
OSMIN: I won't go until you obey me.
On this very spot I am stuck.
BLONDE: No, never, you'll never persuade me, not ever!
not if you were High Muck-a-muck!
(Herman and Apter, 1979a)

Our translation allows Osmin to get comically "stuck" when the music seems
to bog down on a low E-flat (Figure 12.10); and Blonde, after first singing
her words in a descending line similar to Osmin's, to cap the joke by singing
"High" on high notes (Figure 12.11).

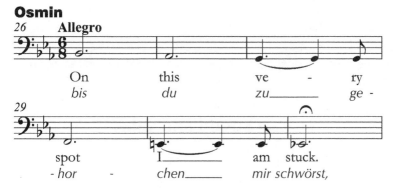

FIGURE 12.10 Die Entführung aus dem Serail, *No. 9, mm. 26–31.*
Source: Herman and Apter (1979a).

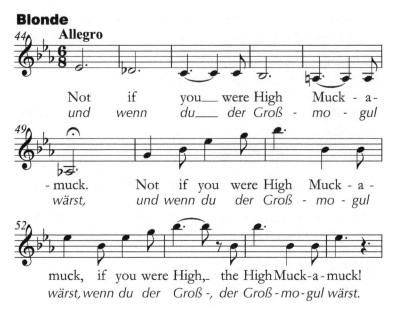

FIGURE 12.11 Die Entführung aus dem Serail, *No. 9, mm. 44–55.*
Source: Herman and Apter (1979a).

12.2.2 Tongue twisters

Like very high and very low notes, tongue twisters present a challenge to singers. Their humor depends on the physical effort needed to pronounce them at the speed indicated: the audience is amused by so much agility expended to achieve so frivolous a result. Czech, hard enough to pronounce in general, is triple trouble in tongue twisters. In a passage in *Dvě vdovy* (*Two Widows*) (1874/77), composer Smetana's *Vivace* shows that he was aware of the comic possibilities of librettist Züngel's lyrics. Ladislav and Mumlal try to keep from stumbling over each other and their words. The alternating *b*'s and *bl*'s of the Czech are almost impossible to get out. So, performers have assured us, is our English (see Figure 12.12).

12.3 Sound and sense

According to Sandra Corse:

> Some of the difficulties in determining the relationship of words to music in opera arise from the fact that language in opera is used in two distinct ways. Language always has a double function: as communication, in which meanings must often be as precise as possible; and as literature, in which the indeterminate, rhetorical, and metaphorical aspects of language tend to be emphasized. (Corse, 1987: 13–14)

FIGURE 12.12 Dvě vdovy (Two Widows), *I.iv*: 67–68.
Source: Herman and Apter (2003).

Words also function in a third way: as sound. Corse recognizes this when she later says, "the words are both language and music" (Corse, 1987: 150). In fact, words can be exclusively music:

> While operatic and vocal music played with the dual use of signified and signifier, words could transcend their semantic meaning in a musical or poetic context and be pure sound, removed from their linguistic sense. (Desblache, 2009: 73)

The use of words as pure sound is rare; it occurs, for instance, when a work is written in a language *no one* understands: Philip Glass's *Satyagraha* (1979) with a text in Sanskrit, or Igor Stravinsky's *Oedipus Rex* (1927/49) with a text in Latin. Neither language is likely to be spoken or understood by many members of the audience. Words may also register as pure sound if set to music that renders them incomprehensible, as some have accused Stravinsky of doing in *The Rake's Progress* (1951).

More typically, words set to music continue to carry semantic meaning, even when composers consciously take their sounds into account. When composers such as Mozart or Rossini do set words incomprehensibly, as when they give sopranos high rapid coloratura, they usually do so only when the words are repeated, after an initial setting in which they are easily understood.

No two languages incorporate exactly the same sounds. Even within a single language, both spoken and sung, different consonants color the vowels they are next to. Therefore, any attempt to keep sounds the same in a translation as they are in the original would seem to be an exercise in futility. However, there are still instances when translators should try to match the original sounds as closely as possible, such as when an onomatopoeic word in the original has an equivalent in the target language. For example, in the lines cited in Chapter 11, English "boom" is the translation of Italian "*bum*" (Herman and Apter, 1983a, *Un giorno di regno,* No. 19, mm. 130–32). And then there is the *Duetto buffo di due gatti (Comic duet for two cats)* (1825), the complete lyrics of which are "*miau*" ("meow"). (The *Duet* is often attributed to Gioacchino Rossini (1792–1868), but many believe that it was composed by someone else drawing on Rossini's music. The identity of the actual composer is still open to speculation.)

Music can create an onomatopoeic effect even for words otherwise lacking it. In *Die Entführung*, Belmonte's heart is so full of love that the word "*liebevolles*" ("love-filled") overflows into a cadenza. "Overflowing" is obviously a good English word to depict this overflow, and has a vowel, the second *o*, to match the decorated *o* of "*liebevolles*" (see Figure 12.13). Mozart suggests the character's emotional state (and his heartbeat) by inserting rests between the syllables of his words. Translators should follow the original and render Belmonte breathless with excitement and love.

12.4 The right word on the right note

Sometimes, word-music interaction demands that a particular word or group of words be set on a particular note or group of notes (see, e.g., Tråvén, 2005). The need for such a setting is perhaps most obvious in comical works. According to Lehman Engel, it is possible for music to give

> the lyrics a framework which . . . makes the place of the joke . . . predictable . . . [;] the audience will wait for it expectantly, hopefully, and then will

Belmonte

FIGURE 12.13 Die Entführung aus dem Serail, *No. 4, mm. 5–18.*
Source: Herman and Apter (1979a).

respond to it in the spot when the music allows "space" for such a reaction.
(Engel, 1972: 63–64)

Consider the American call-and-response folk song "Oh you can't get to
Heaven." (Other names for this song include "Oh the deacon went down," the first
phrase of the traditional first stanza, and "I ain't gonna grieve my Lord no more,"
the last line of every stanza which is then repeated six times for the refrain.) The
song was collected in the Ozark Mountains in 1962 by John Logan, but is much
older, and was in fact sung by one of us at summer camp during the early 1950s.
In one of the many lyrical and musical variants, "Oh you can't get to Heaven" is the
first phrase of most of the stanzas. The next three phrases are at the discretion of
a solo singer, the fourth phrase being the comic zinger explaining just why "you
can't get to Heaven." Then, while the refrain is being sung, the same or a different
soloist thinks of a new stanza, one already known or one newly made up.

There is nothing special about the music for the fourth phrase, but it
nonetheless makes an expected "space" for the joke, as shown by one
variant of one stanza (see Figure 12.14).

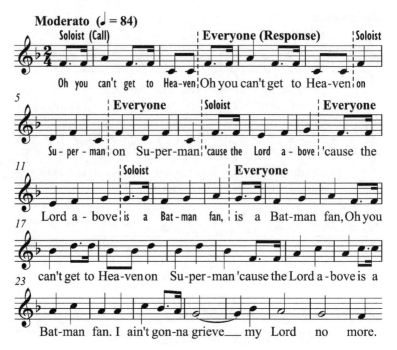

FIGURE 12.14 *"Oh you can't get to Heaven."*
Source: Logan (1962).

Like "Oh you can't get to Heaven," many comic songs make use of the stanza form to reserve a designated spot for a joke. Typically, such songs repeat the same music for each stanza and vary the words. An example is the Political Song from Lecocq's *La fille de Madame Angot* (*Madame Angot's Daughter*) (1872), in which the final two lines of each stanza are reserved for the joke. Unlike "Oh you can't get to Heaven," which includes no special music for the joke, the music for the Political Song emphasizes the joke in three ways, by a *rallentando* (that is, slowing up) beginning with the fifth syllable of the last line, grace notes on the sixth syllable, and a hold on the final syllable (see Figure 12.15).

FIGURE 12.15 La fille de Madame Angot, *No. 6b, mm. 92–94.*
Source: Herman and Apter (1989).

Table 12.1 gives the complete first stanza, including the original French lyrics and literal and singable translations. The final two lines are funnier in the original French than they appear in the literal translation because of the rhymes, among other things. In the singable translation, some of the literal meaning is eliminated to make room for explanatory "footnotes" and to point the joke in English.

TABLE 12.1 *La fille de Madame Angot*, No. 6b, mm. 78–94

Original French lyrics	Literal English translation
Jadis, les rois, race proscrite,	Formerly, kings, a banished race,
enrichissaient leurs partisans,	kept enriching their supporters,
ils avaient mainte favorite,	they had many a favorite,
cent flatteurs, mille courtisans.	a hundred flatterers, a thousand sycophants.
Sous le Directoire, tout change;	Under the Directory, everything has changed;
pourtant ne vous y fiez pas:	but do not be fooled:
On dit Mademoiselle Lange	Mademoiselle Lange is said to be
la favorite de Barras.	the favorite of Barras.

Singable English translation
There was a time we had a king and
a queen who bled the people white.
The court was full of fops and flatterers
granting favors day and night.
Now it's seventeen ninety-seven,
the king and queen and court are gone.
Now Barras will direct the nation
and, with his mistress, carry on.
(Herman and Apter, 1989)

A punchline can cap an entire narrative rather than just a single stanza. In Weber's *Der Freischütz* (1821), Ännchen tells Agathe a scary story about a "monster," which builds and builds until the final three words reveal the "monster" to be "*Nero, der Kettenhund*" ("Nero, the watchdog") (No. 13, mm. 41–42). Somehow, a three-syllable dog needs to be found to match "*Kettenhund*." The word cannot be moved somewhere else. Our solution, after consulting a thesaurus, was "basset hound."

Funny lyrics are not the only words that must go on specific musical notes. Arias expressing rage frequently include words, especially insults, which must, for one reason or another, stay on the same notes in translation as they are in the original. Table 12.2 shows an excerpt from Donizetti's *Maria Stuarda* (1835), in which Mary is insulting Queen Elizabeth. Included are performable translations by both Amanda Holden and us. Some re-arrangement of the thoughts in the first four lines may be allowable, but the climactic statement about the profanation of the English throne should come at the end for dramatic effect. The word "bastard" should stay on the same notes as "*bastarda*" because the word must come very near the end; it is unlikely that Elizabeth would let Mary say much more after the word "bastard."

TABLE 12.2 *Maria Stuarda*, No. 6, mm. 258–70

Original Italian lyrics	Literal English translation
Meretrice	Whore
indegna	unworthy
oscena,	indecent woman,
in te cada il mio rossore . . .	on you let fall my shame . . .
profanato	profaned
è il soglio inglese,	is the English throne,
Vil bastarda,	vile bastard,
dal tuo piè.	by your foot.
Singable English translation (Herman and Apter, 1997)	**Singable English translation (Holden, 1998)**
You ignoble	You disgusting,
usurper,	abusive
you harlot,	old viper!
on your head my shame has fallen!	I'm ashamed to be your cousin . . .
England's proud throne	You discredit
too long has been profaned,	the crown of England,
Tudor bastard,	royal bastard,
by your feet.	at your cost!

Sometimes, a specific word must go on a specific note because of musical word-painting. In Verdi's *Luisa Miller* (1849), Luisa sings:

> Lo vidi, e il primo palpito
>   il cor senti d'amore:
>   mi vide appena, e il core
> balzó del mio fedel.
>   (Verdi, *Luisa Miller*, 1849, No. 2, mm. 204–12)

> (I saw him, and the first beat
> of my heart felt love:
> He just saw me, and the heart
> leaped of my faithful one.)

On "*balzó*" ("leaped") in mm. 210–11, Verdi leaps up an octave, making it mandatory that some form of "leap" be set on those notes. The setting of the four lines, including our singable translation, is shown in Figure 12.16.

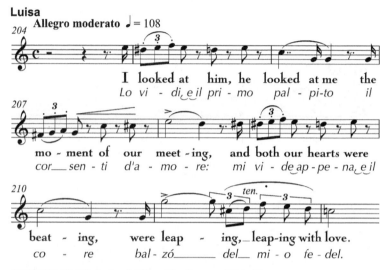

FIGURE 12.16 Luisa Miller, No. 2, *mm. 204–12.*
Source: Herman and Apter (2004).

Sometimes, putting certain words on certain notes is not required, but is useful to point a musical-verbal joke. In Act II of *Die Entführung*, Konstanze enters a stage already occupied by Blonde and sings an aria (No. 10). According to the stage directions, Konstanze sings it "*ohne Blonde zu bemerken*" ("without noticing Blonde"). Blonde gets her revenge for being ignored in a subsequent aria. Blonde has noticed, as has the theater audience, that Konstanze makes musical sighs in her aria while singing the word "*Klagen*" ("lamentation, moaning, complaining"). One prominent sigh consists of holding a single note for a long time, dropping down a minor third and then coming back up. So as to make everything clear to a contemporary audience, translators should supply a suitable word, such as "sighing" (see Figure 12.17).

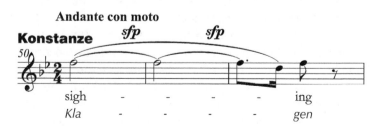

FIGURE 12.17 Die Entführung aus dem Serail, *No. 10, mm. 50–52.*
Source: Herman and Apter (1979a).

In her own aria, Blonde sings that Konstanze's sadness will soon be over. While doing so, she takes Konstanze's musical figure and satirizes it by inverting it, going up, not down. Blonde's word is not "*Klagen*" but "*Herzen*" ("heart"), but, again, it helps a contemporary audience to get the joke if Konstanze's word, "sighing," is also given to Blonde (see Figure 12.18).

FIGURE 12.18 Die Entführung aus dem Serail, *No. 12, mm. 107–12.*
Source: Herman and Apter (1979a).

The exact right word is also required when the composer has set it on particular notes in order to depict character. As mentioned above, Konstanze's self-absorption is revealed by her singing an aria while not noticing that Blonde is on stage with her. It is also revealed in her earlier Act I introductory aria (No. 6), during which she repeatedly sings the line "*Kummer ruht in meinem Schoß.*" The literal meaning of this line may be approximated in English as "Grief/sorrow/sadness rests/pauses/stands still in my lap/womb/bosom." The common German cliché words "*Herz*" ("heart") and "*Brust*" ("breast") are avoided. Konstanze is weeping to her physical core, and the sadness is *real*, but at this point in the opera she has yet to transcend her not very noble self-absorption. Mozart, after setting this line in a relatively undecorated way so that the audience can understand every word, repeats the line with excessively florid high coloratura. The coloratura is known to have satisfied the lead soprano's demand for a showoff piece. Mozart himself admitted to "sacrific[ing] the aria a bit to Mlle. Cavalieri's glib gullet" (letter to his father, September 26, 1781, in Anderson, King, and Carolan, 1966, II: 768–70). The decorated word, "*meinem*" ("my"), is a good choice because the "ah" vowel, the first part of the "*-ei-*" diphthong in "*meinem*," is an especially good one for musical runs. However, to assume that that is the only reason for *"meinem,"* as some critics do, is to ignore much of Mozart's dramatic genius. Certainly Arthur Sullivan knew what Mozart was doing, and copied the device to point out Mabel's vanity in *The Pirates of Penzance* (see Figure 12.19).

FIGURE 12.19 The Pirates of Penzance, No. 7, *mm. 76–78.*
Source: Gilbert and Sullivan (1879).

Obviously, translators must put a self-referential word on the *"meinem"* runs. Some measures from the last part of the aria, with our "I" and Amanda Holden's "my," are shown in Figure 12.20 on the next page.

The right words can be the wrong words. In *Die Entführung,* later in the aria cited in Figure 12.13 above, Belmonte is so bemused with love that he sings the words *"O wie ängstlich, o wie feurig"* on the notes previously reserved for *"klopft mein liebevolles Herz"* (see Figure 12.21 on page 239). As the composer has done, so should the translators.

Translators for the musical stage must always be aware that their words will be sung rather than spoken. There is no such thing as a generic translation of a lyric, such as a poem, which will fit all possible musical settings. The particular musical setting is as important an element of the original as is the meaning of the words, and a translation not accounting for it is bound to be a failure.

This book discusses the many maddening, frustrating constraints facing translators for the musical stage. What makes the effort worthwhile is the joy of finding the right words for the right notes, of creating a musical-verbal experience in the target language analogous to that of the original.

FIGURE 12.20 Die Entführung aus dem Serail, *No. 6, mm. 98–115.*
Source: (a) Herman and Apter (1979a) and (b) Holden (1999/2009).

FIGURE 12.21 Die Entführung aus dem Serail, *No. 4, mm. 94–98.*
Source: Herman and Apter (1979a).

Afterword

Those who object to singable translations mainly cite the difficulty of creating such translations, the impossibility of reproducing the sounds of the original, and the failure of some singers to be understood in any language. The objectors also claim that singable translations have been made unnecessary by the advent of projected captions. More understandably, major opera companies think it better not to require international stars to learn a work in more than one language. The last, according to Nikolaus Bachler, Artistic and General Director of the Bavarian State Opera in Munich, is more a loss than a gain:

> The singer sings as the person he or she is, just as the actor acts like they [*sic*] are. At the Volksoper, I learned what it meant to understand the texts. Even if you cannot hear all the words, an opera sung in your language is a different experience. We now have a sort of esperanto in opera—which is not really "original language" at all. The way even the best artists sing different languages is seldom authentic or credible—and the so-called benefits of an opera being performed as the composer wrote it takes us a long way from communicating with the real local public . . . We have an advantage in opera in that we can cast great voices from anywhere in the world: but in doing so, we lose the authentic spirit of the art.
>
> (Bachler, quoted by Tom Sutcliffe, 2010: 25)

The prejudice against performable translations has unfortunately been re-inforced by the long history of bad ones, especially of bad translations into English. As evidenced by the frontispiece to this book written by Joseph Addison in 1711, critics have railed against such translations for over 300 years. More recent criticisms include those of Deems Taylor (1885–1966), who expostulated in 1937:

> Mention opera in English to the average operagoer, and he thinks you mean the curious doggerel into which operas are generally translated.
> (Taylor, 1937: 580)

What Taylor craved was

> an English version . . . that has the same literary and poetic distinction as
> the original. (Taylor, 1937: 580–81)

Oscar Hammerstein is of the same mind. In addition to being an original
lyricist, Hammerstein is the creator of *Carmen Jones* (1943), an English
adaptation of Bizet's *Carmen* (1875). Here are his views, taken from the
Introduction to the published libretto of that adaptation:

> To the plea for opera in English there is a stock answer. "It has always
> failed". This happens to be true and it seems like pretty crushing evidence
> against our side. But there's a joker hidden in this answer. The sad fact is
> that when you hear opera in English it is in pretty bad English. These great
> works, originally written by distinguished dramatic poets, are translated by
> scholarly but untalented gentlemen [and women] who know nearly nothing
> about the science of writing phonetic, singable lyrics. They are not poets,
> nor dramatists, nor showmen. A good adaptation of an opera requires a
> librettist who is all of these.
>
> Thus, when opera in English has failed, it is the translations that have been
> rejected, and rightly so. The public has not rejected "opera in English", because
> it has never had a skillful English version of an opera submitted to it.
>
> I feel in my bloodstream the approach of that choleric indignation that
> invariably seizes me when I discuss this topic. I am beginning to sweat, and
> this is not a hot day. I must control myself, else I will be taking wild swipes
> at my list of very special hates: the dear singing teachers who instruct their
> pupils to broaden every "a" so that a lovely word like "romance" becomes
> "romonce"—no word at all; the foreign singer whose accent makes English
> less intelligible than his own tongue; the conductor who thinks there is
> more entertainment in a blast from a horn than in any English word that
> could possibly be sung. But I must forbear. This is not the day for me to
> handle these opera-house barnacles as they should be handled.
>
> (Hammerstein, 1945: xiv–xv)

> *Carmen Jones*[, though only an adaptation,] is an indication, if not positive
> proof, that opera in English may be popular if the lyrics are singable,
> understandable, and dramatic. A more complete proof would be [a true
> translation] of the original, keeping the scene in Spain and all details the
> same except for the exigencies of translation. Some day someone who
> understands music and the theatre will write a straight English version of
> some opera, and some courageous director will force the singers to act in
> a sensible manner—and the result will be astounding.
>
> (Hammerstein, 1945: xvii)

We end this book with our own plea, for more and better translations and performances in English translation, leading to more and better original English librettos, leading to more . . . so that finally the English-speaking world can claim all musical-stage genres as its own. Even as contemporary composers, 400 years after the invention of opera, are breaking down whatever barriers may have existed between operas and musicals, opera still remains a foreign entity on the English-speaking stage. Translation has made William Shakespeare the most popular playwright in the world. If the Russians and Japanese and Germans can own Shakespeare, surely English speakers can own opera and art song. Without such ownership many supreme artistic creations are denied them:

Operas of the past . . . can live again, not only in our imagination, but also on the stage, where their movement, color, and sound can still exalt us.
(Grout and Williams, 1988: 728)

Bibliography

1. Original works

The works are alphabetized by the composer's last name, if there is a composer, except when the librettist is customarily given first, as for "Gilbert and Sullivan."

Adams, J., composer, and A. Goodman, librettist (1991), *The Death of Klinghoffer*. London: Boosey & Hawkes.

Ariosto, L. (1516–32), *Orlando furioso*, Marcello Turchi and Edoardo Sanguineti (eds). Milan: Garzanti, 1974.

Arodin, S., composer, and H. Carmichael, arranger and modifier of lyrics (1930), "Up a Lazy River." Many publications and recordings.

Austen, J. (1798 written, 1803 revised, 1818 published), *Northanger Abbey*. Many editions available.

Bach, J. S., composer (before 1725, published 1867), (Great) Prelude (Fantasia) and Fugue in G minor, BWV 542, score available at: https://musopen.org/sheetmusic/3556/johann-sebastian-bach/fantasia-fugue-in-gm-bwv-542/, accessed June 30, 2014.

Berlin, I., composer and lyricist (1926), "Blue Skies," first published 1927. Many editions available.

Bernart de Ventadorn (twelfth century), *A Bilingual Edition of the Love Songs of Bernart de Ventadorn in Occitan and English: Sugar and Salt*, R. Apter (trans.). Lewiston, NY: The Edwin Mellen Press, 1999. This book includes the original lyrics, translations, commentary, and an article discussing the milieu in which Bernart composed his songs.

Bernstein, L., composer, S. Sondheim, lyricist, A. Laurents, book, and J. Robbins, choreographer (1957), *West Side Story*. n.p.: G. Schirmer and Chappell. This is a piano-vocal score. The complete text of *West Side Story* may be found in S. Richards (1973), *Ten Great Musicals of the American Theatre*, Vol. I: 349–412.

Bizet, G., composer, and H. Meilhac and L. Halévy, librettists (1875), *Carmen*, Robert Didion (ed.), (2000), Mainz: Schott Musik International. Based on the novella *Carmen* by Prosper Mérimée.

Blanchard, T., composer, and M. Cristofer, librettist (2013), *Champion*. Available at: <http://en.wikipedia.org/wiki/Champion_(opera)>, accessed September 13, 2014.

Bock, J., composer, S. Harnick, lyricist, and J. Stein, playwright (1964), *Fiddler on the Roof*, based on stories by Sholem Aleichem. In S. Richards (1973), Vol. 1: 489–555. This is the text of the musical.

Boieldieu, F., composer, and C. de Longchamps, librettist (1803), *Ma tante Aurore, ou le roman impromptu* (*My Aunt Aurore, or the Impromptu Novel*). Nashville: Herman and Apter (published 1982).

Borodin, A. (Бородин, А.), composer (1887, incomplete), *Князь Игорь* (*Knyaz' Igor' [Prince Igor]*). Information on available scores at: <http://imslp.org/wiki/Prince_Igor_(Borodin,_Aleksandr)>, accessed September 2014.

Britten, B., composer, and P. Pears, co-librettist (1960), *A Midsummer Night's Dream*, adapted from the play by William Shakespeare. London: Boosey & Hawkes.

Carmina Burana (*Songs of Buran*) (twelfth century), Hilka, A., Schumann, O., and Bischoff, B., eds., Heidelberg: Carl Winter Universitätsverlag, 1930–71. There are recordings of the original lyrics sung to reconstructions of the original music: The Clemencic Consort: Harmonia Mundi HMU 335 and HMU 336, and Telefunken SAWT 9455-A. Also see "Orff" below.

Carroll, L. (1871), *Through the Looking-Glass, and What Alice Found There*, in The Complete Works of Lewis Carroll. New York: The Modern Library, 133–271.

Catullus, (First Century BCE), *C. Valerii Catulli Carmina*, R. A. B. Mynors (ed.). Oxford: Oxford University Press, 1958.

Cavalli, F., composer, and A. Aureli, librettist (1655), *Erismena*. Scores available at: <http://imslp.org/wiki/L'Erismena_(Cavalli,_Francesco)>, accessed in Septemer 2014.

Cercamon (twelfth century), *The Poetry of Cercamon and Jaufre Rudel*, G. Wolf and R. Rosenstein (eds.) and (trans.). New York and London: Garland, 1983.

Cervantes, M. de (1605, 1615), *El ingenioso hidalgo don Quijote de la Mancha* (*The Ingenious Nobleman Don Quijote de la Mancha*), Edición del IV centenario, Real Academia Española (400th Anniversary Edition, The Royal Spanish Academy). Miami, FL: Santillana USA Publishing Company, 2004).

Chaikovskiy, P. I. (Чайковский, П. И.), composer, with a libretto by the composer and Konstantin Shilovsky, after the novel in verse by Alexander Pushkin (1879), *Eugene Onyegin (Евгений Онегин)*. n.p.: Dover Publications (Full Score, published 1997).

Clemencic, R., (1992) *Carmina Burana: Version Originale & Integrale*. Volumes 1 and 2 are two recordings by the Clemencic Consort of the original lyrics to reconstructions of the original music: Harmonia Mundi HMU 335 and HMU 336. Another recording of *Carmina Burana* with reconstructed music is Telefunken SAWT 9455-A.

Collins, F. Jr., R. F. Cook, and R. Harmon, eds. (1982), *A Medieval Songbook: Troubadour and Trouvère*. Charlottesville: University of Virginia Press.

Dante Alighieri (1304–7), *Convivio* (*The Banquet*), original Italian and English translation (2008) by A. S. Kline. Available at: <http://www.poetryintranslation.com/PITBR/Italian/Convivioll.htm>, accessed July 20, 2015.

Davenson, H., ed. (1967), *Les Troubadours*. Paris: Éditions du Seuil.

Donizetti, G., composer, and G. Bardari, librettist (1835), *Maria Stuarda*, ed. A. Wiklund (1989). Milan: Ricordi (Ricordi 134916).

Donizetti, G., composer, and G. Bardari, librettist (1976), *Maria Stuarda*, Recording, Richard Bonynge (conductor). London: Decca 425 410–2. Reissued as a set of CD's by London Records in 1990.

Dessau, P. composer, and B. Brecht, lyricist and playwright (with significant contributions by Margarete Steffin) (1939, first performed 1941), *Mutter*

Courage und ihre Kinder: Eine Chronik aus dem Dreißigjährigen Krieg (*Mother Courage and Her Children: A Chronicle of the Thirty Years' War*). Berlin: Suhrkamp Verlag (published 1964).

Dryden, J. (1667), *Sir Martin Mar-All, or The Feign'd Innocence*. London: H. Herringman.

Duval, A., *Le faux Stanislas: Comédie en trois actes et en prose* (1809). In *Oeuvres complètes d'Alexandre Duval* (1823). Paris: J. N. Barba Libraire, 7: 73–182.

Dumas, A., *fils* (1848, novel; 1852, play), *La Dame aux camélias* (*The Lady of the Camellias*). Paris: G. Havard (published 1858).

Ferrero, L., composer, and M. Ravasini, librettist (1981, revised 1991), *La figlia del mago* (*The Sorcerer's Daughter*). Milan: Ricordi (Ricordi 137776).

Gay, J., librettist (1728), *The Beggar's Opera*. London: Boosey & Hawkes (revised edition, 1926). This is a piano-vocal score (musical numbers only) arranged by Frederic Austin. The edition published by The Heritage Press (New York: 1937) includes the complete text, vocal lines for the music, and illustrations by Mariette Lydis.

Gershwin, G., composer, and DuBose Heyward, lyricist (Ira Gershwin is also sometimes credited as co-lyricist) (1935), "Summertime," from the opera *Porgy and Bess*. New York: Gershwin.

Gershwin, G., composer, and I. Gershwin, lyricist (1935), "It Ain't Necessarily So," from the opera *Porgy and Bess*. New York: Gershwin.

Gilbert, H. (1912), *Robin Hood and the Men of the Greenwood*, republished as *Robin Hood* (2009). Rockville, MD: Wildside Press.

Gilbert, W. S., librettist and Sullivan, A., composer (1878), *H.M.S. Pinafore, or The Lass that Loved a Sailor*, new score edition (2002), C. Simpson and E. H. Jones (eds.). Mineola, NY: Dover.

Gilbert, W. S., librettist and Sullivan, A., composer (1879), *The Pirates of Penzance*, new score edition (2001), C. Simpson and E. H. Jones (eds.). Mineola, NY: Dover.

Gilbert, W. S., librettist and Sullivan, A., composer (1882), *Iolanthe*, libretto and some music in Green (1961).

Gilbert, W. S., librettist and Sullivan, A., composer (1885), *The Mikado, or The Town of Titipu*, new score edition (1999), C. Simpson and E. H. Jones (eds.). Mineola, NY: Dover.

Gilbert, W. S., librettist and Sullivan, A., composer (1889), *The Gondoliers*, libretto and some music in Green (1961).

Glass, P., composer and librettist, the latter with Constance DeJong (1979), *Satyagraha*, opera in three acts for orchestra, chorus, and soloists. The text is taken from the *Bhagavad Gita*, and sung in the original Sanskrit. Translated supertitles are usually provided during performances.

Gounod, C. F., composer, and P. J. Barbier and M. Carré, librettists (1958), *Le médecin malgré lui* (*The Doctor in Spite of Himself*). Nashville: Herman and Apter (published 1979).

Gounod, C. F., composer, and M. Carré, librettist (1864), *Mireille*. n.p.: Book on Demand (published 2014).

Green, M., ed. and annotator (1961), *Martyn Green's Treasury of Gilbert & Sullivan*. New York: Simon and Schuster.

Gruber, F. X., composer, and J. Mohr, librettist (1818), "Stille Nacht, heilige Nacht" ("Silent night, holy night"). Available at: <www.stillenacht.at/en/text_and_music.asp>, accessed May 10, 2014.

Halévy, F., composer, and E. Scribe, librettist (1835), *La Juive* (*The Jewess*). Paris: Maurice Schlesinger.

Handel, G. F., composer (1738), *Serse* (*Xerxes*), libretto adapted from an earlier one by Silvio Stampiglia adapted from an even earlier one by Nicolò Minato, Friedrich Chrysander (ed.). Leipzig: Deutsche Händelgesellschaft (published 1884).

Handel, G. F., composer (1741, first performed 1742, first published 1767), *Messiah*. Many editions.

Hilka, A., O. Schumann, and B. Bischoff, eds. (1930–71), *Carmina Burana* (*Songs of Buran*) (twelfth century). Heidelberg: Carl Winter Universitätsverlag.

Hoffman, A., M. David, and J. Livingston, composers and librettists (1948), "Bibbidi-Bobbidi-Boo," introduced in the 1950 Walt Disney film *Cinderella*. n.p.: Walt Disney Music Company.

Jagger, M. and K. Richards, composers and lyricists (1965), "(I Can't Get No) Satisfaction." New York: Immediate Music.

Jaufre Rudel (1983), *The Poetry of Cercamon and Jaufre Rudel*, G. Wolf and R. Rosenstein (eds.) and (trans.). New York and London: Garland.

Jonson, B. (1616), "To Celia." Complete text and information available at: <http://www.poetryfoundation.org/poem/173729>, accessed September 2014.

Joyce, J. (1939), *Finnegans Wake*. London: Faber and Faber. Critical edition published by Penguin in 2012 (*The Restored Fnnegans Wake*, London: Penguin Modern Classics).

Juster, N. (1961), *The Phantom Tollbooth*, with illustrations by Jules Feiffer. New York: Knopf.

Kander, J., composer, F. Ebb, lyricist, and J. Masteroff, playwright (1966), *Cabaret*. Milwaukee, WI: Hal Leonard. Adapted from the play *I Am A Camera* (1951) by John Van Druten, based on *Goodbye to Berlin* (1939), later incorporated into *The Berlin Stories* (1945) by Christopher Isherwood.

Lecocq, C., composer, and Clairville, Siraudin, and Koning, librettists (1872), *La fille de Madame Angot* (*Madame Angot's Daughter*). Nashville: Herman and Apter (published 1989).

Lehrer, T., composer and librettist (1953/4), "The Hunting Song," in Lehrer (1981) *Too Many Songs*, 30–32.

Lehrer, T., composer and librettist (1954), "A Christmas Carol," in Lehrer (1981), *Too Many Songs*, 60–62.

Lehrer, T., composer and librettist (1965/66), "The Vatican Rag," in Lehrer (1981), *Too Many Songs*, 139–41.

Lehrer, T., composer and librettist (1981), *Too Many Songs by Tom Lehrer with Not Enough Drawings by Ronald Searle*. New York: Random House.

Loesser, F., composer and lyricist, J. Swerling and A. Burrows, playwrights (1950), *Guys and Dolls*. New York: Frank Music Corp. This is a piano-vocal score. The complete text may be found in Eric Bentley (ed.), (1955), *The Modern Theatre*, Vol. 4. Garden City, NY: Doubleday Anchor Books, 283–380. The book of the musical is usually attributed to both Jo Swerling and Abe Burrows, but almost all of the final result is by Abe Burrows.

Loewe, F., composer, and A. J. Lerner, librettist (1960) *Camelot*, in Richards (1976) *Ten Great Musicals*, Vol. 2, 396–469. This is the text of the musical. *Camelot* is based on the legend of King Arthur as recounted in *The Once and Future King* (written 1938–41, published 1958) by T. H. White.

Logan, J., collector, "Oh you can't get to Heaven," traditional American folk song from the Ozark Mountains, collected in 1962, in the University of Arkansas Libraries, Ozark Folksong Collection, available at:<http:// digitalcollections.uark.edu/cdm/ref/collection/OzarkFolkSong/id/891#img_ view_container>, accessed June 19, 2015. Other websites also show lyrics and/or music for this song.

Marcabru (twelfth century), *Poésies Complètes du Troubadour Marcabru*, J. M. L. de Jeanne (ed.). Toulouse: Imprimerie et Librairie Édouard Privat, 1909.

Marot, C. (sixteenth century), "Ma mignonne." For text and translations, see Hofstadter (1997), *Le Ton beau de Marot* under "Translations and Adaptations" in this bibliography.

Massenet, J., composer, and L. Gallet, librettist (1893), *Thaïs*. Score available at: <http://imslp.org/wiki/Tha%C3%AFs_(Massenet,_Jules)>.

Meyerbeer, G., composer, and E. Scribe and E. Deschamps, librettists (1836), *Les Huguenots* (*The Huguenots*). Paris: Brandus & Cie (published about 1860).

Molière (pen name of Jean Baptiste Poquelin) (1666), *Le médecin malgré* lui (*The Doctor in Spite of Himself*). Paris: Librairie Larousse (published 1970).

Molloy, J. L., composer, and G. C. Bingham, lyricist, (1884), "Love's Old Sweet Song." This song includes the well-known line "Just a song at twilight," has been recorded many times, and was mentioned in James Joyce's novel *Ulysses*.

Monteverdi., C., composer, and G. F. Busenello, librettist (1643), *L'incoronazione di Poppea* (*The Coronation of Poppea*), Raymond Leppard (ed.). London: Faber Music (published 1966).

Moore, M. (2003), *The Poems of Marianne Moore*, Grace Schulman (ed.). New York: Penguin.

Mozart, W. A. (1781), Letter to his father, Leopold Mozart, September 26, 1781, in *The Letters of Mozart and His Family,* 2 vols., Emily Anderson (ed. and trans.); 2nd edition, ed. by A. Hyatt King and Monica Carolan. New York: St. Martin's Press, 1966, II: 768–70.

Mozart, W. A., composer, and G. Stephanie, the younger, librettist, adapted from an earlier libretto by C. F. Bretzner (1782), *Die Entführung aus dem Serail* (*The Abduction from the Seraglio*), K. 384, critical edition, G. Croll, (ed.) and J. Sommer (piano reduction of the orchestral score) (1982). Kassel: Bärenreiter (BA 4591).

Mozart, W. A., composer, and L. Da Ponte, librettist (1786), *Le nozze di Figaro, ossia la folle giornata* (*The Marriage of Figaro, or The Day of Madness*), K. 492, critical edition, L. Finscher (ed.) and E. Epplée (piano reduction of the orchestral score) (2001). Kassel: Bärenreiter (BA 4565).

Mozart, W. A., composer, and L. Da Ponte, librettist (1787), *Il dissoluto punito, ossia il Don Giovanni* (*The Libertine Punished, or Don Giovanni*), K. 527, critical edition, H. Moehn (ed.) (1968). Kassel: Bärenreiter (BA 4550).

Mozart, W. A., composer, and L. Da Ponte, librettist (1790), *Così fan tutte, ossia La scuola degli amanti* (*The Way They're Made, or The School for Lovers*), K. 588, critical edition, F. Ferguson and W. Rehm (eds.) (1991). Kassel: Bärenreiter (BA 4606).

Mozart, W. A., composer, and E. Schikaneder, librettist (1791), *Die Zauberflöte* (*The Magic Flute*), K. 620, critical edition, G. Gruber and A. Orel (eds.) and H. Moehn (piano reduction of the orchestral score) (1970). Kassel: Bärenreiter (BA 4553).

Musicals, *Ten Great Musicals of the AmericanTheatre*, S. Richards (ed.). Radnor, PA: Chilton Book Company, 1973, Vol. 1; 1976, Vol. 2.

Musorgskiy, M. (Мусоргский, М.), composer and librettist (1869 and 1872), *Борис Годунов (Boris Godunov)*, based on *Boris Godunov* by Aleksandr Pushkin, and *The History of the Russian State* by Nikolai Karamzin. There is a critical edition of the orchestral score of the 1869 version edited by Yevgeniy M. Levashev (Moscow: Muzyka and Schott, 1996); and a decent version of both the 1869 and 1872 versions, edited and translated by David Lloyd-Jones. London: Oxford University Press, 1975.

Offenbach, J. composer, and P. J. Barbier, librettist (1880), *Les Contes d'Hoffmann (The Tales of Hoffmann)*, after the play by Barbier and Michel Carré (1851), based on the stories of E. T. A. Hoffmann. Many "rewritten" scores. No definitive critical edition as yet.

Offenbach, J. composer, and D.-L.-E. Nuitter,. librettist (1864), *Les fées du Rhin (The Fairies of the Rhine)*. First performed in Vienna in a truncated version, as *Die Rheinnixen*, translated into German by Alfred von Wolzogen. The first complete concert performance occurred in 2002, the first fully staged performance in 2005.

Orff, C., composer (1936, first performed 1937), *Carmina Burana: Cantiones Profanae (Songs of Buran: Secular Songs)*. Mainz: B. Schott's Söhne.

Porter, C., composer and lyricist (1928), "Let's Do It," from the musical *Paris*. New York: Harms.

Poulenc, F., composer and librettist (1957) *Dialogues des Carmélites (Dialogues of the Carmelites)*. Milan: Ricordi. Italian translation by Flavio Testi.

Pound, E. (1940), *Cantos LII–LXXI* (1940). Norfolk, CT: New Directions.

Prokofiev, S. S. (Прокофьев, С. С.), composer, with a spoken text by the composer (1936), *Peter and the Wolf: A Symphonic Story for Children (Петя и волк: Симфоническая сказка для детей)* (Op. 67), available online at: <http://petruccilibrary.ca/download.php?file=files/imglnks/caimg/0/0c/IMSLP00347-Prokofiev_-_Peter_And_The_Wolf.pdf>.

Puccini, G., composer, and G. Giacosa and L. Illica, librettists (1896), *La bohème*, critical edition. Milan: Ricordi, to be published. After the novel *Scènes de la vie de bohème* (1845–49) by Henri Murger and the play *La vie de bohème* (1849) by Murger and Théodore Barrière.

Puccini, G., composer, and G. Adami and R. Simoni (librettists) (1924 incomplete) *Turandot*.

Purcell, H., composer, and N. Tate, librettist (1688), *Dido and Aeneas*. London: Musical Antiquarian Society (published 1841, edited by George Alexander Macfarren). The earliest extant score dates from no earlier than 1750, over sixty years after the opera was actually composed.

Pyle, H. (1883), *The Merry Adventures of Robin Hood of Great Renown in Nottinghamshire*. New York: Charles Scribner's Sons.

Rachmaninoff, S. V. (Рахманинов, С. В.), composer (1895), *Six Choral Songs for Treble Voices and Piano (Шесть хоров для женского хора с фортепьяно)*. San Diego: Musica Russica (published 2009). The libretto consists of six Russian poems. Sample pages of the score may be seen and samples of the songs sung in Russian may be heard at <http://www.musicarussica.com/collections/ra-6ch>.

Radcliffe, A. W. (1794), *The Mysteries of Udolpho*. Available for free at <http://www.gutenberg.org/files/3268/3268-h/3268-h.htm>, accessed September 2014.

Raimbaut (twelfth century) *The Life and Works of the Troubadour Raimbaut d'Orange*, W. T. Pattison (ed.). Minneapolis: The University of Minnesota Press, 1952.

Richards, S., ed. (1973, Vol. 1; 1976, Vol. 2), *Ten Great Musicals of the American Theatre*. Radnor, Pennsylvania: Chilton Book Company.

Rodgers, M., composer, M. Barer, lyricist, and J. Thompson, D. Fuller, and M. Barer, playwrights (1959), *Once Upon A Mattress*, after "The Princess and the Pea" by Hans Christian Andersen. Milwaukee, WI: Hal Leonard.

Rodgers, R., composer, and O. Hammerstein II, librettist (1943), *Oklahoma!*, based on the play *Green Grow the Lilacs* (1931) by Lynn Riggs. Milwaukee, WI: Hal Leonard.

Rodgers, R., composer, and O. Hammerstein II, librettist (1951), *The King and I*, based on the novel *Anna and the King of Siam* by Margaret Landon (1944), derived from the memoirs of Anna Leonowens about her years in Siam in the 1860s. Milwaukee, WI: Hal Leonard.

Rodgers, R., composer, and L. Hart, librettist (1940), *Pal Joey*, based on a character and situations created by John O'Hara.

Rossetti, D. G. (1961), *Rossetti's Poems*, Oswald Doughty (ed.). London: J. M. Dent & Sons; New York: E. P. Dutton.

Rossini, G., composer, and L. Prividali, librettist, after a play by Eugène Scribe (1812), *L'occasione fa il ladro* (*Opportunity Makes the Thief*), G. C. Ballola, P. B. Brauner, and P. Gossett (eds.) (1994). Milano: Ricordi (Ricordi 134552).

Rossini, G., composer, and C. Sterbini, librettist (1816), *Il barbiere di Siviglia [Almaviva o sia L'inutile precauzione]* (*The Barber of Seville [Almaviva, or the Useless Precaution]*), P. B. Brauner (ed.) (2008). Kassel: Baerenreiter (BA 10506).

Rossini, G., composer (1825), *Duetto buffo di due gatti* (*Comic duet for two cats*) (1825). Often attributed to Rossini, many believe it was composed by someone else drawing on Rossini's music.

Salieri, A., composer, and G. B. Casti, librettist (1786), *Prima la musica e poi le parole* (*First the Music and Then the Words*), Thomas Betzwieser and Adrian La Salvia (eds.) (2013). Kassel: Bärenreiter.

Satie, E., composer (1923), *Scènes Nouvelles pour Le médecin malgré lui de Charles Gounod*, Robert Orledge (ed.) (2001). Liverpool: Aerial Kites Press.

Scarlatti, A., composer, and S. Stampiglia, librettist (1700), *Eraclea*, Donald Jay Grout (ed.) (1974). Cambridge, MA: Harvard University Press.

Schiller, F. v. (1800), *Maria Stuart*. Stuttgart: Philipp Reclam Jr., GmbH (1965).

Schubert, F., composer (1824), *Die schöne Müllerin, ein Zyklus von Liedern, gedichtet von Wilhelm Müller* (*The Beautiful Girl of the Mill, a song cycle set to poems by Wilhelm Müller*), available at: <http://imslp.org/wiki/Die_S ch%C3%B6ne_M%C3%BCllerin,_D.795_(Schubert,_Franz)>, accessed September 2014.

Shakespeare, W., playwright (1600), *The Tragedy of Hamlet, Prince of Denmark*. The speech of Polonius paraphrased is Act II, Scene 2, lines 379–81.

Sherman, R., M., and R. Sherman, composers and librettists (1964), "Supercalifragilisticexpialidocious," introduced in the 1964 Walt Disney film *Mary Poppins*, available at: <http://www.musicnotes.com/sheetmusic/ mtdFPE.asp?ppn=MN0057105&ref=google>, accessed September 2014.

Silcher, F., composer or arranger, (1837), "Die Lorelei," available at: <http://www.
      musicnotes.com/sheetmusic/mtdFPE.asp?ppn=MN0128789&ref=google>,
      accessed September 2014. The melody of "Die Lorelei" is either a genuine
      folk song arranged by Friedrich Silcher or was composed by Silcher. It is a
      setting of a poem by Heinrich Heine.
Smetana, B., composer, and K. Sabina, librettist (1866–70), *Prodaná nevěsta*
      (*The Bartered Bride*), F. Bartoš (ed.) (1953). Prague: State Publishing House
      for Literature, Music, and Art.
Smetana, B., composer, and E. Züngel, librettist (1874, rev. 1877), *Dvě vdovy*
      (*Two Widows*), F. Bartoš (ed.) (1950). Prague: National Music Publishing
      House. Libretto based on *Les deux veuves* (*The Two Widows*) (1860) by J. P.
      F. Mallefille.
Sondheim, S., composer and librettist, and H. Wheeler, book (1979), *Sweeney
      Todd: The Demon Barber of Fleet Street*. New York: Rilting Music.
Strauss, R., composer and librettist (1905), *Salome*. London: Boosey & Hawkes.
      Based on Hedwig Lachmann's German translation of the French play *Salomé*
      by Oscar Wilde.
Strauss, R., composer, and C. Krauss, librettist (with the composer, after Stefan
      Zweig and Joseph Gregor) (1943), *Capriccio*. London: Boosey & Hawkes.
Stravinsky, I., composer (1927, rev. 1948), *Oedipus Rex*, with a Latin libretto
      translated by Abbé Jean Daniélou from Jean Cocteau's French adaptation of
      Sophocles' Greek tragedy. London: Boosey & Hawkes.
Stravinsky, I., composer (1951), *The Rake's Progress*, libretto by W. H. Auden
      and Chester Kallman, based on the eight paintings and engravings *A Rake's
      Progress* (1733–1735) by William Hogarth. London: Boosey & Hawkes.
Tiomkin, D., composer, and N. Washington, librettist (1952), "The Ballad of *High
      Noon*." New York: Leo Feist.
Troubadours (Davenson), (1967), *Les Troubadours*, H. Davenson (ed.). Paris:
      Éditions du Seuil.
Troubadours (van der Werf, H.) (1984), *The Extant Troubadour Melodies:
      Transcriptions and Essays for Performers and Scholars*. Rochester, NY: van
      der Werf.
Troubadours and Trouvères (Collins et al.), (1982), *A Medieval Songbook:
      Troubadour and Trouvère*, F. Collins Jr., R. F. Cook, and R. Harmon, (eds.).
      Charlottesville: University of Virginia Press.
Twain, M., (1884, United Kingdom; 1885, United States), *Huckleberry Finn*,
      Critical edition, Thomas Cooley (ed.) (1998). New York: W. W. Norton.
van Breen, E., composer, and K. Ligtelijn and M. Okrand, librettists
      (2010), "*u*," a Klingon opera. The quotation marks around "*u*"
      indicate that the pronunciation begins and ends with a glottal stop.
      An article about this opera may be found at: <http://en.wikipedia.org/
      wiki/%E2%80%99u%E2%80%99>.
van der Werf, H. (1984), *The Extant Troubadour Melodies: Transcriptions and
      Essays for Performers and Scholars*. New York: Rochester.
Verdi, G., composer, and F. Romani, librettist (1840), *Un giorno di regno, od
      Il finto Stanislao* (*A Day in the Reign, or The False Stanislas*), F. Izzo (ed.)
      (expected 2016). Chicago: University of Chicago Press. Felice Romani's
      libretto, based on a French play, *Le faux Stanislas*, by Alexandre Vincent
      Pineu-Duval, had been previously set to music in 1818 by Adalbert Gyrowetz,
      and may have been modified for Verdi's use by Temistocle Solera.

Verdi, G., composer, and Temistocle Solera, librettist (1842), *Nabucco (Nabucodonosor; Nabuchadnezzar)*, R. Parker (ed.) (1988). Chicago: University of Chicago Press.

Verdi, G., composer, and F. M. Piave, librettist (1844), *Ernani*, C. Gallico (ed.) (1985). Milan: Ricordi (Ricordi 133716).

Verdi, G., composer, and Temistocle Solera, librettist (1847), *I Lombardi alla prima crociata (The Lombards on the First Crusade)*. Based on the poem of the same name by Tommaso Grossi. The critical edition is not yet available. The only currently available edition seems to be a Kalmus orchestral score (no date).

Verdi, G., composer, and S. Cammarano, librettist (1849), *Luisa Miller*, J. Kallberg (ed.) (1991). Milan: Ricordi (Ricordi 134605). After the play *Kabale und Liebe (Intrigue and Love)* (1784) by Friedrich von Schiller.

Verdi, G., composer, and F. M. Piave, librettist (1851), *Rigoletto*, M. Chusid (ed.) (1983). Milan: Ricordi (Ricordi 133359).

Verdi, G., composer, and S. Cammarano, librettist (1853), *Il trovatore*, D. Lawton (ed.) (1992). Milan: Ricordi (Ricordi 136183).

Verdi, G., composer, and F. M. Piave, librettist (1853), *La traviata*, F. D. Seta (ed.) (1996). Milan: Ricordi (Ricordi 137341). After the play *La dame aux camélias* by Alexandre Dumas *fils*.

Verdi, G., composer, and A. Somma, librettist (1859), *Un ballo in maschera (A Masked Ball)*, Narici, I. (ed.) (n.d.). Milan: Ricordi (only available as a rental). After the libretto *Gustave III, ou Le bal masqué*, by Eugène Scribe.

Verdi, G., composer, and A. Boito, librettist (1887), *Otello*. Critical edition not yet available.

Wagner, R., composer and librettist (1869), *Das Rheingold (The Rhinegold)*, the "Preliminary Evening" of *Der Ring des Nibelungen (The Ring of the Nibelung)* (1876). New York: Dover, 1985. This is a reprint of the 1873 edition of the full score originally published by B. Schott's Söhne, Mainz. In the passages quoted, the German spelling has been modernized.

Wagner, R., composer and librettist (1869), *Die Walküre (The Valkyrie)*, the "First Day" of *Der Ring des Nibelungen (The Ring of the Nibelung)* (1876). New York: Dover, 1978. This is a reprint of the 1910 edition of the full score originally published by C. F. Peters, Leipzig, Mainz. In the passages quoted, the German spelling has been modernized.

Wagner, R., composer and librettist (1876), *Siegfried*, the "Second Day" of *Der Ring des Nibelungen (The Ring of the Nibelung)* (1876). New York: Dover, 1983. This is a reprint of the 1876 edition of the full score originally published by B. Schott's Söhne, Mainz. In the passages quoted, the German spelling has been modernized.

Wagner, R., composer and librettist (1876), *Götterdämmerung (Twilight of the Gods)*, the "Third Day" of *Der Ring des Nibelungen (The Ring of the Nibelung)* (1876). New York: Dover, 1982. This is a reprint of the 1877 edition of the full score originally published by B. Schott's Söhne, Mainz. In the passages quoted, the German spelling has been modernized.

Wallace, S., composer, and M. Korie, librettist (1994), *Harvey Milk*. New York: Sidmar Music (administered by Schott Music Corporation, New York), material availabe for rent only, not for sale.

Weber, C. M. v., composer, and F. C. Hiemer, librettist (1811), *Abu Hassan*, critical edition piano-vocal score, J. Veit (ed.) (2003). Mainz: Schott.

Weber, C. M. v., composer, and J. G. Kind, librettist (1821), *Der Freischütz*. New York: Dover (1977).

Weill, K., composer, and B. Brecht, lyricist and playwright (with significant contributions by Elisabeth Hauptmann) (1928), *Die Dreigroschenoper* (*The Threepenny Opera*), based on Elisabeth Hauptmann's German Translation of John Gay's *The Beggar's Opera* (1728). Critical Edition Piano-Vocal Score (EA 4002 PV) by Edward Harsh, based on the critical edition of the orchestral score (Kurt Weill Edition, Series I, Volume 5), Stephen Hinton and Edward Harsh (eds.). Miami, FL: European American Music Corporation, Copyright 2000. A website, <http://www.threepennyopera.org>, includes much information about translations and productions, including reviews and comments by Lotte Lenya (1898–1981), Kurt Weill's widow who was in the original off-Broadway cast as Jenny, and Bertolt Brecht himself. The website was viewed during September 2014. The complete text of *Die Dreigroschenoper* may be found in Bertolt Brecht's *Dreigroschenbuch*. Frankfurt am Main: Suhrkamp Verlag, 1960.

Wharton, E. (1920), *The Age of Innocence*, Stephen Orgel (ed.) (2006). Oxford: Oxford University Press.

Wilder, B., director and producer (1959), *Some Like It Hot*, screenplay by Wilder and I. A. L. Diamond, produced by the Mirisch Company, distributed by United Artists.

Wolf, G. and R. Rosenstein, eds. and trans. (1983), *The Poetry of Cercamon and Jaufre Rudel*. New York and London: Garland.

2. Translations and adaptations

Anderson, M. (2005), "The Saami Yoik: Translating Hum, Chant, or/and Song," in Gorlée (2005a) *Song and Significance: Virtues and Vices of Vocal Translation*, 213–33.

Anonymous, trans. (1982), The English National Opera, Puccini's *La bohème*. London: John Calder.

Anonymous, trans. (no date), Weber's *Der Freischütz*. New York: Fred Rullman.

Apter, R., trans. (1999), *A Bilingual Edition of the Love songs of Bernart de Ventadorn in Occitan and English: Sugar and Salt*. Lewiston, NY: The Edwin Mellen Press. This book includes the original lyrics, translations, commentary, and an article discussing the milieu in which Bernart composed his songs.

Armour, M., trans. (1911), Wagner's *The Ring of the Niblung [sic]*. New York: Garden City.

Auden, W. H., and C. Kallman, trans. (1955), Mozart's *The Magic Flute*. New York: Random House.

Belov, A., trans. (2004), *Libretti of Russian Operas, Vol. 1: Operas Based on the Poetry and Prose of Alexander Pushkin*, with International Phonetic Alphabet Transcriptions and Word-for-Word and Sentence-for Sentence Translations. Geneseo, NY: Leyerle.

Bentley, E., translator of the lyrics, D. Vesey, trans. of the book (1949), Brecht and Weill's *Die Dreigroschenoper*. New York: Grove Press (published 1964).

Bergman, I., dir. (1975), Mozart's *Die Zauberflöte (Trollflöjten; The Magic Flute)*. Performed in Swedish translation, subtitled with an uncredited English verse translation. Originally shown on Swedish television, later released to movie theaters.

Bernofsky, S., trans. (2004), "Über die verschiedenen Methoden des Übersetzens" ("On the Different Methods of Translating") (1813) by Friedrich Schleiermacher. In Venuti (2004), *The Translation Studies Reader*, 2nd Edition. London and New York: Routledge, 43–63.

Biern, B., adapter (2013), Mozart's *The Abduction from the Seraglio*. Information available at: <http://www.baribiern.com/>, accessed September 13, 1914.

Blitzstein, M., trans. (1954), Original Cast Recording of *The Threepenny Opera* (Brecht and Weill's *Die Dreigroschenoper*), MGM Records E3121 (monoaural) and MGM Records SE3121 (stereo). Some of Blitzstein's translation was published in Vocal Selections from *The Threepenny Opera*, New York: Warner Bros, 1984.

Bloch, J., trans. (1957), Mozart's *The Abduction from the Seraglio*. New York: G. Schirmer (published 1962).

Bowles, D. (2014), "Translating 'An Otomi Song of Spring' from the Nahuatl Codex *Songs of Mexico*," *Translation Review*, 88: 37–44.

Branagh, K., dir. and S. Fry, trans. (2006), Mozart's *Die Zauberflöte* (*The Magic Flute*), West Hollywood, CA: Revolver Entertainment (DVD Released 2012).

Brewster, J. J., trans. (1991), *Carmina Burana*, available at: <http://www.providencesingers.org/Concerts06/Season10–11/Apr11Carmina1.php>, accessed September 2014.

Byron, H. J., trans. (no date), Lecocq's *La fille de Madame Angot*. London: Boosey.

Castel, N., trans. (ongoing series), Many Operas, Libretti with International Phonetic Alphabet Transcriptions and Word-for-Word and Sentence-for Sentence Translations. Geneseo, NY: Leyerle.

Cheek, T. (2010), The Bartered Bride / Prodaná nevěsta: *Performance Guide with Translations and Pronunciation*. Lanham, MD: The Scarecrow Press.

Cochran, G. and J. Krimsky, trans. (1933), Brecht and Weill's *Die Dreigroschenoper*, in Stage works of Kurt Weill: librettos and other text-related materials in the Weill-Lenya Research Center. Information available at: <http://www.kwf.org/introduction>, accessed September 2014. The text of this translation has been lost.

Cross, J. and E. Crozier, trans. (1945, revised 1978), Smetana's *The Bartered Bride*. London: Boosey & Hawkes. This is an English-only piano-vocal score.

Csonka, P. and A. Theslöf, trans. (1968), Smetana's *The Bartered Bride*. n.p.: Kalmus. German-English piano-vocal score. This piano-vocal score is a reprint of the 1936 Peters edition of Max Kalbeck's loose German adaptation of 1893, *Die verkaufte Braut*. To Kalbeck's German has been added Csonka and Theslöf's performable English translation of Kalbeck's adaptation, not of Smetana's opera. Missing from this edition are the names of the translators, the text of the actual opera (i.e., the Czech text), and an English translation of the actual opera.

Dean, A., trans. and adaptor (1935), *The Frantic Physician, or Three Drams of Matrimonium* (adaptation of Gounod's *Le médecin malgré lui*). New York: Silver, Burdett.

Dent., E. J., trans. (1952), Mozart's *The Abduction from the Seraglio*. London: Oxford University Press.

Farquhar, M., trans. (1956), Smetana's *The Bartered Bride*. New York: Schirmer. This is an English-only piano-vocal score. Farquhar's translation is mostly of Max Kalbeck's 1893 German adaptation rather than of Smetana's opera.

Feingold, M., trans. (1989), *Die Dreigroschenoper*. Included in the critical edition of 2000 (see Weill and Brecht (1928).

Fielding, H. (1732), *The Mock Doctor; or, the Dumb Lady Cur'd*. Critical edition by Marti J. Brewerton. Grand Forks: University of North Dakota Press (published 1971)

Fry, S., trans. and K. Branagh, dir. (2006), Mozart's *Die Zauberflöte* (*The Magic Flute*), West Hollywood, CA: Revolver Entertainment (DVD Released 2012).

Glowacki, J. M., trans. and adapter (1930), Smetana's *The Bartered Bride*. Boston, MA: Tracy Music.

Guerriero, V., trans. and adapter (2013), Mozart's *The Marriage of Figaro*. A review by James Jorden may be found at <http://nypost.com/2013/06/13/morningside-operas-updating-of-mozarts-figaro-is-as-timely-as-it-is-sexy/>, accessed September 2014.

Harrison, T., trans. and adapter (1978), Smetana's *The Bartered Bride*. New York and London: G. Schirmer. This is an English-only libretto.

Herman, M. and R. Apter, trans. (1977, revised 2013), *Carmina Burana*. Nashville: Herman and Apter.

Herman, M. and R. Apter, trans. (1979a), Mozart's *Die Entführung aus dem Serail*. Nashville: Herman and Apter.

Herman, M. and R. Apter, trans. (1979b), Gounod's *Le médecin malgré lui*. Nashville: Herman and Apter.

Herman, M. and R. Apter, trans. (1980), Weber's *Abu Hassan*. Nashville: Herman and Apter.

Herman, M. and R. Apter, trans. (1981), Verdi's *La traviata*. Nashville: Herman and Apter.

Herman, M. and R. Apter, trans. (1982a), Boieldieu's *Ma tante Aurore*. Nashville: Herman and Apter.

Herman, M. and R. Apter, trans. (1982b, revised 2015), Mozart's *Die Zauberflöte*. Nashville: Herman and Apter.

Herman, M. and R. Apter, trans. (1983a), Verdi's *Un giorno di regno*. Nashville: Herman and Apter.

Herman, M. and R. Apter, trans. (1983b), Wagner's *Das Rheingold*. Nashville: Herman and Apter.

Herman, M. and R. Apter, trans. (1984), Smetana's *Dvě vdovy*. Nashville: Herman and Apter.

Herman, M. and R. Apter, trans. (1986), Weber's *Der Freischütz*. Nashville: Herman and Apter.

Herman, M. and R. Apter, trans. (1989), Lecocq's *La fille de Madame Angot*. Nashville: Herman and Apter.

Herman, M. and R. Apter, trans. (1992b), Scarlatti's *Eraclea*. Nashville: Herman and Apter.

Herman, M. and R. Apter, trans. (1993), Ferrero's *La figlia del mago*. Milano: Ricordi.

Herman, M. and R. Apter, trans. (1994), Verdi's *Ernani*. Chicago: University of Chicago Press and Milano: Ricordi.

Herman, M. and R. Apter, trans. (1997), Donizetti's *Maria Stuarda* (Mary Stuart). Milano: Ricordi.

Herman, M. and R. Apter, trans. (2002), Verdi's *Il trovatore*. Chicago: University of Chicago Press and Milano: Ricordi.

Herman, M. and R. Apter, trans. (2003), Smetana's *Prodaná nevěsta*. Nashville: Herman and Apter.

Herman, M. and R. Apter, trans. (2004), Verdi's *Luisa Miller*. Chicago: University of Chicago Press and Milano: Ricordi.

Herman, M. and R. Apter, trans. (2007), Rossini's *L'occasione fa il ladro* (A Thief by Chance). Milano: Ricordi.

Herman, M. and R. Apter, trans. (2009), Rachmaninoff's *Six Choral Songs for Treble Voices and Piano*. San Diego: Musica Russica.

Herman, M. and R. Apter, trans. (in press), Puccini's *La bohème*. Milano: Ricordi.

Hofstadter, D. R. (1997), translator of Marot's "Ma mignonne," in *Le Ton beau de Marot: In Praise of the Music of Language*. New York: Basic Books.

Holden, A., trans. (1998), Donizetti's *Maria Stuarda* (*Mary Stuart*), personal communication from Amanda Holden.

Holden, A., trans. (1999, revised 2009), Mozart's *The Abduction from the Seraglio*, personal communication from Amanda Holden.

Holden, A., trans. (2006), Smetana's *The Bartered Bride*, personal communication from Amanda Holden.

Holden, A., trans. (2007), Mozart's *The Magic Flute*, personal communication from Amanda Holden.

Holden, A., trans. (2009), Puccini's *La bohème*, personal communication from Amanda Holden.

Jameson, F., trans. (1896), Wagner's *Das Rheingold*. London: Schott. Page numbers are to the Kalmus reprint (New York: Edwin F. Kalmus [no date]).

Kalbeck, M., adapter (1893), Smetana's *Prodaná nevěsta (Die verkaufte Braut)*. Leipzig: C. F. Peters (published 1936). Kalbeck's German adaptation is included in the Kalmus edition listed above for "Csonka and Theslöf."

Kenney, C. L., trans. (no date), Gounod's *Le médecin malgré lui* (*The Mock Doctor*), Arthur Sullivan and J. Pittman (eds.). London: Boosey.

Klein, A. S., trans. (2008), *Convivio* (*The Banquet*) (1304–7) by Dante Alighieri, original Italian and English translation freely available at: <http://www.poetryintranslation.com/PITBR/Italian/ConvivioII.htm>, accessed July 20, 2015.

Machlis, J., trans. (1956, published 1958), Puccini's *La bohème*. New York: W. W. Norton.

Machlis, J., trans. (1962), Verdi's *La traviata*. Milan: Ricordi (Ricordi 133060).

Macfarren, N., trans. (n.d.), Mozart's *The Magic Flute*. New York: Edwin F. Kalmus (reprinted in 1967).

Macfarren, N., trans. (1898), Verdi's *La traviata*. New York: G. Schirmer, online at: <https://archive.org/stream/latraviataoperai00verd#page/142/mode/2up>, accessed June 28, 2014.

Macfarren, N., trans. (1898), Verdi's *Il trovatore*. New York: G. Schirmer.

Macfarren, N. and T. Baker, trans. (1904), Weber's *Der Freischütz*. New York: G. Schirmer, later reprinted by Edwin F. Kalmus. This edition omits an entire dialogue scene: Act III, Scene 1.

Manheim, R. and J. Willett, trans. (1976), Brecht and Weill's *Die Dreigroschenoper*. New York: Arcade Publishing (published 1994).

Manheim, R. and J. Willett, trans. "Jealousy Duet" from Brecht and Weill's *Die Dreigroschenoper*, available at: <https://www.youtube.com/watch?v=pxFS42xzFBY>, posted October 20, 2011, accessed September 2014.

Mann, W., trans. (1964), Wagner's *Ring*, Vol. 1, *Das Rheingold* and *Die Walküre*. London: The Friends of Covent Garden.

Martin, R. and T. Martin, trans. (1941, revised 1951), Mozart's *The Magic Flute*. New York: G. Schirmer.

Martin, R. and T. Martin, trans. (1944, revised 1962), Mozart's *The Abduction from the Seraglio*. London: Boosey & Hawkes.

Martin, R. and T. Martin, trans. (1946, revised 1961), Verdi's *La traviata*. New York: G. Schirmer.

Martin, R. and T. Martin, trans. (1954), Puccini's *La bohème*. New York: G. Schirmer.

McClatchy, J. D., trans. (2011), *Seven Mozart Librettos: A Verse Translation*. New York: W. W. Norton. These are non-singable verse translations.

McClatchy, J. D., trans. (2004), Mozart's *The Magic Flute*. Directed by Julie Taymor. Broadcast on National Public Television in 2007. This is an abridged singable translation.

Newman, F. W., trans. (1856), Homer's *Iliad*, available at: <https://archive.org/details/iliadhomerfaith00newmgoog>, accessed September 2014.

Newmarch, R., trans. (1934), Smetana's *The Bartered Bride*. London: Hawkes and Son. This is an English-only piano-vocal score.

Parlett, D., trans. (1986), *Selections from the* Carmina Burana: *a verse translation*. London: Penguin Classics. Also see <http://richardgard.com/carmina-urana/>, accessed September 2014.

Pippin, D. (ongoing), *The Donald Pippin Collection*, available at: <http://library.stanford.edu/collections/donald-pippin-collection>, accessed September 2014.

Pippin, D., trans. and adapter (2003), Smetana's *The Bartered Bride*, performed at the Pocket Opera. In D. Pippin (ongoing), *The Donald Pippin Collection*.

Pippin, D., trans. and adapter (2013), Mozart's *The Abduction from the Seraglio*, performed at the Pocket Opera. In D. Pippin (ongoing), *The Donald Pippin Collection*.

Porter, A., trans. (1976), Wagner's *The Ring of the Nibelung*. New York: W. W. Norton.

Porter, A., trans. (1980), Mozart's *The Magic Flute*. London: Faber Music; New York: G. Schirmer.

Porter, A., trans. (1986), Mozart's *The Abduction from the Seraglio*. St. Louis: Opera Theatre of Saint Louis Guild. Sung lyrics only, the spoken English dialogue in this edition is by Elkhanah Pulitzer and dates from 2003.

Pulitzer, E., trans. (2003), Mozart's *The Abduction from the Seraglio*. St. Louis: Opera Theatre of Saint Louis Guild. Spoken dialogue only, the sung English lyrics in this edition are by Andrew Porter and date from 1986.

Robb, S., trans. (1960), Wagner's *Der Ring des Nibelungen*. New York: E. P. Dutton.

Robinson, D., trans. (1997), "Über die verschiedenen Methoden des Übersetzens" ("On the Different Methods of Translating") (1813) by Friedrich Schleiermacher. In D. Robinson (ed.) (1997), *Western Translation Theory from Herodotus to Nietzsche*, Manchester, UK: St. Jerome, 225–38.

Sams, J., trans. (1987), Mozart's *The Magic Flute*. Santa Fe, New Mexico: The Santa Fe Opera.

Sams, J., trans. (1994), Brecht and Weill's *Die Dreigroschenoper*, CD recording. Canada: Jay (published in 1997).

Sams, J., trans. (2002), Wagner's *The Rheingold*, no publisher listed.

Sellars, P., dir. (1989), Mozart's *The Marriage of Figaro*, DVD New York: London Records (published 1992).

Sellars, P., dir. (1989), Mozart's *Don Giovanni*, DVD. London: Decca (published 2005).

Sellars, P., dir. (1989), Mozart's *Così fan tutte*, DVD London: Decca (published 1991).

Siegel, M. and W. Lyman, trans. (1956), Mozart's *The Abduction from the Seraglio*. New York: International Music Company.

Smythe, B., trans. (1911), *Trobador Poets: Selections from the Poems of Eight Trobadors*, translated from the Provençal with introduction and notes by Barbara Smythe. London: Chatto and Windus. Reprinted (1966), New York: Cooper Square. Republished (2000), Cambridge, Ontario, as .html and .pdf, In Parenthesis Publications, Old Occitan Series. Available online at: <http://www.yorku.ca/inpar/trobador_smythe.pdf>.

Spencer, D. adapter and lyricist (1984, revised 2002), *La bohème*: New English Adaptation and Lyrics. For further information, contact the author's agent, Patricia McLaughlin c/o Beacon Artists Agency / 1501 Broadway, Suite #1200 / New York, NY 10036; (212) 736–6630, <beaconagency@hotmail.com>.

Stokes, R., ed. (2000), *J. S. Bach, The Complete Cantatas in German-English Translation*. Lenham: Long Barn Books/Scarecrow Press.

Symonds, J. A., trans. from *Carmina Burana* (1884), *Wine, Women and Song: Students' Songs of the Middle Ages*. London: Chatto & Windus; reprint edition, Mineola, NY: Dover (2002).

Weaver, W., trans. (1963, reprinted 1977), *Seven Verdi Librettos*. New York: W. W. Norton.

Whicher, G. F., trans. (1949), *The Goliard Poets: Medieval Latin Songs and Satires*. New York: New Directions.

Wilhelm, J. J., ed. and trans. (1971), *Medieval Song: An Anthology of Hymns and Lyrics*. New York: E. P. Dutton.

Zeydel, E. H., ed. and trans. from *Carmina Burana* (1966), *Vagabond Verse: Secular Latin Poems of the Middle Ages*. Detroit: Wayne State University Press.

Zukofsky, C. and L. Zukofsky, trans. (1969), *Catullus*, Cape Golliard Press, in association with Grossman Publishers.

3. Other

Addison, J. (1711), *The Spectator*, no. 18, March 21.

Adler, K. (1965), *Phonetics and Diction in Singing*. Minneapolis: University of Minnesota Press.

Alfaro, M. J. M. (June–December 1996), "Intertextuality: Origins and Development of the Concept," *Atlantis* 18.1/2: 268–85.

Anonymous, (1986), Introduction to Andrew Porter's translation of Mozart's *The Abduction from the Seraglio*. In Porter, A. (1986), Mozart's *The Abduction from the Seraglio*. St. Louis: Opera Theatre of Saint Louis Guild. Sung lyrics only, the spoken English dialogue in this edition is by Elkhanah Pulitzer and dates from 2003.

Apter, R. (1982), "Romanticism and Revolution in Mozart's *The Abduction from the Seraglio*," *The Opera Journal*, XV.3: 15–24.

Apter, R. (1984), *Digging for the Treasure: Translation After Pound*. New
    York: Berne, Frankfurt am Main: Peter Lang Publishing; reprint ed.
    (1987), New York: Paragon House Publishers. References are to the
    reprint edition.
Apter, R. (1999), *A Bilingual Edition of the Love songs of Bernart de Ventadorn in
    Occitan and English: Sugar and Salt*. Lewiston, NY: The Edwin Mellen Press.
    This book includes the original lyrics, translations, commentary, and an article
    discussing the milieu in which Bernart composed his songs.
Apter, R. and M. Herman (1995), "The Worst Translations: Almost Any Opera in
    English," *Translation Review*, 48/49: 26–32.
Arnold, M. (1860–61), *On Translating Homer*, in *The Complete Prose Works*, R.
    H. Super (ed.), 11 vols., Ann Arbor: University of Michigan Press (1960–77).
    Part of *On Translating Homer* may also be found in Robinson (1997: 250–55).
Ashbrook, W. (1992), "*Maria Stuarda*," in Sadie (1992), III: 213–14.
Bartoš, F. (1953), Předmluva (Foreward) to the Critical Orchestral Score of
    The Bartered Bride. Prague: Museum Bedřicha Smetany (Bedřich Smetana
    Museum); and Státní nakladatelství krásné literatury, hudby a umění (State
    Publishing House for Literature, Music, and Art).
Benjamin, W. (1923), "*Die Aufgabe des Übersetzers*" ("The Task of the Translator"),
    English translation by Harry Zohn (1968: 15–23) reprinted in Venuti (2000b)
    together with "A note on Harry Zohn's translation" by Steven Rendall, 23–25.
Billiani, F. (2011), "Censorship," in *The Routledge Encyclopedia of Translation
    Studies*, 2nd edition, M. Baker and G. Saldanha (eds.). New York: Routledge,
    28–31.
Bosseaux, C. (2008), "Buffy the Vampire Slayer: Characterization in the Musical
    Episode of the TV Series," in Susam-Sarajeva (2008), 343–72.
Bosseaux, C. (2011), "The Translation of Song," in K. Malmkjær and K. Windle
    (2011) *The Oxford Handbook of Translation Studies*. Oxford: Oxford University
    Press, 183–97.
Bosseaux, C. (2013), "Some Like It Dubbed: Translating Marilyn Monroe," in
    Minors (2013), 81–92.
Brisset, A. (1996), "The Search for a Native Language: Translation and Cultural
    Identiy." Chapter 4 in *A Sociocritique of Translation: Theatre and Alterity in
    Quebec, 1968–1988*, by Annie Brisset, translated into English by Rosalind Gill
    and Roger Gannon. Toronto: University of Toronto Press, 162–94. Reprinted
    in Venuti (2000b): 343–75.
Brower, R. A. ed. (1959), *On Translation*. New York: Oxford University Press.
Brown, F. (1968), *An Impersonation of Angels: A Biography of Jean Cocteau*.
    New York: Viking Press.
Brown-Montesano, K. (2007), *Understanding the Women of Mozart's Operas*.
    Berkeley: University of California Press.
Burrows, D. (1990), *Sound, Speech, and Music*. Amherst: The University of
    Massachusetts Press.
Chalmers, K. (2013), "Assistance or Obstruction: Translated Text in Opera
    Performances," in Minors (2013), 49–57.
Chapman, R. L., ed. (1986), *New Dictionary of American Slang*. New York:
    Harper & Row.
Chozick, A. (2011), *The New York Times*. December 12.
Churnside, C. (2014), "Text-Music Relations in the Early Settecento: The Case of
    Il trionfo della carità," *Ars Lyrica* 21 (2012, actually published 2014): 41–69.

Clément, C. (1979), *L'Opéra ou la Défaite des femmes*. Paris: Éditions Grasset & Fasquelle. Published in an English translation by Betsy Wing as *Opera, or the Undoing of Women* (1988), Minneapolis: University of Minnesota Press. Page numbers refer to the 1989 British edition published in London by Virago Press, Ltd.

Clinkscale, M. N. (1992), *"Erismena,"* in Sadie (1992), II: 63–64.

Clüver, C. (2008), "The Translation of Opera as a Multimedia Text," in Susam-Sarajeva (2008), 401–9.

Corse, S. (1987), *Opera and the Uses of Language: Mozart, Verdi, and Britten*. Cranbury, NJ; London; and Mississauga, Ontario: Associated University Presses.

Cowan, I. B. (1971), *The Enigma of Mary Stuart*. New York: St. Martin's Press.

Deane-Cox, S. (2014), *Retranslation: Translation, Literature and Reinterpretation*. London: Bloomsbury.

de Landes, L. (1861), *Glossaire érotique de la langue française depuis son origine jusqu'a nos jours*, Brussels.

Denomy, A. J. (1947), *The Heresy of Courtly Love*, Boston College Candlemas Lectures on Christian Literature. New York: McMullen.

Desblache, L. (2004) "Low Fidelity: Opera in Translation, II," *Translating Today*, available online at: <http://www.translatingtoday.com/low-fidelity-opera-in-translation/>.

Desblache, L. (2007), "Music to My Ears, But Words to My Eyes? Text, Opera and Their Audiences," in A. Remael and J. Neves (eds.), *A Tool for Social Integration? Audiovisual Translation from Different Angles, Linguistica Antwerpiensi*. New Series, 6. Antwerp: Artesis University College 155–70.

Desblache, L. (2008), "The Turn of the Text? Opera Libretto and Translation: Appropriation, Adaptation and Transcoding in Benjamin Britten's *The Turn of the Screw* and *Owen Wingrave*," *Quaderns de Filologia. Estudis literaris. Traducció Creativa*, 13, 105–124.

Desblache, L. (2009), "Challenges and Rewards of Libretto Adaptation," in J. Díaz-Cintas et al. (eds.) (2009), *Audiovisual Translation: Language Transfer on Screen*. Basingstoke: Palgrave Macmillan, 71–82.

Desblache, L. (2013), "Tales of the Unexpected: Opera as a New Art of Glocalization," in Minors (2013), 9–19.

DiDonato, J. (July/August 2014), quoted in *Opera Now*, p. 5.

Dryden, J. (1680), Preface to *Ovid's Epistles*, in Hooker and Swedenberg (1956–74).

Dryden, J. (1685), Preface to *Sylvae*, in Hooker and Swedenberg (1956–74).

Elzeer, N. (2010), "Language-Based Humour and the Untranslatable: The Case of Ziad Rahbani's Theatre," in *Translation, Humour and Literature*, Delia Chiaro (ed.). London: Bloomsbury, 196–208.

Engel, L. (1972), *Words with Music: The Broadway Musical Libretto*. New York: Schirmer Books Division of Macmillan.

Ferrari-Fontana, E., *Musical America*, February 7, 1914.

Forssell, Jonas composer and librettist (2008), *Death and the Maiden*, an opera based on a play by Ariel Dorfman.

Folkart, B. (2007), *Second Finding: A Poetics of Translation*. Ottawa: University of Ottawa Press.

Frame, D. (1989), "Pleasures and Problems of Translation," in *The Craft of Translation*, John Biguenet and Rainer Schulte (eds.). Chicago: The University of Chicago Press.

Franzon, J. (2005), "Musical Comedy Translation: Fidelity and Format in the Scandinavian *My Fair Lady,*" in Gorlée (2005a), 263–97.

Franzon, J., Mateo M., Orero, P., and Susam-Sarajeva, Ş. (2008), "Translation and Music: A General Bibliography," in Susam-Sarajeva (2008), 453–60.

Fraser, A. (1969), *Mary Queen of Scots*. New York: Dell.

Gass, W. H. (1999), *Reading Rilke: Reflections on the Problems of Translation*. New York: Basic Books.

Gennrich, F., ed. (1958), *Der musikalische Nachlass der Troubadours, Summae Musicae Medii Aevi*. Darmstadt: no publisher.

Goldin, F. (1967), *The Mirror of Narcissus in the Courtly Love Lyric*. Ithaca, NY: Cornell University Press.

Goldin, F. (1975), "The Array of Perspectives in the Early Courtly Love Lyric," in *In Pursuit of Perfection: Courtly Love in Medieval Literature*, Joan M. Ferrante and George Economou (eds.). Port Washington, NY: Kennikat, 51–100.

Golomb, H. (2005), "Music-Linked Translation [MLT] and Mozart's Operas: Theoretical, Textual, and Practical Perspectives," in Gorlée (2005a), 121–61.

Gorlée, D. L. (1994), *Semiotics and the Problem of Translation: With Special Reference to the Semiotics of Charles S. Peirce* (Approaches to Translation Studies 12). Amsterdam and Atlanta, GA: Rodopi.

Gorlée, D. L. (1996), "Opera Translation: Charles Peirce: Translating Richard Wagner," in *Musical Semiotics in Growth* (Acta Semiotica Fennica 4) E. Tarasti (ed.). Bloomington, IN and Imatra: International Semiotics Institute, 407–25.

Gorlée, D. L. (1997a), "Intercode Translation: Words and Music in Opera," *Target* 9.2: 235–70.

Gorlée, D. L. (1997b), "Bridging the Gap: A Semiotician's View on Translating the Greek Classics," *Perspectives: Studies in Translatology* 5.2: 153–69.

Gorlée, D. L. (2002), "Grieg's Swan Songs," *Semiotica* 142.1/4: 142–210.

Gorlée, D. L. (2004a), *On Translating Signs: Exploring Text and Semio-Translation* (Approaches to Translation Studies 24). Amsterdam and New York: Rodopi.

Gorlée, D. L. (2004b), "Horticultural Roots of Translational Semiosis," in *Macht der Zeichen, Zeichen der Macht (Signs of Power, Power of Signs)* (TRANS-Studien zur Veränderung der Welt 3), G. Withalm and J. Wallmannsberger (eds.). Vienna: INST Verlag, 164–87.

Gorlée, D. L. (ed.) (2005a), *Song and Significance: Virtues and Vices of Vocal Translation*. Amsterdam and New York: Rodopi.

Gorlée, D. L. (2005b), "Prelude and Acknowledgements," in Gorlée (2005a), 7–15.

Gorlée, D. L. (2005c), "Singing on the Breath of God: Preface to Life and Growth of Translated Hymnody," in Gorlée (2005a), 17–101.

Gossett, P. (2006), *Divas and Scholars: Performing Italian Opera*. Chicago: The University of Chicago Press.

Gottlieb, R. and R. Kimball (eds.) (2000), *Reading Lyrics*. New York: Random House.

Graham, A. (1989), "A New Look at Recital Song Translation," *Translation Review* 29: 31–36.

Graham, C. (1986), Quoted in the Introduction to Andrew Porter's translation of Mozart's *The Abduction from the Seraglio*, in Porter, A. (1986).

Green, M., ed. and annotator (1961), *Martyn Green's Treasury of Gilbert & Sullivan*. New York: Simon and Schuster.

Groos, A. and Parker, R. eds. (1988), *Reading Opera*. Princeton, NJ: Princeton University Press.

Grout, D. J. with H. W. Williams (1988), *A Short History of Opera*. 3rd edition. New York: Columbia University Press.

Hall, R. A. Jr. (1964), *Introductory Linguistics*. Philadelphia: Chilton.

Hammerstein II, O., librettist (1945), Introduction to *Carmen Jones* (1943). New York: Alfred A. Knopf.

Herman, M. and Apter, R. (1992a), "Words and Music: A Theatrical Partnership," *The Opera Journal* 25.4: 3–24.

Herman, M. and Apter, R. (2012), "Translating Art Songs for Performance: Rachmaninoff's *Six Choral Songs*," *Translation Review* 84 (2012): 27–42.

Hilson, J. (2013), "Homophonic Translation: Sense and Sound," in Minors (2013), 95–105.

Hoch, M. (2014), *A Dictionary for the Modern Singer*. Lanham, MD: Rowman & Littlefield.

Hofstadter, D. R. (1997), *Le Ton beau de Marot: In Praise of the Music of Language*. New York: Basic Books.

Holt, Tom (1987), *Expecting Someone Taller*. London: Macmillan and New York: St. Martin's Press. E-book version, 2012, New York: Orbit.

Hooker, E. N., and H. T. Swedenberg Jr., eds. (1956–74), *The Works of John Dryden*, 18 vols., Berkeley and Los Angeles: University of California Press.

Jacobs, A. (1992), "Translation," in Sadie (1992), IV: 786–90.

Jakobson, R. (1959), "On Linguistic Aspects of Translation," in Brower (1959), 232–39.

Johnson, S. (1779/81), *Lives of the Most Eminent English Poets*. Information on editions is viewable at <http://en.wikipedia.org/wiki/Lives_of_the_Most_Eminent_English_Poets>, accessed September 2014.

Kaindl, K. (1995), *Die Oper als Textgestalt: Perspektiven einer interdisziplinären Übersetzungswissenschaft*, Studien zur Translation, V. 2, Tübingen: Stauffenburg Verlag Brigitte Narr. Claus Clüver (2008) has written an extensive review of this book in English.

Kaindl, K. (2004), "Die Welt ist schön, Milord: Zum Genre- und Diskurstransfer in der Popularmusik," in *Und sie bewegt sich doch . . . Translationswissenschaft in Ost und West. Festschrift für Heidemarie Salevsky zum 60. Geburtstag*, I. Müller (ed.). Frankfurt: Peter Lang, 177–96.

Kaindl, K. (2005), "The Plurisemiotics of Pop Song Translation: Words, Music, Voice and Image," in Gorlée (2005a), 235–62.

Kerman, J. (1956), *Opera as Drama*. New York: Alfred A. Knopf; (1988), Revised ed., Berkeley and Los Angeles: University of California Press. Page references are to the revised edition.

Kivy, P. (1988), *Osmin's Rage: Philosophical Reflections on Opera, Drama, and Text*. Princeton, NJ: Princeton University Press.

Koestenbaum, W. (1993), *The Queen's Throat: Opera, Homosexuality, and the Mystery of Desire*. Cambridge, MA: Da Capo Press (reprint edition, 2001).

Lamb, A. (1992), "*Les Contes d'Hoffmann*," in Sadie (1992), I: 925.

Landers, C. E. (2001), *Literary Translation: A Practical Guide*, Topics in Translation 22. Clevedon: Multilingual Matters.

Langer, S. K. (1953), *Feeling and Form: A Theory of Art Developed from Philosophy in a New Key*. New York: Charles Scribner's Sons.

Lefevere, A. (1982), "Mother Courage's Cucumbers: Text, System and Refraction in a Theory of Literature," *Modern Language Studies*, 12.4: 3–20; reprinted in Venuti (2000b), 233–49.

Lefevere, A. (1992), *Translating, Rewriting, and the Manipulation of Literary Fame*. New York: Routledge.

Levine, J. (1991), Introduction to the *Metropolitan Opera Book of Mozart Operas*, The Metropolitan Opera Guild. New York: Harper Collins, p. x.

Loos, H. (1992), "Originalsprache oder Übersetzung? Zu einem Problem in der Aufführungsgeschichte der Oper," *Festschrift Hubert Unverricht zum 65. Geburtstag*, Eichstätter Abhandlungen zur Musikwissenschaft 9 ("Original Language or Translation? About a Problem in the Performance History of Opera," *Publication in Honor of Hubert Unverricht's 65th Birthday*, Reference Papers on Musicology). Tutzing: Hans Schneider, 153.

Low, P. (2005), "The Pentathlon Approach to Translating Songs," in Gorlée (2005a), 185–212.

Low, P. (2013), "Purposeful Translating: The Case of Britten's Vocal Music," in Minors (2013), 69–79.

Matamala, A. and P. Orero (2008), "Opera Translation: An Annotated Bibliography," in Susam-Sarajeva (2008), 427–51.

Midgette, A., *The New York Times*, January 16, 2001.

Milton, J. (May 1, 2009), "Between the Cat and the Devil: Adaptation Studies and Translation Studies," *Journal of Adaptation in Film & Performance* 2.1: 47–64.

Minors, H. J., ed. (2013), *Music, Text and Translation*. London: Bloomsbury.

Montgomery, A. (2006), *Opera Coaching: Professional Techniques and Considerations*. New York: Routledge, 169.

Mordden, E. (2012), *Love Song: The Lives of Kurt Weill and Lotte Lenya*. New York: St. Martin's Press.

Morgan, C. (1994), *Don Carlos and Company*, Julia MacRae. New York: Oxford University Press, reprint 1996.

Mossop, B. (2013), "Singing in Unknown Languages: A Small Exercise in Applied Translation Theory," *The Journal of Specialised Translation*, 20 (July 2013): 33–48.

Nabokov, V. (1955), "Problems of Translation: *Onegin* in English," *Partisan Review* 22: 496–512, reprinted in Venuti (2000b): 71–83.

Newmark, P., completed by Minors, H. J. (2013), "Art Song in Translation," in Minors (2013), 59–68.

Newman, F. W. (1861), *Homeric Translation in Theory and Practice*. A major section, "The Unlearned Public Is the Rightful Judge of Taste," is reprinted in Robinson (1997), 255–58.

Nida, E. A. (1964), *Toward a Science of Translating: With Special Reference to Principles and Procedures Involved in Bible Translating*. Leiden: Brill.

Noriega, C. "Something's Missing Here!: Homosexuality and Film Reviews during the Production Code Era, 1934–1962," *Cinema Journal* 30.1 (Autumn 1990): 20–41.

North, M. (2013), "The Making of 'Make It New,' *Guernica*, August 15, available at: <https://www.guernicamag.com/features/the-making-of-making-it-new/>, accessed October 2014.

Okrent, A. (2010), *In the Land of Invented Languages: Adventures in Linguistic Creativity, Madness, and Genius*. New York: Random House.

Opera News (February 1999).

Orr, C. W. (October 1941), "The Problem of Translation," *Music & Letters* 22.4: 323.

Osborne, C. (2004), *The Opera Lover's Companion*. New Haven, CT: Yale University Press.

Osborne, R. (1992), "*L'occasione fa il ladro*," in Sadie (1992), III: 644.

Page, J. (2013), "Surtitling Opera: A Translator's Perspective," in Minors (2013), 35–47.

Palmer, J. (2013), "Surtitling Opera: A Surtitler's Perspective on Making and Breaking the Rules," in Minors (2013), 21–33.

Parker, R. (1992), "*Il trovatore*," in Sadie (1992), IV: 824–27.

Pérez-González, L. (2014), "Multimodality in Translation and Interpreting Studies," in *A Companion to Translation Studies*, S. Bermann and C. Porter (eds.). Chichester: Wiley-Blackwell: 119–31.

Pérez-González, L. (2015), *Audiovisual Translation: Theories, Methods and Issues*. New York: Routledge.

Peyser, H. F. (July 1922), "Some Observations on Translation," *The Musical Quarterly* 8.3: 354.

Pippin, D. (ongoing), *The Donald Pippin Collection*, available at: <http://library.stanford.edu/collections/donald-pippin-collection>, accessed September 2014.

Pippin, D. (1984), Introduction to translation of Weber's *Der Freischütz*. In Pippin, D. (ongoing).

Pippin, D. (1998), "Turning Opera into English," A talk given February 22, 1998 at the Bocce Cafe in San Francisco, site of the Old Spaghetti Factory. In Pippin, D. (ongoing).

Pippin, D. (2002), in "PROFILE / DONALD PIPPIN / Piano man makes opera Pocket-sized / Key milestone on horizon for S.F. company and its founder," in http://www.sfgate.com/performance/article/PROFILE-DONALD-PIPPIN-Piano-man-makes-opera-2848215.php by Joshua Kosman *[San Francisco Chronicle]*, Music Critic, April 22, 2002.

Pippin, D. (2010), in "Pippin of the Pocket," by Janos Gereben, in San Francisco Classical Voice, a website. https://www.sfcv.org/article/pippin-of-the-pocket, dated April 13, 2010, accessed May 22, 2014.

Plowden, A. (1999), *Two Queens in One Isle*, Phoenix Mill, Stroud. Gloucestershire: Sutton Publishing Ltd. First published in 1984 by Harvester Press Ltd.

Pleasants, H. (1989), *Opera in Crisis: Tradition, Present, Future*. New York: Thames & Hudson.

Pound, E. (1935), *Make It New: Essays by Ezra Pound*. New Haven, CT: Yale University Press.

Pound, E. (1968), *Literary Essays of Ezra Pound*, T. S. Eliot (ed.). New York: New Directions.

Preston, K. K. (Autumn 2003), "Between the Cracks: The Performance of English-Language Opera in Late Nineteenth-Century America," *American Music* 21.3: 349–74.

Pym, A. (1998), *Method in Translation History*. Manchester: St Jerome.

Racz, G. J. (2013), "No Anxiety of Influence: Ethics in Poetry Retranslation after Analogical Form," in *Translation Review* 85.

Raffel, B. (1988), *The Art of Translating Poetry*. University Park: The Pennsylvania State University Press.

Raw, L., ed. (2012), *Translation, Adaptation and Transformation*. London: Bloomsbury.

Robinson, D. ed. (1997), *Western Translation Theory from Herodotus to Nietzsche*. Manchester: St. Jerome.

Rodgers, R., composer, and O. Hammerstein II, librettist (1958), Introduction to *The Rodgers and Hammerstein Song Book*. New York: Simon and Schuster and Williamson Music.

Rosand, E. (1991), *Opera in Seventeenth-Century Venice: The Creation of a Genre*. Berkeley: University of California Press.

Rutschman, K. (2013), "Swedish Opera in Translation," *Ars Lyrica* 22 (published 2014): 95–130.

Sadie, S. ed. (1992), *The New Grove Dictionary of Opera*, 4 vols. London: Macmillan; New York: Grove's Dictionaries of Music.

Savory, T. (1968), *The Art of Translation*. Boston, MA: The Writer.

Schleiermacher, F. (1813), "*Über die verschiedenen Methoden des Übersetzens*" ("On the Different Methods of Translating"). Originally a lecture delivered to the Royal Academy of Sciences in Berlin. English translation by Douglas Robinson in Robinson (1997), 225–38. English translation by Susan Bernofsky in Venuti (2004): 43–63.

Schmalfeldt, J. (2012), "Brahms, Again the 'Master of Allusion', with his Godson in Mind," *Ars Lyrica* 21 (2012, actually published 2014): 115–54.

Schön, D. A. (1983), *The Reflective Practitioner: How Professionals Think in Action*. New York: Basic Books.

Scott, R. (1872), "The Jabberwock Traced to Its True Source," *MacMillan's Magazine*, February.

Sellar, W. C., and R. J. Yeatman (1931) *1066 And All That*. New York: E. P. Dutton.

Smith, N. B., and Bergin, T. G. (1984), *An Old Provençal Primer*. New York: Garland.

Smith, P. J. (1970/75), *The Tenth Muse: A Historical Study of the Opera Libretto*; Reprint: New York: Schirmer Books, division of Macmillan.

Spencer, D. (June 1990), "Collaborating With the Dead, or: How I Rewrote *La Bohème*," *Opera Monthly*: 20–25.

Stageberg, N. C. (1965), *An Introductory English Grammar*. New York: Holt, Rinehart and Winston.

Steiner, G. (1975), *After Babel: Aspects of Language and Translation*. New York: Oxford University Press.

Sullivan, J. P. (1964), *Ezra Pound and Sextus Propertius: A Study in Creative Translation*. Austin: University of Texas Press.

Susam-Sarajeva, Ş. ed. (2008), "Translation and Music," Special Issue of *The Translator*, 14.2.

Sutcliffe, T. (Sept/Oct 2010), "Going Native," *Opera Now*: 25.

Taylor, D. (1937), "The Case for Translated Opera," in *The World Treasury of Grand Opera: Its Triumphs, Trials and Great Personalities*, G. R. Mareck (ed.). New York: Harper.

Thomson, V., composer (1982), "On Writing Operas and Staging Them," *Parnassus: Poetry in Review*, 10.2: 4–19.

Thomson, V., composer (1989), *Music With Words: A Composer's View*. New Haven, CT: Yale University Press.

Thorne, J. V., librettist (2000), commenting in *Opera America Newsline* 9.5 (February).

Toury, G. (1980), *In Search of a Theory of Translation*. Tel Aviv: The Porter Institute for Poetics and Semiotics, Tel Aviv University.

Toury, G. (1995), *Descriptive Translation Studies and Beyond*. Amsterdam: John Benjamins.

Tråvén, M. (1999), Dissertation, University of Stockholm, *Om översättning av musikaliskt bunden text: en studie av Mozarts Da Ponte-opera Don*

Giovanni *i sex svenska översättningar* (On the translation of musical bound text: a study of the Mozart-Da Ponte opera Don Giovanni in six Swedish translations).

Tråvén, M. (2005), "Musical Rhetoric—the Translator's Dilemma: A Case for *Don Giovanni*," in Gorlée (2005a), 103–20.

Trowell, B. (1992), "'Libretto (ii)," in Sadie (1992), II: 1191–1252.

Tunbridge, L. (2013), "Singing Translations: The Politics of Listening between the Wars," *Representations* 123.1 (August 1): 53–86.

Turner, H., *[Brighton] Uproar*, May 23, 1997.

Tyrrell, J. (1992), "*The Bartered Bride*," in Sadie (1992), I: 331–34.

Tyrrell, J. (2003), personal communciation.

Venuti, L. (1993), "Translation as Cultural Politics: Regimes of Domestication in English," in *Textual Practice* 7.2: 208–23.

Venuti, L. (1995/2008), *The Translator's Invisibility: A History of Translation*, 2nd edition. Abingdon, UK: Routledge.

Venuti, L. (2000a), "Translation Community, Utopia," in Venuti (2000b): 468–88.

Venuti, L. ed. (2000b), *The Translation Studies Reader*. London and New York: Routledge.

Venuti, L. ed. (2004), *The Translation Studies Reader*, 2nd edition. London and New York: Routledge.

Venuti, L. (2009), "Translation, Intertextuality, Interpretation," *Romance Studies* 27.3 (July 1): 157–73.

Wagner, R. (1850), "*Das Judenthum in der Musik*" (literally, "Jewdom [cf. Christendom] in Music," most often translated as "Judaism in Music," though it has nothing to do with Judaism [that is, the religion] per se), Leipzig, *Die Neue Zeitschrift für Musik*. Written under the pseudonym K. Freigedank (K. Freethought). Followed up by an expanded version in 1869, written under Wagner's own name, and subsequent anti-semitic essays and newspaper articles.

Warburton, T. (2003), *Efter 30 000 sidor: från en översättares bord* (*After 30,000 Pages: From a Translator's Desk*). Söderström (Stockholm) and Atlantis (Helsinki).

Warren, F. L. (1931), *The New Yorker* (January 10).

Wormald, J. (1988, revised 2001), *Mary Queen of Scots: Politics, Passion and a Kingdom Lost*. London and New York: Tauris Parke Paperbacks.

Wuilmart, F. (1995), "*Översättaren som förlossare ur den babyloniska språkförbistringen*" ("The Translator as a Redeemer from the Babylonian Confusion of Tongues"), in the Swedish journal *Dialoger*, 33. The Swedish text was translated from the German by Leif Janzon.

Index

Mateo, M. 4
McClatchy, J. D., translator,
  Mozart's *Die Entführung aus dem
  Serail* 53, 110, 123
  Mozart's *Die Zauberflöte* 92,
  118–19, 122
*Le médecin malgré lui (The Doctor
  in Spite of Himself)*, music
  composed by C. Gounod,
  libretto by Barbier and Carré
  after the play by Molière 32,
  51, 59, 64–5, 76, 98–100, 102,
  107–8, 120–1, 135–8, 144–6,
  186, 204–5
Meilhac, H., librettist, Bizet's
  Carmen 42, 75
Mérimée, P. *see Carmen*
Merlin 24
Meso-American music 177
Messiah see Handel
The Metropolitan Opera xvii, 12, 14,
  121–3
Met titles *see* electronic librettos
Meyerbeer, G., composer, *Les
  Huguenots* 123
Midgette, A. 96
Milton, J. 57
Minors, H. J. 3–4
Mireille, music composed by C.
  Gounod 64
Mohr, J., lyricist, "*Stille Nacht, heilige
  Nacht*" 25
Molière (stage name of Jean-Baptiste
  Poquelin), playwright, *Le
  médecin malgré lui* 76, 98–9,
  120–1, 135, 144–5
Monroe, Marilyn (professional persona
  assumed by Norma Jeane
  Mortenson) 5
Monteverdi, C., composer 7, 143
Moore, M., poet 43
Mordden, E. 104
Morris, W. 36
Mossop, B. 14
*Mother Courage and Her Children
  see Mutter Courage und ihre Kinder*
Mozart, W. A., composer 79, 91, 230
  Così fan tutte 60, 81, 91

Die Entführung aus dem Serail 13,
  52–3, 80, 91, 110–12, 123–4,
  190–4, 203–4, 207, 218–20,
  226–8, 230–1, 235–9
Don Giovanni xiv, 60
Le nozze di Figaro xiv, xvi, 8, 60,
  113, 155–6, 220
Die Zauberflöte 34, 38, 59, 80–1,
  91–2, 117–22, 223
Musorgskiy, Modest (Модест
  Мусоргский), composer,
  *Boris Godunov (Борис
  Годунов)* 14, 59
Muti, R. xv
*Mutter Courage und ihre Kinder
  (Mother Courage and Her
  Children)*, play by B. Brecht,
  music composed by P.
  Dessau 59–60
My Aunt Aurore see Ma tante Aurore
The Mysteries of Udolpho by A. W.
  Radcliffe 133

Nabokov, V. 32–3
Nabucco (Nabuchadnezzar), music
  composed by G. Verdi 123
Nabuchadnezzar see Nabucco
Newman, F. W. 31–2
Newmarch, R., translator of Smetana's
  Prodaná nevěsta 63
Newmark, P. 217
New York City Opera 13
Nida, E. 16–17
non-local translation
  see compensation in translation
North, M. 139
Northanger Abbey by J. Austen 133
Northern Opera of Sweden xvi
Le nozze di Figaro (The Marriage of Figaro),
  music composed by W. A. Mozart,
  libretto by L. Da Ponte xiv, xvi, 8,
  60, 113, 155–6, 220

Oberlin, R. 178
*L'occasione fa il ladro (Opportunity
  Makes the Thief, or, A Thief By
  Chance)*, music composed by
  G. Rossini, libretto by